*Degraded Work*

# Degraded Work

## *The Struggle at the Bottom of the Labor Market*

Marc Doussard

University of Minnesota Press
Minneapolis | London

The University of Minnesota Press gratefully acknowledges financial assistance provided for publication of this book by the Campus Research Board at the University of Illinois at Urbana–Champaign.



Published by the University of Minnesota Press
111 Third Avenue South, Suite 290
Minneapolis, MN 55401-2520
http://www.upress.umn.edu

Library of Congress Cataloging-in-Publication Data

Doussard, Marc.
Degraded work : the struggle at the bottom of the labor market / Marc Doussard.
Includes bibliographical references and index.
ISBN 978-0-8166-8139-6 (hc : alk. paper) — ISBN 978-0-8166-8140-2 (pb : alk. paper)
1. Unskilled labor—United States. 2. Labor—United States. 3. Working poor—United States. 4. Wages—United States. 5. Labor market—United States. I. Title.
HD8072.5.D68 2013
331.7'980973—dc23

2013010386

Printed in the United States of America on acid-free paper



20 19 18 17 16 15 14 13 10 9 8 7 6 5 4 3 2 1

# Contents

Introduction: The Boom in Poorly Paid and Precarious Jobs vii

1. New Inequalities: The Deterioration of Local-Serving Industries 1
2. Beyond Low Wages: The Problem of Degraded Work 23
3. The City That Sweats Work: Growth and Inequality in Post-Fordist Chicago 49
4. Oases in the Midst of Deserts: How Food Retailers Thrive in Disinvested Neighborhoods 81
5. "They're Happy to Have a Job": Midsize Supermarkets and Degraded Work 107
6. Building Degradation: Dangerous Work and Falling Pay during a Construction Boom 143
7. A Perfectly Flexible Workforce: Day Labor in a Precarious Industry 171
8. New Answers to New Problems: The Creative Work of Reversing Degradation 203

Conclusion: Building a Fair Labor Market in Postmanufacturing Economies 225

Acknowledgments 237

Notes 241

Bibliography 247

Index 263

Introduction

# The Boom in Poorly Paid and Precarious Jobs

Most of us know the image well. Dozens of men stand on a street corner or maybe at the edge of a park looking simultaneously bored and anxious. Many of them wear baseball caps against the sun, but they are otherwise clad in paint-spattered pants, heavy work boots, and other clothing poorly suited to the hot day. The sleepy lull of the day labor corner seems permanent until a white van approaches, and torpor turns to chaos. The men leap forward, their bodies crushing against the van the instant it pulls to a stop. The driver, a construction contractor on his way to the day's job, had practiced the question, *¿Quién quiere trabajar?* on the way to the corner, but he does not need it now. Before he can offer work, a dozen day laborers are pledging their labor: "Painting! Drywall! Demolition!"

The contractor could pause to bargain down wages, but as often as not, he doesn't bother. At eight to ten dollars per hour for basic jobs, day labor comes cheap, and most of the *jornaleros* on the corner have preemptively cut their bids to move to the top of the queue. Besides, negotiation means delay, and there is work to be done. The shotgun courtship between contractor and day laborers sometimes lasts as little as ten to fifteen seconds, but it lies at the center of a broad set of conflicts and questions about a changing labor market. The immigrant and often undocumented status of most day laborers, combined with the unscheduled repurposing of public space initiated by the street corner shape-ups, has led many cities to ban the practice or restrict the activities of not-for-profit organizations devoted to assisting the day labor workforce. As is common in contemporary U.S. politics, the racialized discourse about day laborers' immigration status overlaps with a clear set of class-based concerns about work in an increasingly perilous labor market. The *fact* of day labor provides an acute visual reminder of the increasing insecurity of all employment. The multiple uncertainties day laborers face every day—whether they will be hired, whether they will be paid, whether they will be retained—are exaggerated versions of the uncertainties inscribed in a growing number of all professional, manufacturing, and service jobs. Day labor draws our attention because it dramatizes a series of surprisingly widespread threats to the experience of work as it has long been understood.

We know the image of the day labor corner well, and its vivid specificity stands in sharp contrast to the vague picture of what happens after the contractor's van pulls away. While day labor corners themselves ignite fierce debate, the work day laborers actually perform remains curiously invisible and beyond substantial scrutiny. It is thoroughly unpleasant work—fast-paced, physically dangerous, and generally devoid of breaks—even when compared with other types of manual labor. Working under extreme contingency and in the absence of formal employment agreements, day laborers share in little of their employers' good fortune but absorb a disproportionate amount of risk. Even amid the once-in-a-generation housing boom in the 2000s, they received none of the on-the-job training, overtime pay, or vacation days most of us associate with paid work. Quite often, they failed to be paid at all—a crucial development for an industry that saw hourly wages stagnate during a historically unprecedented expansion.

Our failure to generate a clear picture of the day laborer's work experience is a telling symbol of our inability to come to terms with the remaking of work itself over the past forty years. Day labor provides a common point of analytical entry into questions surrounding the decimation of wages, the immiseration of working conditions, and the institutionalization of precarious employment for a broad swath of the U.S. workforce, native-born and immigrant alike. Yet the most commonly repeated tropes on the issue—that undocumented workers take jobs away from hard-working Americans or, incompatibly, that they do jobs those Americans no longer want to do—betray the underrealized conceptual apparatus through which the lay public and experts alike attempt to untangle the reorganization of labor markets. The predominantly immigrant (and predominantly undocumented) day labor workforce faces problems that workers of *all* backgrounds and citizenship statuses increasingly confront. Cleaning staff in hotels, for example, have seen their wages flatline or fall even as their daily workloads grow. A surprisingly large share of retail employees reports that management fails to pay the legally mandated time-and-a-half rate for overtime and that work schedules shrink, swell, and shift at a moment's notice. Labor scholars have documented in painstaking detail that these problems constitute much more than a series of isolated incidents of management malfeasance. As workplace regulatory agencies have lost funding and experimentation with cost-cutting measures has become the norm, the conditions of employment itself and the expected rewards for hard work have been degraded.

This book defines the combination of low wages, poor working conditions, and frequent employer violations of labor laws as the distinctive problem of *degraded work.* Frequently marginalized or understated in broad measures of income inequality, degraded work problems are most visible at the level of the workplace. A characteristic story related by a recent immigrant whom I will call Jaime, one of the fifty-four day laborers I interviewed, conveys the difference between simple low-wage work and degraded work. When I met with Jaime, he had recently returned from an especially frustrating construction job. The job wasn't bad in and of itself or, at least, not worse than others. He and another worker had been asked by a contractor to tear out the old fixtures in a kitchen being prepared for an expensive face-lift. For Jaime demolition was an unexceptional job, one that he often accepted, especially when the hourly pay rate—an above-market twelve dollars an hour on the day in question—warranted the effort. Instead of pointing to the difficult work itself, Jaime complained to me of a bind in which he was placed by another day laborer's actions. Day laborers are paid by the hour, a practice that incentivizes them to work slowly in order to draw a bigger end-of-the-day payout. But every one-day job contains the potential for renewed employment in the future, a fact that incentivizes day laborers to work quickly in order to impress contractors. It is a frustrating bind. On the day in question, the other day laborer working alongside Jaime was new to the shape-up. Optimistically, he determined that working quickly would secure him future work with the same contractor. Jaime described him as working like a burro, tearing out drywall, digging up floorboards, and pulling apart cabinets at crushing speed—all without pausing for lunch or a break. The job promised to pay Jaime an agreeable one hundred dollars or more at the beginning of the day, but he left the work site with less than sixty dollars in his pocket. Neither worker saw the contractor again.

Viewed through the conceptual frame of low-wage work, Jaime's day does not pose any readily evident problems. After all, his hourly wage rate was more than double the day's federal minimum wage of $5.15. But Jaime had to queue at the day labor shape-up for days to obtain the job, and he was unemployed as soon as it ended. The work was physically demanding—the crooked postures and restricted hand movements of many of the day laborers I met conveyed the toll construction work had taken on them—and had none of the rest periods, comforts, or nonwage benefits office workers take for granted. If Jaime had been injured on the job, he would have footed his own medical bill. And if the homeowner had refused to pay the contractor, Jaime would have gone home with empty pockets. Low-wage work becomes a problem when employees struggle to make ends meet. But the problems of *degraded* work begin in the workplace and stretch far beyond the question of hourly pay rates.

These problems take us quickly from a focus on workers themselves to the contractors who employ them. Behind Jaime's high-productivity and low-cost workday lies a contractor who benefited from the flexibility day labor provides. That contractor in turn negotiated with a homeowner and a network of subcontractors, all of whose work and costs were impacted by the presence of Jaime and other day laborers. Despite the curious invisibility of labor degradation in popular discourse, the analytical path to making sense of it has few complications. In order to understand degraded work, we need to understand workplaces. And in order to understand workplaces, we need to understand the employers and industries that sweat labor.

## Placing Employers at the Center of Inequality

This book is a response to the ongoing degradation of low-wage labor markets—problems that have intensified despite the growth of organizations working to improve workplaces and the establishment of the once-marginal issue of income inequality as central in political debate at all levels. The popularization of the issue of inequality represents a crucial step forward in grappling with a rapidly changing U.S. political economy. But it is more starting point than fully realized analysis. Though problematically low, hourly pay levels in retail trade, personal services, residential construction, and other local-serving industries typically associated with undesirable jobs are declining much less rapidly than the increasingly fast-paced, unreliable, and threat-laden conditions under which that work is performed. Redefining the labor market problem not as low-wage work or the abstract development of polarization but rather as the workplace-based problem of degraded work clarifies important aspects of both the analytical and the practical challenges posed by the ongoing deterioration of low-wage jobs.

Focusing on employers and the profit-making paths they pursue frames the problems facing low-wage workers in an actionable way. Community organizations, unions, and other actors troubled by the spread of degraded working arrangements have few tools with which to regulate international migration or the restructuring of the U.S. economy writ large. But they have a rich and sophisticated history of pressuring employers and industries. From Saul Alinsky's Industrial Areas Foundation to neighborhood responses to deindustrialization to the community–labor coalitions forming today, community organizations have at their disposal an intricate, field-tested repertoire of strategies and tactics for compelling employers to provide better pay and better work. Today, these organizations and their allies face a formidable challenge. Their efforts to pressure law-breaking employers in local-serving industries, about which scholars know comparatively little, amount to a local-level response to a far larger structural problem. The outsize mismatch between minimally funded community organizations and seemingly global workplace problems suggests the eventual inadequacy of even the smartest and most forceful campaigns. Many of these organizations understand that basic mismatch all too well and increasingly look to augment intensive organizing drives against individual employers with the transformation of the institutions and practices regulating those industries. Individual organizations and networks have made real and substantial progress along these lines as a movement, but worker centers and community–labor coalitions lack a synthetic framework with which to systematically categorize employers' strategies and identify pressure points for organizing campaigns and legal action.

Focusing on the unique characteristics of the place-bound, local-serving industries that degrade work the most aggressively, this book develops such a framework. The need to focus on local-serving industries neglected in historical studies of manufacturing brings us to an important theoretical problem. The theories, policies, and life experiences we use to make sense of employment inequalities arose directly or indirectly from the Fordist economic settlement of the postwar years. They continue to bear the stamp of that era, even when the discussion begins with the assumption that postwar political-economic arrangements have been voided. The most commonly used tools of urban economic analysis derive from an empirical focus on manufacturing industries. For orthodox economists like Charles Tiebout, this yielded optimistic, market-based theories of equilibrium in exporting industries. The critical theories developed by David Harvey and the economic geographers who engaged the problem of deindustrialization carried mirror-opposite assumptions and conclusions but shared an underlying concern (rooted in the historical materialism of Marx) with dynamic manufacturing industries. As a result, critics of urban economic transformation today have little choice but to draw on core theories that reify the dynamism of manufacturers and treat hotels, retail, industrial laundries, and other industries in which labor degradation flourishes as afterthoughts. Under an export-driven understanding of economic production, aerospace firms and other manufacturers are understood to restructure in fascinating ways, combining and recombining technology, skilled labor, and innovative firm organization to remake regions, markets, and economies. But retailers, janitorial firms, and landscapers are treated primarily as remainders: static, labor-sweating, cost-competitive industries that operate in the stylized competitive world of an economics textbook.

Building from these traditions, the most influential scholarly and popular accounts treat the problem of employment inequality as a problem of service sector *growth.* Historically and experientially, this emphasis resonates. In New England and the Upper Midwest, fleeing manufacturers left in their wake a two-tier economy built on a sharp division between highly skilled, high-paying professionals and low-wage work in consumption industries. But the narratively tidy story of service sector growth now obscures more than it reveals. Our nostalgia for a manufacturing-based economy naturalizes the conditions and political-economic arrangements that made manufacturing jobs so appealing in the postwar years. The news that manufacturing jobs offer superior wages, working conditions, and job security would have surprised the industrial workers of the 1910s and 1920s, who worked long hours in miserable conditions for subsistence-level pay. The manufacturing jobs that are the object of our current nostalgia resulted from profound and hard-fought changes, changes inaugurated by firms who saw economic benefits to Fordism, by workers who organized unions, and by New Deal political-economic bargains that ensured vigorous regulation and created a social safety net. Wages and working conditions in the worst service industries today are superior to most of the manufacturing jobs of old, yet we treat them as intrinsic to the industry and beyond the reach of regulation.

Recasting low-wage sectors as dynamic industries similar to the manufacturing firms around which public authorities design economic policy opens up new possibilities for action. In our current imagination, workers' advocates have at their disposal the threat of (unlikely) state or federal regulation and little else. The research in this book points to other tools in their repertoire and suggests that these organizations possess a significant and still-unrealized capacity for further strategic and tactical innovation. I spent portions of five years researching labor degradation in the food retail and the residential construction industries in Chicago. The picture of these industries that emerges contrasts sharply with the received wisdom about the supposedly unmitigated cost-based competition among local-serving firms. The firms that degrade work in Chicago do not compete in an undifferentiated marketplace. They prefer certain neighborhoods and consumer populations to others, use subcontracting to increase flexibility in addition to lowering labor costs, rely on appeals to ethnic solidarity to protect market share, and seek public sector support to assemble their businesses and regulate competition. These are among the many industry traits and actions that provide organizers and regulators with valuable leverage to change industry practices. Organizations that insert themselves at key points in the production process—at the day labor corner, where contractors assemble work crews with haste; in the multiple planning permissions new businesses need to open their doors; in the employer–consumer relationship on which customer-facing firms depend—use their leverage to push, prod, and pull employers toward a different approach to their workers. At this point, few concrete plans of action suggest themselves, a point I stress in a necessarily speculative evaluation of community-organizing tactics that remain tentative and experimental. Yet despite their numerous limitations, the creative strategies workers, organizers, and unions have developed to reregulate low-wage industries represent the most tangible hope for policies that reverse the decline in wages and working conditions and help to restore the shrinking American middle class. The path forward begins with asking a new set of questions.

Labor degradation thrives for many reasons, but indifference to the problem is not one of them. Theories about economic inequality have proliferated in the past twenty years, but policy approaches to the problem remain unchanged. Accordingly, chapter 1 examines our current paralysis in the face of labor degradation. Globalization, once a marginal concept, appears on syllabi across the social sciences, and vague treatises about a "new" economy have given way to a much more promising discussion about international divisions of labor, corporate geographies, and the unique inequalities produced in the central business districts of globally connected cities. Despite their promise, an enduring focus on transnational corporations and manufacturing firms limits the purchase of these analyses, most of which infer rather than document working conditions and business practices in low-wage service industries. Deepening our understanding of labor degradation means reconceptualizing low-wage industries as active producers of inequality rather than as manifestations of a problem that originates in multinational firms.

The internal workings of these industries have changed at a greater pace than most of us realize. Chapter 2 reviews the workplace practices of low-wage employers in order to sharpen the understanding of the problem at hand. Our limited understanding of nonmanufacturing industries springs in substantial part from the highly stylized and incomplete notion of low-wage work. Wage cuts and deteriorating working conditions have spread so completely across the bottom of the labor market that we need a fresh perspective on the problem. Where the concept of low-wage work suggests marginal changes within an existing set of economic arrangements, my concept of degraded work denotes a more far-reaching set of transformations to working conditions and the day-to-day negotiation of power between employers and employees. After mapping key dimensions of the problem, I turn to the questions of explanation: Why have these changes occurred, and how do firms profit from them? The theories of economic restructuring scholars use to assess transformation and plant relocation in manufacturing industries provide a sound basis for understanding service industries and the ends to which firms degrade work. Paying particular attention to the local market orientation of low-wage service industries suggests a series of distinctive market strategies we can test and evaluate.

The day-to-day particulars of pursuing profit within an industry matter to employers, workers, and policy makers. Place is crucial in these locally oriented industries, and this means scrutinizing the local economy within which they operate. Chapter 3 introduces the food retail and residential construction cases and the dynamic Chicago economy in which employers remade these industries. By the early 2000s the supposedly paradigmatic Chicago of urban studies legend had disappeared, if it ever in fact existed. The economy in which degraded work arrangements thrived was characterized not by Fordist stability but by *instability.* Ongoing deindustrialization, spatially specific social, racial, and economic divisions, and the Richard M. Daley administration's aggressive embrace of commercial and residential redevelopment all unsettled longtime competitive practices in construction and retail. Evaluating the industries against this backdrop suggests targeted questions about firm-level strategy and the organization of the workforce and, ultimately, about approaches to regulating employment abuses. Because traditional methods of economic analysis provide minimal information on these firms (they remain unstudied in large part because they frustrate efforts to use national-level datasets), I also introduce a methodological discussion that outlines the evidence, assumptions, and basis for making conclusions about these sectors.

This leads to the cases themselves. Chapter 4 details the food retail industry's evolution away from a pseudo-Fordist competitive model based on unionized labor, economies of scale in purchasing, market expansion, and homogeneity among consumers. In Chicago the income inequalities resulting from deindustrialization sped the dissolution of this model. Today, the unionized chain supermarkets that long dominated the city have given away to competitors who make Chicago's social and economic fragmentation the basis of their business models. Even as scholars in Chicago and elsewhere have fretted over the emergence of food deserts in which urban populations lack access to food, big-box firms, neighborhood bodegas, and a rapidly expanding set of midsize supermarkets have pushed into areas of the city long abandoned by large chain supermarkets. These firms reverse long-standing practice in the industry, targeting immigrant and "ethnic" populations and relying on the sale of low-cost meat and produce to lower-income households with a strong incentive to economize.

The conventional wisdom on low-wage employers suggests they follow a straightforward competitive model built around cheap product costs and cheap labor costs. Chapter 5 documents a more complex set of relationships, showing that degraded work supports competitive strategy in food retail in varied ways. The new, thriving food retailers undersell chain supermarkets by 50 percent or more on many products, and they use low-cost, highly productive labor to move those goods. Employers draw these high productivity rates out of workers through a number of innovative strategies, each of which I detail. Yet despite the clear linkage between low-wage labor and low-cost goods, firms in the industry erect a number of distinctive barriers, many of them geographic, to naked cost-based competition. This complicates our assumptions about low-wage employers and their business models and at the same time frustrates community actions against employers with whom many low-income populations identify as consumers. To demonstrate this last point, I compare a pair of organizing campaigns at low-wage food retailers on Chicago's Southwest Side. Because the organizers misread the firms' competitive strategies, these campaigns did not proceed as expected. They offer distinctive lessons about the industry and the need to understand these firms in detail.

The book then turns to residential construction. Chapter 6 examines the seeming paradox of the Chicago construction boom in the first decade of the twenty-first century. The volume of residential construction rose by more than 50 percent between 2000 and 2006. Normally, industry expansion of this magnitude triggers substantial pay increases and concessions to labor. But the opposite occurred. Construction wages *fell* during the boom, and street corner day labor hiring institutionalized multiple employment abuses. The changing structure—the restructuring—of residential construction illuminates these developments. On the heels of a long-term push for subcontracting, general contractors responded to cheap construction money and ample work by reconfiguring their subcontractor relationships to incorporate vulnerable day labor workers at multiple points. What appears on the surface to be a straightforward story of contractors sweating immigrant labor on closer inspection plays out as the deliberate and strategic restructuring of long-standing industry arrangements.

The omnipresence of bidding and subcontracting in residential construction suggests that contractors will use the cost savings from labor sweating to make cheaper bids on jobs and win extra market share. But this is not the case. Chapter 7 explores this disconnect and its implications for practice. From a distance the residential construction industry appears to operate in the manner suggested by economics textbooks. Contractors bid against one another for jobs, with the lowest price theoretically winning. This suggests significant benefits to undercutting competitors. Yet few of the contractors employing day laborers behaved this way. I document the poorly understood bidding process and show that the increasingly elaborate articulation of subcontracting chains militated against contractors incorporating labor cost savings into their bids. This reverses the conventional wisdom and implies new targets for organizers and lawmakers eager to stem abuses in a notoriously abusive industry.

Reviewing the pressure points, profit potential, and distribution of risk within residential construction and food retail provides a fresh opportunity to evaluate the fledgling strategies that community organizations, labor unions, and elected officials use to redress problems with degraded work. The ideal solutions—such as improving enforcement of labor laws or strengthening the National Labor Relations Act—lie at the federal level, beyond the grasp of locally oriented workers' advocates and, frankly, beyond the reach of current political will. But the strategies and tactics local organizations have used to combat the problem are inventive and surprisingly diverse. Chapter 8 analyzes some of the most promising responses to the problem and provides a framework that makes clear the shared characteristics of and limits to these approaches. National advocacy networks such as the National Day Laborer Organizing Network and Restaurant Opportunities Centers United play a crucial role in disseminating strategies, but adapting policy ideas to the specifics of industries, local labor markets, and local political opportunities ideally begins with an extra set of institutional analyses. Surprisingly, an industry focus often shifts workers' organizations onto a terrain where they are better organized than their employers. This is promising for the future.

I conclude the book by addressing the broader implications of the concept of degraded work for scholars engaged in the problem of urban inequality. Defining working conditions, in addition to wages, as a central component of workplace inequality suggests several new lines of inquiry into the problem. I hope the questions raised here will help to identify the elusive answer to the signature problem of contemporary cities.

# 1

# New Inequalities

## *The Deterioration of Local-Serving Industries*

Deep inequalities have become such a fundamental part of U.S. cities that it is increasingly hard to see them. From the late 1930s until 1973, income convergence was a central fact of American life. The growth of the middle class seemed as natural as the seasons. Recessions, including steep ones in 1948 and 1969, slowed the expansion of the middle class but did not halt it, much less reverse it. But we now stand amid a forty-year period in which these trends have been reversed. Real wages began to stagnate in the 1970s. They continued to stagnate in the 1980s as upper-income earners pulled away. Instead of narrowing these gaps, the record-setting expansion of the 1990s drove the poor further away from the wealthy. And the 2000s' boom—a strong one by many macroeconomic metrics—delivered such paltry rewards to the bottom nine-tenths of wage earners that many thought there was no boom at all.

Perhaps more disturbing, the 2001–7 business cycle was characterized in many areas by the proliferation of jobs that offered few of the rewards typically associated with employment. These jobs paid low wages—at and often *below* the legal minimum—and subjected workers to a variety of risks, employer abuses, and safety concerns long thought to have been extinguished in the U.S. labor market. These jobs are best encapsulated in the figure of the day laborer, a solitary construction worker who lines up before dawn every morning in the hope of receiving eight to ten dollars per hour for a day of physically intense work. Within the growing world of low-wage work, day laborers are fairly well paid on an hourly basis. But on any given day, they are as likely to go home without work as they are to find a job. They routinely work without safety equipment, breaks, or proper instruction on techniques to mitigate the often devastating physical impacts of construction work. There is more. Construction contractors dangle the promise of continued employment to guarantee maximal effort every day: work hard enough and don't complain, and you'll have a job tomorrow. And when homeowners withhold pay from those contractors—a common response to dissatisfaction with their work—the day laborers go unpaid altogether. Quantitative and income-based conceptualizations of inequality do not come close to adequately describing these problems.

One of the more distressing aspects of these changes has been the fact that they were so obvious to so many. The rising wave of critical social sciences research on inequalities in Western market economies has, like inequality itself, grown so steadily as to become monotonous. In urban studies, engagement with the issue has understandably come back time and again to the question of deindustrialization and the growth of an (inconsistently defined) service economy. The leading scholars disagree on the places, industries, and sociopolitical developments behind these growing inequalities but find consensus on a central point: economic inequalities in U.S. cities can be traced to the disappearance of highly paid manufacturing jobs and the growth of low-wage, low-skill jobs in service sectors.

The changing structure of the economy—the dwindling share of employment comprised by skilled manufacturing jobs, as opposed to labor-intensive service jobs—marks a clear starting point for understanding the problem. Described by potent neologisms such as *dual city, global city,* and *partitioned city,* this structure is shaped, if not defined, by the gulf between skilled finance employees and low-wage deliverers of services, just as the network society and the hourglass and two-tier economies are shaped by the mobility of manufacturing capital and the dwindling employment options of workers with limited skills and labor market credentials (see Mollenkopf and Castells 1991; Sassen 2001; Van Kempen and Marcuse 1997; Castells 1996). The core assumption uniting these competing accounts of transformation is that the shift from manufacturing-based to services-based economies is the primary mechanism producing this long-run slide into mass economic inequality. Industries may change their day-to-day operations and restructure in significant ways, but it is the restructuring of the economy writ large that pushes these inequalities forward.

This book challenges that dominant perspective. I argue that the shift from a manufacturing-dominated to a services-dominated employment base offers a weaker explanation of economic polarization than does the obvious—and for the most part ignored—fact of *job downgrading* across place-bound industries. Service sector employment has indeed grown as a share of all employment, and it has done so across U.S. urban areas of every description. And low-skill service jobs do tend to offer fewer financial rewards than the manufacturing jobs that have departed American shores. But the reality that these service sector jobs have long been less preferable than higher-skilled jobs in manufacturing tends to obscure the fact that employment in most service industries has become overwhelmingly less preferable in recent decades. Compared with the imagined heyday of stable, year-round, and highly paid manufacturing employment, the growth of service sectors is indeed a problem. But the consistent downgrading of those service jobs is a much bigger problem.

Conceptualizing service jobs—or more accurately, low-wage jobs across retail, entertainment, construction, and a range of sectors lumped together under the rubric of services—as static in terms of quality leads to a significant misunderstanding of the nature of urban inequality and of the tools that can combat it. If the dominant employment problem is the *growth* of the service sector and if that growth is inevitable, then there is little that we can do, especially with the modest resources urban social movements possess. But if the dominant problem is the *downgrading* of service jobs and if that downgrading is itself the result of a series of specific policies, institutional rearrangements, and business strategies, then the low-income workers of today, much like the displaced manufacturing workers of a generation ago, have at their disposal a wide array of tools that can reorder the contest between capital and labor in their favor.

Arguing in favor of the malleability of wages and working conditions in today's low-wage industries stands the conventional wisdom on its head. If wages and working conditions in place-based industries can change, then organizing and political strategies supporting that goal should be pursued much more aggressively than were the oft-celebrated community-organizing efforts against runaway manufacturing shops. Manufacturers almost always had a credible threat to pick up their business and leave; the second deindustrialization of the United States, taking place today, and the mass industrialization of China and India attest to this. Ironically, the retailers, the cleaning agencies, the construction contractors, and the panoply of other low-wage businesses ignored in urban policy cannot run away. In short, the conventional wisdom suggests that low-wage employees in local-serving industries have scant bargaining power. But their employers' dependence on local markets suggests the opposite. Their profit-making strategies and day-to-day operations are built around locally specific end markets, regulations, and labor markets, and if for some reason they do flee to a different locale, a replacement business will quickly step in to take their place.

The idea that these locally oriented industries (as they are subsequently referred to) might be superior targets for organizing raises several important questions. As ever, the practical details matter. How can community organizations, labor unions, and progressive policy advocates campaign effectively to force these industries into a more favorable set of workplace practices? How can they adapt their current organizing and advocacy approaches, the majority of which are derived from past community–labor campaigns designed to check the power of well-capitalized, footloose manufacturers? These questions are crucial, and this book addresses each of them in turn. The pressing issues are to confirm that jobs in these industries have changed for the worse and to confirm that alternate paths to employer profit are possible. This takes us to classic questions about firms, industrial organization, and economic restructuring. How did we get here? And why does the idea that local industries are a distraction—a minimally important afterthought to the far more important workings of multinational firms—persist?

## The Globalization Trap

The dominant narratives of urban economic polarization tell a vivid story in which local industries play a secondary role. These narratives provide theoretically and empirically sophisticated explanations of the radical shift in the composition of the U.S. economy over the past thirty-plus years. This is a valuable contribution: deindustrialization has fundamentally remade labor markets and cities. It has done this so thoroughly and for so long that we often fail to grasp its ongoing relevance.

Early in the postwar boom, U.S. manufacturers began investing their profits in offshore development. The deindustrialization of America began in the 1950s in New England, spread across the Northeast and the Midwest in the 1970s and 1980s, and moved into the South and the West in the 1990s and 2000s (Harrison 1984; Bluestone and Harrison 1982; Doussard and Schrock 2012). The political-economic contest underpinning deindustrialization amplified the differences between the stagnating Rust Belt of shuttered factories and the thriving Sun Belt of lower-wage nonunion manufacturing employment in right-to-work states (Perry and Watkins 1977). Once a zero-sum game between different regions of the United

States, deindustrialization is now a negative-sum game for the country as a whole. Manufacturing accounted for 16 percent of the jobs in the U.S. economy in 1990, but its share fell precipitously thereafter. The nation shed manufacturing jobs at a greater rate in the 2000s than in the 1970s or 1980s, and by the time the national recovery from the Great Recession began in 2009, only one out of every eleven workers was employed in the sector.[1]

The scholarship on the impact of this change verges on consensus. Deindustrialization has been devastating to midwage households, and the loss of skilled manufacturing jobs—which provided family wages to workers with limited educational backgrounds—has left behind a two-tier labor market characterized by a small number of highly paid jobs for skilled professionals, a growing number of entry-level jobs for the unskilled, and a rapidly dwindling intermediary tier of midwage jobs (generally in the twelve-to-twenty-dollars-per-hour range). The best statistical evaluations of this shift frame the results in striking terms. For example, Eric Olin Wright and Rachel Dwyer's examination of changing job-growth patterns shows that the expansions of the U.S. economy since the 1960s have produced a progressively polarized set of employment opportunities (Wright and Dwyer 2003). The Economic Policy Institute's annual updating of basic employment measures unfailingly depicts mounting inequality and deteriorating conditions for the lowest-income households (see Mishel, Bernstein, and Allegretto 2006 for the particulars at the end of the last business cycle). Mirroring these analyses, the Gini coefficient, a basic (and conservative) economist's measure of inequality, shows that the U.S. income structure more closely resembles that of Mexico and China than it does the UK's, Canada's, or that of any other industrialized nation (Organization for Economic Cooperation and Development 2011). No matter the metric, the story of manufacturing job loss fundamentally is a story of growing inequality.

These inequalities are most apparent in cities—and especially in large cities—where the social structure, employment base, and built environment increasingly reflect a massive divide in income. This has led to a sustained engagement with the question of urban poverty, albeit in terms that often stray far from the straightforward question of job loss at hand. The notion that deindustrialization creates a new underclass of unemployed and, subsequently, unemployable workers forcefully entered urban scholarship with William Julius Wilson's *When Work Disappears*. Wilson's text, which first invokes manufacturing job loss as a cause of diminished opportunity for urban African Americans and then attributes ongoing unemployment to problematic "ghetto-related behavior" among that population, illustrates the recurrent problems attached to this type of analysis. In *When Work Disappears,* as elsewhere, structural accounts of economic change powerfully explain basic shifts in economic composition. Yet those same accounts underconceptualize the city itself, leaving urban space as a black box onto which scholars project unrelated analyses. Regrettably, these structural narratives also push the employers responsible for job losses to the margins of the discussion. A uniquely important object of study in and of itself, polarization often becomes a secondary jumping-off point for other observations.

This difficulty in moving back and forth between accounts of structural and place-specific economic change blunts the ability of much of this scholarship on inequality to speak effectively to the real and pressing problem of polarization, particularly in terms of policy and local action. If the U.S. economy as a whole has become inequitable on a level unseen since the 1920s, then its largest urban areas—especially New York, Chicago, Boston, San Francisco, and Los Angeles—manifest levels of inequality that challenge the theoretical and empirical vocabularies through which we understand the issue. Both ends of the income spectrum are pulling apart in these cities: pay for top earners has soared, whereas the bottom one-fifth of earners makes significantly less today than it did a generation ago (Doussard, Peck, and Theodore 2009). This polarization is reflected everywhere: in a housing market caught between supergentrification on the one hand and a foreclosure epidemic on the other (Lees 2003; Ashton 2009), in the increasingly uneven and erratic provision of basic social services (Lake and Newman 2002), and in the aggressive use of public power to secure the real estate goals of politically influential developers (Sites 2003).

As inequality became the new normal in urban areas after the 1980s, social scientists focused on a basic question, why? In most analyses changes to the structure of large corporations provide the answer. The theories supplied to address this question are rooted in intricate readings of Marxian political economy and world systems theory. But they broadly resonate across disciplines and outside the academy because they communicate a commonsense logic and—crucially—provide a linear narrative of polarization in which the mysteries of international economic restructuring take form in the everyday activities of the skilled professionals who flock to large metropolitan areas and the career opportunities they offer.

The basic components of this narrative have saturated urban studies. Moving manufacturing production offshore may cut labor and environment costs, but it entails a massive amount of work—new kinds of work—for corporations. These corporations now need to coordinate production across time zones and across a varying series of legal and regulatory environments, and to do that they need clearly defined channels through which to circulate capital and contracts across borders. Decades ago, David Harvey identified the rise of urban command-and-control centers through which firms could centralize these byzantine practices (Harvey 1985). John Friedmann and Saskia Sassen subsequently traced the social and spatial forms that took hold in the "global cities" that were homes to command and control (Friedmann 1986; Sassen 2001). In recent years formal debate on these questions has evaporated, not because of the obsolescence of the concepts but rather because the basic story about command and control centers has ascended to the status of conventional wisdom, an unexamined commonplace that shapes the way urbanists of all dispositions understand inequality.

That makes it crucial to reexamine this seemingly settled debate. The architecture of the globalization story shapes the way we understand urban economic change, often for the worse. Popular globalization narratives prioritize the specialized needs of large manufacturing firms, whose engagement with international markets requires them to make a dizzying number of deals to finance and import or export new products. These deals require a host of highly specialized technical skills too large and varied for any one firm to house. From this functional challenge to manufacturing firms springs the bustling professional marketplace of the modern downtown. The "high end" of polarization springs from central business districts in which firms can assemble, disassemble, and juggle ever-changing combinations of lawyers, financiers, and consulting experts whose skills fit the unpredictable challenges of the day (Sassen 2001, 32).

Most accounts make these well-paid and creative professionals the authors of low-wage job growth, as well. The narrative proceeds through a nearly mechanical analysis of consumption, and this is where the overly structural, top-down understanding of employment problems becomes clear. Most accounts of globalization point out that law firms, financiers, and upscale downtown businesses consume large amounts of services from other businesses and that those services—cleaning, catering, messenger services—typically employ low-wage workers. Home and leisure contribute to low-wage job growth, as well. The lawyers and MBAs who toil for these firms are long on money but short on time. They sensibly compensate by spending ever-growing sums on dry cleaning, restaurants, cleaning services, and high-status social items—condominiums in converted manufacturing spaces and custom furniture, clothing, and other consumer goods—whose production is labor intensive. At work and at home, the activities of this skilled class stimulate demand for the types of labor-intensive products that have long been associated with low-wage and poor labor practices. Saskia Sassen's *The Global City* conveys this logic forcefully, sketching a shift toward the growth of deskilled low-wage jobs in services, small-batch manufacturing, and residential construction. Whereas the postwar middle class steered its disposable income toward mass-produced products, the wealthy financiers produced by contemporary capitalism favor products generated by a less equitable process.

> High-income gentrification is labor intensive, in contrast to the typical middle-class suburb, which represents a capital-intensive process—tract housing, road and highway construction, dependence on private automobile or commuter trains, heavy reliance on appliances and household equipment of all sorts. . . . High-income gentrification in a city, on the other hand, is labor-intensive: Renovation of townhouses and storefronts and designer furniture and woodwork all require workers, directly and indirectly. Behind the gourmet food stores and specialty boutiques lies an organization of the work process that differs from that of the self-service supermarket and department store. (Sassen 2001, 285)

Sassen's influential narrative of urban employment polarization persuades for many reasons. It yokes a clear-cut, empirically verifiable tale about job growth (which has moved to the top and bottom of the income spectrum) and about income polarization (which reflects the mass replacement of midwage manufacturing jobs with retail, janitorial, and security jobs paying near the legal minimum) to a historically specific reading of capitalist development.

This book primarily concerns itself with the globalization narrative's treatment of low-wage industries. Formally, structuralist interpretations of polarization argue for the analytical importance of low-wage service industries, whose growth accelerates the growth of an American underclass.

But functionally, they treat those industries as analytical dead ends, emphasizing the shift in consumption from mass-produced goods to goods made through labor-intensive work processes. In this view low-wage industries explain inequality because they are *growing*. Mapping the growth of these sectors is indeed a crucial step in charting the changing nature of workplace inequalities. But the story does not end there. I argue that *changes* in these industries—in their organization of work, in management techniques for extracting maximum labor at minimum cost, in business owners' structural advantage in the day-to-day negotiation of pay, working standards, and work rates—go further toward explaining the boom in urban inequalities than does the simple fact of industry growth.

The food retail industry, cited by Sassen and others as paradigmatic of these changes, provides an example of the questions scholars currently fail to ask. The top-down narrative of polarization suggests that employment in food retail has worsened as a result of newly wealthy consumers shifting their purchases from large (and often unionized) supermarkets to small corner stores with less leeway to provide stable jobs, high pay, and good benefits. As the theory suggests, working conditions in these businesses are grim (Ness 2005). But the degradation of work extends into large chain supermarkets, big-box stores, and midsize retailers—none of whom explicitly targets high-end consumers. In fact, as my case studies show, sweating labor often goes hand in hand with efforts to lure spending from cost-conscious middle-class households eager to reconcile their historic standard of living with falling real wages. In food retail as elsewhere, the deterioration of wages and working conditions in consumer-oriented industries stretches far beyond the few industry segments impacted by the consumption tastes of wealthy financiers. Understanding and responding to these changes means moving beyond the useful but incomplete narrative of high-end consumption.

In taking this approach, I echo critics who note that globalization theories' underlying focus on transnational corporations and international business geographies effectively renders the world of local economies, policy, and organizing as a secondary, remaindered category with little room to accommodate analytical innovation (Therborn 2011). As these critiques establish, the global cities construct treats high-wage and low-wage industries as very different theoretical objects. High-wage industries and the jobs they provide are treated as dynamic. Formulations as distinct as a world system of cities, a rising network society, and splintering urbanism emphasize the fluidity and reinvention of these industries (Knox and Taylor 1995; Castells 1996; Graham and Marvin 2001). The who, the what, and the where of work all change, as do the terms on which individuals are employed. Firms in these industries are scrutinized with the full rigor of a careful and historically specific Marxian analysis.

Local-serving service firms, by contrast, are treated as simple organisms that mechanically cut product and labor costs. It is a tremendous shortcoming, and the practical question is what to do about it. Abu-Lughod, Brenner, and others have charted crucial methodological and theoretical restrictions that hamper the ability to accurately read the details of particular cities and institutional problems from the global restructuring template (Abu-Lughod 2001; Brenner 2001). My aim is both to deepen these critiques and to provide an alternative research program capable of identifying firm-level strategies, restructuring trends, and—consequently—regulatory and organizing opportunities in the locally oriented service industries whose low wages and immiserated working conditions we have been persuaded to take for granted.

Absent a working model of these industries, scholars and activists alike default to treating low-wage employers as sweatshops with undifferentiated competitive strategies. The logic behind this approach is clear: employers in labor-intensive industries such as residential construction, retail, and food service stand to gain more from low labor costs than do firms in capital-intensive industries. But this intuitive approach to the issue has two significant flaws. First, it provides disappointingly few regulatory tools for dealing with labor degradation. When the typical employer in an industry *needs* low labor costs to compete in a cost-competitive market, policy makers have few levers to pull and few carrots to dangle. From the organizer's perspective successes are often short lived and may be better described as failures in the long run. If firms face truly competitive end markets, then organizing can backfire: the firm that grudgingly raises its wages today could quickly find itself with a diminished market share and slim or negative profit margins. This pressure has hardened firms in many service industries that have attempted competitive models based on higher wages and improved working conditions.

Fortunately, my research suggests that this problem is insignificant for the simple reason that employers in these thriving locally oriented industries do not follow a straightforward, cost-cutting business model. The employers who drive down wages and working conditions for unskilled workers deploy an intricate and highly varied set of techniques to insulate themselves from straightforward, cost-based competition. This means that we can and should treat local industries as dynamic, strategic, and capable of pursuing multiple paths to profit. In short, we should treat them like the dynamic transnational firms who shift their competitive practices and employment standards in responses to changes in regulation and organizing strategy.

## A Solvable Problem: Job Downgrading in Place-Bound Firms

The theories of globalization that dominate urban scholarship on economic inequality today draw much of their power from the concept of economic restructuring. Open-ended, diverse, and process based, restructuring theories treat contemporary capitalism as spatially uneven and inherently unstable (Lovering 1989). At the level of industries, the restructuring approach to reading economies and political economies generates a practical set of empirical questions surrounding firm location, industry structure, technological innovation, and labor practices. Basic questions about restructuring animate the leading scholarship on globalization, which uses these concepts to subject the organization and evolution of manufacturing and finance industries to rigorous analysis.

Unfortunately, local-serving industries rarely receive that same level of scrutiny. At the heart of the argument that service sector growth is the signature problem of deindustrializing cities lies the problematic assumption that those industries are intrinsically low wage. This ever-present assumption contradicts a significant body of empirical work charting the heterogeneity and variability of wages and working conditions in retail, insurance, construction, and other high-employment "local" industries. For example, the retail sector of the mid-2000s—to say nothing of the Internet-driven change in the industry since—appears as an entirely different industry than it did a generation prior. In the 1960s retail functioned as though it existed in an era bypassed by postwar capitalism. Paternalistically organized through small, family-run firms, the majority of the jobs in the industry were relatively well compensated and permanent—in labor market terms, they belonged to the primary labor market of year-round, full-time work that was once presumed to be an irreversible historical development. In the 1970s and 1980s, this landscape changed. Corporate consolidation and the entry into the workforce of workers with limited educational credentials and markers of marginal social status made it feasible for employers to experiment with cost-cutting labor strategies. Over time, part-time employment evolved from an ad hoc relationship designed to provide extra labor hours during seasonal fluctuations in sales to a permanent, industry-wide norm in the organization of employment (Tilly 1996). In other words, the retail jobs that grew as the United States began to deindustrialize grew considerably *worse* by most measures of job quality. Subsequent trends in corporate consolidation and the elimination of nonwage employment benefits have further reduced the quality of jobs in local-serving industries.

A comparative perspective can deepen our appreciation of the issue. Far from confirming the intrinsically poor quality of jobs in these industries, international comparisons show distinct variation in wages and working conditions for countries across the industrialized North (Gautié and Schmitt 2009). The variance depicted in international comparisons is much smaller when the United States is removed from the analysis. But differences in wages and working conditions between Canada and European nations are comparatively small. It is the wide gap in pay rates between the rest of the industrialized world and the United States that stands out. Even Walmart, the preeminent symbol of low-wage dead-end jobs in the U.S. service sector, pays more generously abroad than in the United States (Tilly 2006). It is difficult to escape the conclusion that the poor job quality taken to be inevitable in the United States is in fact an outlier in an international context.

The construction industry provides a more dramatic illustration of these realities. The growth of street corner day labor shape-ups—sites where workers queue in the hope of securing a day's employment from a construction contractor who drives up to request their services—was a divisive social and political issue across the country in the 2000s (Valenzuela Jr. et al. 2006). Day labor marked a remarkable change in the residential construction industry, which saw wages fall even as the overall size of the industry grew by 50 percent during the decade's housing boom. Here again is a case of a growing local industry in which employment changed for the worse as the industry expanded. *Change* perhaps is too mild a word to capture the industry's transformation. A century ago, day labor was a standard form of work organization within construction, and daily lineups of the type seen in the film *On the Waterfront* were the norm (Valenzuela Jr. 2003). In the interim construction employment was reconfigured by the rise of suburbs and mass-produced housing, which facilitated the growth of large firms with stable, year-round workforces and the infusion of capital technologies to change the work process; by the formalization of high-wage employment and internal labor markets in the commercial construction industry; through the Davis–Bacon Act and unionization; and by the passage and the rigorous enforcement of wage, job-training, and occupational safety laws that normalized employment and vastly improved working conditions for substantial portions of the workforce. The spread of day labor working arrangements in the 2000s marked both the *expansion* and the *downgrading* of employment in an industry that had offered significantly more favorable employment opportunities just a decade prior.

Despite this considerable body of evidence to the contrary, policy makers and a majority of urban theorists operate on the assumption that low wages and poor working conditions in these industries are nearly inevitable.[2] This viewpoint finds fertile ground—its conclusions feel normal, conventional—in theories of urban economic development, regardless of whether they are rooted in orthodox economic or heterodox political economy. The foundational theories of urban economic growth mark a clear distinction between an economic base of exporting industries whose success and expansion determine the fate of local economies and a secondary set of nonbasic industries that serve the local market demand generated by the profits and household income those "basic" industries generate (Tiebout 1956; Markusen 1994). Dissenters have pushed back against this formulation almost from the beginning, with Hans Blumenfeld and Ann Markusen and Greg Schrock providing especially thorough critiques of the dichotomy (Blumenfeld 1955; Markusen and Schrock 2006). But the dichotomy endures in practice: as trained by economists, planners, or geographers, the alert student of economic development concerns herself with automakers, electronics manufacturers, or the biosciences—the dynamic businesses that innovate and make things. In this conventional view policy makers who focus on employers and jobs in local industries are akin to engineers who worry more about what color to paint a bridge than about its load-carrying capacity.

The conditions under which scholars developed restructuring theories complicate the problem of pushing past this divide. The critical, politically engaged geographers who patiently worked through the industry- and regional-level implications of Marxian political economy did so in order to come to terms with what is now known as the deindustrialization of the

North and the West of England (Massey and Meegan 1982). In the United States, restructuring theories took off precisely because of their relevance to manufacturing, and they remain popularly associated with it. *The Deindustrialization of America,* Barry Bluestone and Bennett Harrison's assessment of corporate strategy and job loss, introduced critical restructuring theories to an American audience by documenting the crucial role of corporate strategy and federal policy in the epidemic loss of manufacturing jobs in the Northeast and the Midwest (Bluestone and Harrison 1982). The arguments and questions integrated into the problematic of deindustrialization extend far beyond manufacturing industries themselves, but the strong historical association with a particular moment in time excludes them from the assessment of contemporary problems to which the concept of firm-level restructuring can contribute significantly.

Nevertheless, we remain focused on manufacturing and export-oriented industries that constitute an ever-shrinking portion of the urban economy. At the same time, industries with a local market orientation account for a majority of economic activity in U.S. urban areas (Persky, Doussard, and Wiewel 2009). Because their business remains local, they can rarely invoke the threat of fleeing the region in response to changes in the labor or policy climate. Yet the prevailing approach to urban economic restructuring suggests that we ignore these industries in favor steering our analytical and political resources toward footloose, globe-trotting firms who frequently and potently exercise the threat of relocation. At a minimum this represents a substantial misallocation of intellectual and policy resources.

## Driving without a Map: Community Organizations' Struggle to Regulate Local-Serving Industries

Falling wages and worsening working conditions in local industries may remain an abstract concern to economists and scholars focused on transnational corporations, but they are a daily object of struggle for workers and the community and labor organizations who serve them. In response to members' complaints about maltreatment in the workplace, new organizations and social actors across a wide range of urban areas have transformed themselves into advocacy/social service organizations that lobby regulators and push employers to provide improvements to workplace compensation and standards. These activist groups include community-based and immigrant service organizations—sometimes referred to as migrant civil society—community–labor coalitions, and most prominently worker centers, joint social services/advocacy organizations that mobilize their members to pressure individual employers and lobby for legislation that improves the bargaining power of low-wage workers (Theodore and Martin 2007; Ness and Jayaraman 2005; Gordon 2005; Fine 2006).

These organizations respond to the evolving mismatch between workplace regulatory frameworks and the realities of employer activity. Existing labor regulations in the United States take a top-down approach. Passed during the New Deal and overseen by federal agencies tasked with covering nearly all nonagricultural employers in the nation, the Fair Labor Standards Act, the National Labor Relations Act, and the Occupational Safety and Health Act functionally treat each industry and workplace as the same. As detailed in chapter 2, this limits their reach in deconcentrated industries (such as construction, which features millions of employers nationwide) in which the number of workplaces to police is large (Bernhardt and McGrath 2005). Worker centers and their peer organizations address this problem by attempting to regulate from the bottom up. The list of employers and industries in which they organize is determined by foot traffic and their constituents: they go where the problems are. This approach has led to significant legislative victories (including the passage of a legally binding code of conduct for New York's greengrocers), but assessments of worker centers' overall performance suggest uneven and necessarily limited outcomes. Financial resources and the limited organizing capacity of their members—most of whom are low-wage workers with changing work hours and dependents—are the most obvious barriers to the effectiveness of worker centers.

The necessarily local focus of these centers restricts their ability to generate systematic knowledge and approaches to low-wage industries across regions, industries, and labor markets. Like their peers elsewhere, the community–labor organizations who appear in this book undertake their efforts in near isolation. They have few maps, theoretical, practical, or otherwise, to the industries in which they intervene, and just as significant, their limited contact with peer organizations elsewhere makes it clear that the supermarkets and construction contractors they attempt to regulate are organized differently—behave differently—from elsewhere. In a way that again belies the perception that employment in local industries is monolithic and unchanging, low-wage supermarkets and residential contractors in Chicago, where my research was conducted, were organized differently, did their business differently, and targeted different end markets than did supermarkets elsewhere. Just as important, the competitive plans built from these decisions varied from firm to firm and cannot be inferred from national-scale data on income inequality and economic restructuring writ large. As the most detailed studies of restructuring in local-serving industries show, restructuring does more than simply pad profits by cutting labor costs. It allows employers to shift risks to workers, reorganize the work and production process to improve efficiency and flexibility, and develop new strategies for building market share and tapping sales opportunities that previously lay beyond their grasp.

Linking employment restructuring to questions of firm-level strategy is an important step because it suggests specific ways that workers' organizations can take advantage of competitive asymmetries, frictions, and weaknesses within an industry. These frictions and asymmetries point to specific intervention points—weak spots where activists and policy makers can effectively intervene for change. At the same time, the persistent variance in industry organization from one region to the next indicates substantial heterogeneity in local institutions, regulations, labor markets, and employer strategy—it means that the way employers in an industry do business is particular rather than universal and, thus, subject to change through pressure on regulators, consumers and labor market institutions *at the local level.* This important insight helps to clarify the ways that organizations with a regional and urban focus can impact problems that originate in spatial, scalar, and political realms beyond their direct control. Instead, the Chicago advocates found these comparisons discouraging.

The increasingly potent advocacy research on local-serving industries succeeds in drawing attention to the problem of job downgrading, but its laudable emphasis on charting the nationwide extent of the problem necessarily places it in tension with efforts to shape research and advocacy in specific local industry constellations. We now have access to nationwide surveys of day laborers and low-wage workers across industries in New York, Chicago, and Los Angeles that have identified a systemic pattern of employer violations of basic labor laws (Valenzuela Jr. et al. 2005; Bernhardt, McGrath, and DeFilippis 2007; Bernhardt et al. 2009). The studies confirm the low wages of service workers; more than one-quarter of the most recently surveyed employees reported earning less than the minimum wage, and 60 percent of those workers earned more than one dollar less than the legal minimum. But this research necessarily remains focused on the *what* of low-wage employment, the size, scope, and extent of the problem, rather than on the question of *why* (beyond opportunism) employers have been able to grind away in a short amount of time decades' worth of advancements in employment compensation and working conditions. As a result these broad studies typically lack many of the characteristics workers' organizations and regulators would need to put them to use. Most fundamental, they do not provide an explicit theory of how these industries generate profit and the strategic and competitive goals served by degrading everyday work.

Theorizing the day-to-day operation of these industries should support the establishment of a comparative frame to allow the strategic contrasting of different local-serving industries in the same place (or a single industry across multiple urban areas) in order to draw out the ways in which they may be prone to change. Put another way, industry-level studies support a strategy of individualizing comparisons designed to highlight distinctive and actionable aspects of a particular industry's organization in a specific time and place. For advocates dealing with these problems, this is a welcome departure from academics' reflexive pursuit of variation-finding comparisons that seek to blindly import lessons from elsewhere, often without context (Tilly 1984). Systematically articulating how local industries are organized, how they tap workers and markets, and how employers pursue profit should aid scholars, activists, and anyone else engaged with the problems of the low-wage labor market in detailing the policy problems at hand. It should also facilitate the incorporation of compelling scholarship on contingent labor, labor market segmentation, and immigration into the analysis (Peck 1996; Harrison 1994; Hirschman and Massey 2008).

Just as important, theorizing these industries on their own terms will allow us to shine new light on employers—not the reflexively cost-cutting employers implied by the current literature but the actual businesses remaking labor standards and negotiating day-to-day competitive changes that remain poorly understood. As presently constituted, research on low-wage industries focuses primarily on employees (who are generally far more willing to serve as interview subjects than are their bosses), with the end effect being that the firms responsible for the degradation of basic employment remain in the background (chapter 2 takes up this issue in detail). Theorizing the profit-making models in these industries will shift the spotlight from workers to employers, in the process redirecting our attention to the organizing and the regulatory targets at the center of the story. This marks a much-needed improvement (see Markusen 2003).

## How Local-Serving Industries Restructure

The classical theories of economic restructuring once used to explain job loss in manufacturing industries provide an ideal vehicle for building a theory of service sector restructuring. At first the task appears daunting. Restructuring analysis places an empirical premium on firm location: the political, economic, institutional, and social shifts underlying industry upheaval are traced by following the movement of manufacturing plants to new production sites, new labor markets, and new product markets. The very trait of local industries that makes them ideal targets for organizing—their immobility—appears on the surface to nullify restructuring theories' main analytical tool.

But reducing restructuring theories to the question of firm mobility robs them of their most powerful capabilities. The concept of restructuring may have been deployed to address pressing problems in the manufacturing sector, but the project of restructuring theory engages questions about technology, firm organization, labor markets, regulation, and employers that apply to any industry (Hudson 2001). A sophisticated body of political-economic thought underpins the historical focus on firm location. This conceptual work suggests a straightforward approach to analyzing local-serving industries.

These theories identify concrete and productive ways to complicate our current, highly stylized view of service firms. The picture of service employers that emerges from globalization-based accounts of employment polarization is one in which firms cut labor costs simply because it is in their interest to do so; the questions of how they cut those costs, under which circumstances they target different kinds of costs and work rules, and which strategic goals they pursue by remaking the employment relationship are not entertained. A well-developed theory of restructuring moves these crucial context questions from the periphery of the discussion to its center by asking how industry structure, regulation, and a firm's market position enable and incentivize it to choose one competitive path over another.

The long-standing economic development practice of differentiating high-road and low-road profit-making strategies illustrates the conceptual and practical importance of such a distinction. This conceptually limited but practically useful duality exerts a significant impact on the practice of economic development policy for the simple reason that it identifies pressure points for policy makers to address. Because economic development practitioners understand high-road employers to pursue profit through product improvements and differentiation—as opposed to the low-road path of building market share by cutting prices—they favorably distinguish policies that emphasize public services, infrastructure, and education from those that feed the low-road goal of minimizing input costs (Luria and Rogers 1999). This conceptual schism between firm types provides a useful, albeit limited, template for translating the complexities of firms and industries into policy. But its contribution toward making corporate strategy legible to policy makers—and replacing a one-size-fits-all view of firms with subtler questions about individual business establishments and industry segments—pushes policy decisions in the right direction. Workers' organizations and their advocates can benefit from a similar conceptualization clarifying links between competitive models and policy opportunities in local-serving industries.

Practically speaking, considering the firm as a strategic actor puts on the table an extensive set of questions and policy options that a traditional, economistic reading of the firm would not allow. Indeed, it should be noted that the same globalization theories that treat working conditions in local industries as a lost cause use such a restructuring analysis to detail a broad range of policy and regulatory considerations for transnational corporations and producer services firms. In the field of economic development, this nuanced reading of the firm and its motivation led practitioners to replace the crude practice of smokestack chasing—luring or retaining footloose firms through tax breaks and subsidies—with a set of more subtle approaches designed to improve employee skill level, tie firms to clusters of linked industries, and lure high-wage employers to high-performance central business districts (Clarke and Gaile 1998). Practitioners accomplished this by replacing the stylized, cost-minimizing employer of economics textbooks with a far better model. This is precisely what needs to be done today in service industries.

Thinking about industries this way offers auxiliary benefits, especially for industries about which we know little without additional research. By focusing closely on the what of an industry—on the particulars of its production process, market structure, and historical geography—the concept of restructuring provides a detailed template for contemporary research to fill in. Given the field's historical focus on manufacturing, restructuring analysis has generated close studies of electronics, aerospace, and even watch manufacturing, each of which yielded distinct conclusions about the constraints on employers and the strategies available to them. If we apply this approach in no more than a cursory manner, we will still benefit from identifying new questions to answer about service industries (Massey and Meegan 1979; Markusen et al. 1991; Glasmeier 2000).

This approach to the issue makes an industry's otherwise frustrating discontinuities—the highly varied way in which different sectors, industry segments, and firms operate across regions, market segments, and regulatory geographies—an analytical asset rather than a problem to be dispensed with. Consider the example of the construction industry. Construction accounts for around 15 percent of all U.S. jobs but just a small fraction of workplace research, thanks to the tremendous difficulty the U.S. Bureau of Labor Statistics encounters in surveying mobile contractors without fixed business addresses. Additionally, the industry's project-based work arrangements result in a wildly varied organization of contracts, bidding, and labor arrangements across different cities, in individual trade specialties, and in different submarkets within the same urban region (Finkel 1997). This combination of poor quantitative data and ever-changing industry organization confounds efforts to understand construction through the same methods researchers use to scrutinize manufacturing. Quite sensibly, the Marxian political economy underlying restructuring theories responds to these discontinuities by making them the entry point into an industry's competitive structure and potential for change. The economic ruptures and discontinuities that economic models of competition struggle to explain move to the center of the analysis.

Though restructuring theories suggest a template for assessing job downgrading in local industries, the task of applying them to those industries must be approached with care. Because they are immobile and because they do not make their products in the way a manufacturer does, employers in local industries must operate within specific competitive constraints that are often less important for manufacturers. The next chapter undertakes the work of articulating an approach for evaluating these local industries. Rather than pitching the exercise at the level of theory, I start with the employment problems to be explained. Wages and working conditions in local industries have undergone a series of remarkable changes in the past decade, and these changes provide crucial clues to the strategies employers are pursuing—and the counterstrategies community–labor coalitions can undertake in response.

## Finding Leverage in Local-Serving Industries

The strength of the arguments in favor of targeting local-serving industries for job upgrading makes the neglect of these industries especially frustrating. In terms of employment, these industries constitute a majority share of urban economies, and a growing one. Retaining the entrenched focus on manufacturing and conventional exporting industries—and on theories, ideas, and policies fitted to those industries—means allowing an ever-increasing share of the economy to operate beyond the purview of established regulatory practices and social norms. The dissolution of postwar Fordism has now lasted more than forty years—significantly longer than the brief period of postwar industrial capitalism, which remains the essential touchstone for ideas about economic structure and labor markets. The growing slippage between our ideas about urban labor markets and their actual organization increasingly places them beyond the control of workers, regulators, and activists.

The *practical* case for coming to terms with these industries is even stronger. The improving ability of manufacturers to seek out low-cost homes with favorable regulatory arrangements suggests that any community victory that results in luring high-wage manufacturing jobs will be time limited. But the service sector employers who sweat work do not have the luxury of becoming runaway shops. They service local markets—indeed, their competitive geographies often stretch no farther than the neighborhood level—and cannot move to lower-cost climates without forsaking their current market share. The historical evolution of capitalism suggests these firms will continue to evolve and find new strategies for evading regulation in place. Nevertheless, targeting these industries and taking seriously the varied strategies and competitive models they use to build profits promises to produce a more enduring set of employment arrangements.

With the question of whether to focus on local-serving industries settled, the question of how to do it takes prominence. The mounting cases of workplace experiments, labor law violations, and fast-paced work in these industries deserve our attention because of the costs they impose on workers and the broader political-economic renegotiations they signal. But they also deserve our attention because they reveal significant information about employers and industries. Identifying the causes, mechanisms, and results of the mounting degradation of low-wage work forces a useful assessment of economic and institutional transformations that support employers' ongoing experimentation with workplace rules. In turn, the highly uneven outcomes of these changes suggest shifting the investigation to workplaces themselves. Even within the same industry and market segment, employers organize the work process and the rules of employment differently. The variation in these practices—the highly specialized way in which businesses link labor-sweating tactics to strategies for profiting in competitive markets—provides more clues about how scholars and activists can engage these industries than does any abstract reworking of the concepts inherited from economic Fordism. In order to understand these industries, we have to understand the work itself.

# 2

# Beyond Low Wages

## *The Problem of Degraded Work*

In 2001 Boeing announced a peculiar high-stakes auction. After a century in the Pacific Northwest, the aerospace giant put its headquarters up for sale. Announcing its intention to relocate to a commercial air hub with a business-friendly climate, Boeing placed Chicago, Denver, and Dallas on a list of suitor cities and asked them to bid for its services. The ensuing frenzy saw the finalist cities offer hundreds of millions in tax incentives and outdo one another in lavish personal appeals to Boeing's executives, all in an effort to land a uniquely appealing prize in the battle for corporate headquarters. Boeing's attraction stemmed from its status as a thriving, research-driven firm of the type that lies at the center of the conventional globalization narrative. In addition to seeking distance from its unionized production workforce, Boeing sought relocation to a bustling central business district in which an army of financiers and deal brokers and makers waited to serve its increasingly financialized business operations (Muellereile 2009).

Boeing's subsequent acceptance of an estimated $56 million in tax incentives from Chicago and the state of Illinois compactly frames the core misalignment of urban economic development policy in the early twenty-first century. For all of the attention lavished upon it, Boeing offered just 500 new corporate jobs—most of which were to be filled by in-migrants from Washington State—at a price of approximately $100,000 apiece. By virtually every available measure, this represented a slim net benefit to the city and the options of its workers.

As then-mayor Richard M. Daley consummated the long courtship with Boeing, Chicago was beginning a long—indeed, historically unprecedented—construction boom that carried the potential to improve wages and working conditions for more than 100,000 workers. Unlike the rarified world of Boeing's financialized activities, construction jobs were available to working people of limited formal education—indeed, the construction workforce contained many of the displaced manufacturing workers whose reemployment had been a key public policy question in the wake of deindustrialization. Despite its greater potential to improve employment outcomes, elected officials ignored the disturbing reports surfacing about wages and working conditions. In the subsequent half decade, the volume of residential construction work in Chicago would more than double. Nevertheless, hourly wages *fell*—a virtually unprecedented event during an economic boom—and workers began to report a breakneck pace of work, catastrophic workplace accidents, nonpayment of wages, and verbal and physical abuse by their employers. As a growing cadre of community- and worker-based organizations began to seek answers to these problems and to organize the city's dangerous day labor corners, the Daley administration met them with resistance rather than support.

At its core, confronting the problem of urban employment inequality means confronting this glaring contrast in policy priorities and workplace outcomes. Across the United States, wages and working conditions in local-serving industries took a turn for the worse in the 2000s, often glaringly so. In a recent survey of low-wage workers spread across residential construction and various other local-serving industries in New York, Chicago, and Los Angeles, nearly half of all workers reported pay violations, more than a quarter had recently worked for less than the minimum wage, and a clear majority of workers was repeatedly denied meal or rest breaks (Bernhardt et al. 2009). I label this phenomenon of low-wage work characterized by an intensified pace of labor and frequent employer violations of basic labor laws *degraded work.* Although dozens of studies document the (extensive) scope of the phenomenon, it remains an afterthought in discussions of urban economies writ large. To the frustrated activists with whom I worked in Chicago, this irony was nearly unbearable: As elected officials publicly fussed over a small number of jobs for skilled professionals they ignored the evidence of a widespread workplace downgrading that carried a far bigger impact for the workforce.

That was the first irony of the situation. The second frustrated workers' advocates just as fully. The industries in which poor working conditions were the norm had little ability to flee regulators. Boeing and its footloose peers could always announce another auction and relocate again if local government or workers grew too demanding. But the contractors, retailers, and temp agencies paying subsistence-level wages had no choice but to ply their trade in Chicago. In other words, public policy focused on areas that were difficult to change and in which the payoff to change was limited.

This happens for many reasons, including simple inertia, the tendency of policy makers to hold on to existing models and solutions. Currently, degraded work remains outside the public eye due to the widespread belief that service sector jobs simply cannot support high wages and a rising standard of living for workers. Even critics of urban inequality who are otherwise sympathetic to the problem of workplace degradation often show limited enthusiasm for campaigns and policy ideas targeted at place-bound industries. The clear response to this unfortunate neglect of opportunities to improve low-wage industries is to clarify that these industries have changed for the worse and to identify the means through which they can be changed for the better.

## Low Pay, Fast Work, and Employer Threats: The Reality at the Bottom of the Labor Market

In the mid-2000s workers in Chicago's flourishing independent supermarkets generally earned $8 or more per hour—a figure significantly better than the $6.50 minimum wage of the time. But this hourly wage, while low, significantly underrepresents the poor and rapidly declining quality of work. Butchers in these bustling markets were asked to work without training, safety equipment, or scheduled rest periods. Many employers maintained a three strikes system that disciplined workers for requesting vacation time, sick days, bathroom breaks, overtime pay, and many other basic workplace benefits to which they were legally entitled. One of the city's burgeoning chains employed public verbal abuse of workers as a customer relations strategy to appease customers who complained about the cuts of meat they purchased. The degradations varied from workplace to workplace, boss to boss, and worker to worker, but the *fact* of degradation, of new forms of discipline and new technologies to extract greater productivity from workers, was a constant.

These workplace degradations are not confined to food retail. Across cities, industries, and occupations, employers are experimenting with the day-to-day conduct of work itself. Meat-packing plants are increasing hourly quotas without increasing hourly wages. Retail workers who used to work full time and for predictable hours now see their schedules—and total number of hours worked—fluctuate from day to day and week to week, often without notice. Time-and-a-half pay for overtime, though still the law, rarely reaches employees' pockets. And when workers protest these degradations, appeal to the authorities, or seek union representation, they lose their job for their efforts. These changes cannot be easily measured like wages, and they are not visible in the standard workplace surveys scholars use to scrutinize the labor market. Even when the degradation of work is visible and plain to see, we lack a conceptual and practical vocabulary for what is happening. Moving these changes in *nonwaged* aspects of employment from the margins to the center of debates over employment inequality is essential: these degradations have a greater impact on firms' competitive options and profit margins and on the ability of workers to share in the good fortune of their employers than does the slow-but-steady erosion of hourly pay.

Low pay remains a significant problem and a defining element of the U.S. labor market vis-à-vis the labor markets of virtually all other industrialized nations (Mason and Salverda 2010). Yet the very prominence of low-wage work suggests that employers will look away from wages for new opportunities to enhance profits, productivity, and labor control. Entry-level pay rates in the United States already lie below the subsistence level, as the reliance of working-poor families on the Earned Income Tax Credit, Medicaid, various State Children's Health Insurance Programs (colloquially, S-CHIP), Temporary Assistance for Needy Families, food stamps, child care subsidies, and a host of other basic income supplements makes clear (Zabin et al. 2004). Although an enterprising employer may be able to force effective hourly pay rates to the federal minimum of $7.25 or lower, that employer is likely to gain more from engineering new ways to make workers toil harder, work faster, skip lunch, and reflexively say yes to any request from a boss.

In other words, the key problem in these workplaces is not falling wages but degraded work: low-wage employment in which employers intensify the pace of work and routinely violate basic labor laws. Defining the problem as encompassing a broad range of workplace characteristics and practices beyond easily quantifiable hourly wage rates clarifies in useful ways the challenges facing workers, activists, and scholars. Crucially, the concept of degraded work requires a full engagement with the specifics of workplaces, employers, and industries. Though the extent of low-wage work in the United States is striking, emphasizing low pay rates clarifies neither the causes nor the solutions to the problem. All things being equal, employers prefer paying less to paying more. Marxists and neoclassical economists agree on this simple point, which suggests that wage inequality is business as usual or worse, the product of market dynamics over which workers and the community organizations working on their behalf have no control. As I detail, the primary tactic that firms degrading work use to suppress labor costs is outright legal evasion—the payment of subminimum wages, the underpayment of overtime, and the nonpayment of agreed-upon compensation levels for work performed.

It is tempting to think of blatantly unsafe working conditions and flagrant employer violations of labor laws as isolated incidents, problems so extreme they must be the equivalent of statistical outliers. But degraded work practices are widespread across a broad number of industries and occupations. They have been documented in especially minute detail in the New York, Chicago, and Los Angeles labor markets, where the combination of extensive immigration, withering manufacturing economies, and wealthy professionals has entrenched the ground conditions in which local-serving industries and labor-sweating practices flourish. But the specific constellations of degraded work practices that workers encounter vary from city to city, industry to industry, and occupation to occupation—in fact, they often vary under the same employer and within the same workplace. Figure 1 summarizes the key industries in which degraded work practices flourish, as documented by sociologists, geographers, and urban planners during the 2000s.

The existing body of scholarship on degraded work began with a narrow focus on specific industries embedded in single cities. Based on intensive interviews and exhaustive documentation at the industry level, these studies identify the outlines of a broader problem to be charted. As the documented scope of degraded work expanded, scholarship on the problem grew more ambitious. In the mid-2000s researchers launched a series of large-sample-size studies documenting degraded work in a wide range of cities, industries, and occupations. The resulting picture of labor degradation is exhaustive. Across multiple industries, low pay, fast work, and selective compliance with workplace laws are the norm. At the same time, these studies fashion a clear picture of heterogeneous degradation. There is no one-to-one correspondence between working conditions and industries; interview-based and industry-focused work draws out the unique ways that individual employers intensify the work process and hold the line on compensation. But the fact of multiple, overlapping labor

| Author(s) | Year | Key Industries with Labor Violations: Auto Repair | Building Maint. & Security | Child Care | Durable Manufacturing | Food Service | Food Retail | General Retail | Health Services | Laundries & Dry Cleaning | Meatpacking | Nondurable Manufacturing | Personal Services | Residential Construction | Restaurants | Transportation | Common Violations: Subminimum Wages | Unpaid Overtime | Wage Theft | Illegal Dismissal | Health and Safety | Other |
|---|---|---|---|---|---|---|---|---|---|---|---|---|---|---|---|---|---|---|---|---|---|---|
| Bernhardt et al. | 2009 | | ■ | | | | ■ | ■ | | | | ■ | ■ | | ■ | ■ | ■ | ■ | ■ | ■ | ■ | ■ |
| Sassen | 2008 | | | ■ | | | | | | | | ■ | | ■ | ■ | | | | | | | ■ |
| Bernhardt, McGrath, and DeFilippis | 2007 | ■ | ■ | ■ | ■ | | ■ | ■ | | ■ | ■ | | ■ | ■ | ■ | ■ | ■ | ■ | ■ | ■ | ■ | ■ |
| Fine | 2006 | ■ | | ■ | | | | ■ | | ■ | ■ | ■ | | | | | ■ | ■ | ■ | ■ | ■ | ■ |
| Bernhardt et al. | 2006 | | | ■ | ■ | ■ | ■ | ■ | ■ | ■ | | | ■ | ■ | | ■ | ■ | ■ | ■ | ■ | ■ | ■ |
| Valenzuela Jr. et al. | 2006 | | | | | | | | | | | | | ■ | | | ■ | ■ | ■ | ■ | ■ | |
| Mehta and Theodore | 2006 | | | | | | | | | | | | | ■ | | | | | ■ | | ■ | |
| Ness | 2005 | | | | | ■ | ■ | | | | | | | | | ■ | ■ | ■ | ■ | ■ | ■ | ■ |
| Gordon | 2005 | | | | | | | | ■ | | | | ■ | ■ | | | ■ | ■ | ■ | ■ | ■ | |
| Restaurant Opportunities Center of New York | 2005 | | | | | | | | | | | | | | ■ | | ■ | ■ | | ■ | ■ | |
| Weil | 2005 | | | | | | | | | | | | | ■ | | | | | | | ■ | ■ |
| Waldinger and Lichter | 2003 | | | | ■ | | | ■ | | | | ■ | | | | | ■ | ■ | ■ | ■ | ■ | |
| Theodore | 2003 | | | | | | | | | | | ■ | | | | | | | ■ | | ■ | |
| Sassen | 2001 | | | | ■ | | | | | | | ■ | | ■ | | | | | | | | ■ |
| Marcelli, Pastor, and Joassert | 1999 | | | | ■ | | | | | | | | ■ | ■ | | | ■ | | | ■ | ■ | ■ |

*Figure 1. Key Industries and Labor Law Violations Identified in Major Studies of Low-Wage Labor Markets.*

law violations remains a constant: individual cases of labor sweating lie within a broader framework of employer strategies that simultaneously target flexibility, a fast pace of work, and the minimization of labor costs.

## Using Working Conditions to Understand Employer Strategy and Find Leverage

The concept of degraded work suggests a focus on profit maximization rather than just simple labor cost cutting. Profit making provides a bigger window into the workings of firms and industries and fashions a framework that places legal evasion and working conditions in the same conceptual space as simple low wages. When employers add to hourly quotas or browbeat employees into skipping lunch breaks and paid vacation or shuffle a worker's scheduled employment hours to minimize idle time, they enable new competitive strategies and enhance profit margins without cutting pay rates in a readily visible way. Thus, making sense of degraded work means making sense of the strategies, tactics, and market-making practices employers use to maximize the benefits of low-wage work.

The strategic ends to which employer use degraded work vary extensively in some industries and minimally in others, and the ways in which they vary are simultaneously surprising and predictable. For example, manufacturers who contract with temporary help agencies use employment flexibility to hold down wages, evade regulatory responsibility, and minimize the paid employment hours for which they are responsible. This approach is a logical fit for insulating manufacturers in cost-competitive, deskilled industry segments from persistent market risk (Theodore 2003). Day labor, an extreme and informalized form of temporary employment, provides the same cost-cutting advantages to construction contractors. But it also allows them to solve the basic, ever-present problem of assembling project teams whose composition, skills, and availability must shift from day to day to match the ever-changing construction process (Finkel 1997). Shifting the analytical frame from low wages to degraded work and from cost cutting to profit maximizing clarifies that firms gain much more than simple cost reductions from degrading work and that the strategic uses of labor degradation vary with a firm's market position and the type of work it performs.

This shift in thinking matters. An emphasis on labor degradation leads to questions about an employer's competitive stance, market position, and profit-making strategy, all of which help to open up new areas in which to conceptualize responses to the problem. Efforts to reverse labor degradation face substantial barriers in the form of weak regulation, minimal political will, and strong employer opposition. Typically, the push to reregulate these workplaces emanates from worker centers, unions, community-based organizations, and other local actors seeking leverage with which to press individual employers, industry segments, and local industries to upgrade job quality. The more these actors know about a firm's business model, its interaction with regulators, and its market position, the more they can tailor their activities to the particulars of the situation. Perfect policies and organizing campaigns remain elusive, of course, and any community organization attempt to regulate workplaces by itself faces a formidable challenge. But it is easier to regulate specific firms, industries, and markets—and significantly easier to regulate place-bound employers than footloose ones—than to regulate the stylized widget makers of textbooks.

Consider the following examples of two organizing efforts, one aimed at a footloose manufacturer, the other at janitorial services firms tied to a specific submarket. The first, led by a UNITE HERE! Local union against a New Bedford, Massachusetts, plant operated by the military equipment manufacturer Eagle Industries, attempted to secure union representation and a collective bargaining agreement at the site of a high-profile immigration raid. In its previous incarnation as Michael Bianco Inc., the employer (staffed by many of the same managers) had combined threats against the residency status of its primarily undocumented workforce with a fast pace of work and nonpayment of overtime hours to maximize its profits from a fixed contract with the U.S. Department of Defense (Juravich and Williams 2011; Nicodemus 2007).

The ease with which employers violate the National Labor Relations Act during union-organizing campaigns has led most contemporary unions to abandon workplace votes in favor of campaigns encouraging employers to allow outright union recognition at the point that a majority of workers has signed cards declaring its wishes for a union election. Without a clear market relationship to pressure, the workers and UNITE HERE! combined familiar appeals to justice and fairness with political pressure on the Department of Defense agency overseeing the firm's sole-source defense contract.[1] The campaign took advantage of the few pressure points available to the workers, but the threat of capital mobility limited its success. After an out-of-state defense contractor bought the New Bedford facility and moved to close it, the workers successfully delayed the closing and used public outrage against the footloose employer to secure a union contract with the firm New Bedford had hired to take its place. Given the small number of pressure points union advocates were able to target in the campaign, this represented a favorable outcome.

The approaches and outcomes of the military manufacturing campaign stand in sharp contrast to the Los Angeles–based Justice for Janitors campaign. The plan to win union recognition with the Service Employees International Union (SEIU) and, thus, improve wages and working conditions for those employed by low-wage, law-breaking janitorial subcontractors rested on a top-to-bottom analysis of the industry. This analysis showed that the janitorial contractors who hired those subcontractors depended on contracts in downtown buildings—an industry characteristic that suggested clear ways in which the workers could target their efforts. They staged public protests designed to embarrass the well-heeled firms cleaned by subcontracted workers who toiled in miserable conditions. At the same time, they pressured the Los Angeles Community Redevelopment Authority to make building approvals contingent upon fair contracting, and they prevailed on the pension funds for California's unionized public workforce to use their influence as investors. These actions enabled the SEIU to gradually unionize the industry, leading to significant improvements in pay and workplace quality (Milkman 2006). The immobility of employers, combined with a dense network of intervention points for union activists, led to the reregulation of a previously cost-competitive labor market.

As these examples suggest, workers and their advocates already link degraded work conditions to employer strategy and employer strategy to their own plans for action. But an employer's ability to relocate—an ability that manufacturers possess but janitorial firms do not—limits the strategies available to workers, as does an employer's disregard of a positive public image. These small examples hint at the much greater potential to tease out trends, patterns, and distinctions from place- and sector-based organizing campaigns designed to combat degraded work. But the communicative frameworks through which workers, unions, community organizations, and sympathetic regulators can exchange ideas remain limited. Currently, these organizations share knowledge through what scholars label *mimetic isomorphism,* straightforwardly copying the activities of their successful peers (Milkman 2010). This has led to convergence in the general tactics used to improve degraded work arrangements, but no institutionalized vocabulary exists to chart the employer practices, regulatory inflection points, and market fissures to which these practices can be employed. Building that vocabulary requires a broader focus on the institutional regulation of low-wage labor markets and on the unique pressures employers face at the industry level.

## How We Got Here: The Origins and Expansion of Degraded Work

Responses to degraded work face the challenge of addressing an urban-scale problem rooted in multiple political-economic shifts at the national level. Fundamentally, degraded work follows from the increasing latitude employers have to renegotiate wages and working conditions and the diminishment of institutional safeguards allowing workers to bargain on their own behalf. From afar, degraded work looks a lot like contingent work—temporary, contract, or on-call employment performed outside the auspices of the long-term, full-time employer–employee relationship—and this is no accident. The growth of contingent work relationships in the 1990s marked a transformation of employer strategy within the workplace. By the end of the 1990s' expansion, these jobs accounted for nearly 5 percent of total employment and more than 10 percent in the most heavily impacted industries and occupations (Hipple 2001).

Temporary and contract work arrangements were not new, but the aggressiveness with which employers pursued them was. Historically, temporary employment was rooted in the need to match labor hours to highly variable product demand, and temporary workers were mainly employed to provide extra labor power when production needs spiked (Gordon, Edwards, and Reich 1982; Theodore and Peck 2002). The expansion of contingent work transformed these employment arrangements from tactical responses to market fluctuations into strategic instruments of employer control over labor, wages, and benefits (Peck 1996; Appelbaum 2000). In high-wage industries and low, the maintenance of an arm's-length relationship with employees has since restrained workers' ability to push for raises and improved benefits, to challenge the conditions of work, and to organize labor unions (Benner 1996; Mehta and Theodore 2000). Contingent workers enjoy fewer formal legal rights than year-round, full-time employees, and the need to constantly audition for continued employment makes them reluctant to exercise the rights they do possess.

The expansion of contingent work proceeded in tandem with the gradual weakening of the New Deal–era laws that improved workers' footing in the workplace. Among the most prominently weakened laws and institutions was the federal minimum wage, whose inflation-adjusted value fell from more than $10 an hour (in 2011 dollars) in 1968 to $7.25 today. At the same time, the institutionalization of an antiunion political climate and the rise of union-avoidance consulting cut nationwide union density from 29.3 percent in 1964 to 19.1 percent in 1984, 13.6 percent in 2000, and less than 10 percent today. Other measures that had historically allowed workers to sit out bad labor markets were also weakened. Prominent among these was the reduction of welfare benefits (and imposition of workfare requirements) mandated by the Personal Responsibility and Work Opportunities Reconciliation Act of 1996. Cumulatively, these changes have severely restricted workers' bargaining power by curtailing the option to opt out of substandard employment.

These changes are staples of any narrative of inequality. But a less-documented, equally significant shift in *enforcement,* as opposed to legal coverage, is perhaps more important. Employer violation of labor laws is a basic element of degraded work for the simple reason that personnel and budgets at the agencies charged with enforcing the law have absorbed tremendous cuts. Since the mid-1970s enforcement budgets for most labor regulations, particularly wage-and-hour and workplace safety laws, have shrunk in comparison with the size of the economy. The reduction in funding for the U.S. Department of Labor's Wage and Hour Division, which enforces the federal minimum wage, overtime pay, and other basic wage protections, typifies the problem. From 1975 to 2004, the number of business establishments covered by wage-and-hour laws grew by 112 percent, yet the number of workplace inspectors actually decreased by 14 percent (Bernhardt and McGrath 2005). Subsequent improvements in funding levels under the Obama administration have begun to reverse this downward trend, but aggregate enforcement funding remains low compared with postwar standards (Dixon and Evangelist 2011). In the absence of viable enforcement, wage-and-hour violations have become a central feature of labor relations in low-wage, labor-intensive industries.

Enforcement of other federal laws, particularly those administered by the Occupational Safety and Health Administration (OSHA) and the National Labor Relations Board (NLRB), has also been scaled back. In the case of OSHA, this rollback undermines an agency charged with a difficult task even under the best of circumstances. When firm sizes are small, the number of workplaces to monitor in an industry is large. This makes effective safety regulation difficult even when funding is ample. As OSHA assigns fewer and fewer inspectors to a growing number of workplaces (and pursues a formally cooperative, win-win stance with firms) meaningful enforcement of the law increasingly depends on the presence of a collective bargaining unit to educate workers, collect complaints, and protect whistleblowers (Weil 1991). In other words, the decline of one institution can be mitigated only by a similarly declining institution.

The unions that can provide this enforcement are shrinking, and the weakening of the labor movement plays a significant role in the expansion of degraded work practices. Ideally, unions would respond to falling membership numbers by organizing new workers. They try—and try aggressively—but typically fail. In the 2000s, 30 percent of all employers faced with a union election responded by illegally firing workers, an action that the small fines imposed by the NLRB fail to deter (Eaton and Kriesky 2006). Many antiunion activities fall deliberately in a legal grey area. Employers frequently use coordinated, professionalized antiunion campaigns that carefully blend legally permissible actions (mandatory company-wide meetings, one-on-one meetings between management and workers) and illegal tactics (employee dismissal, reduced hours, deliberately unworkable schedules, explicit threats to relocate the company) to undermine union support (Levine 2007). The power of these threats is increased by the fact that the low-wage workforce increasingly consists of immigrants who lack other employment options and cannot afford to be dismissed at any cost. Numerous studies have shown that tight household finances, border crossing debts, and the lack of options for job upgrading make even the threat of illegal termination a powerful tool for employers (Cornelius 2005).

For decades union support and regular workplace inspections insulated many workers from the labor-sweating tactics employers often adopt, whether by opportunity or necessity, in cost-competitive industries. The growing ineffectiveness of these regulatory forces is evident in workplaces in which disputes over pay, working conditions, and workplace safety are frequent, and employer compliance with labor laws is increasingly optional. Today, these changes allow employers to experiment with new work rules in workplaces where many employees are uniquely vulnerable to pressure from their managers.

Little has been documented about the paths through which this experimentation unfolds. How firms respond to cost-cutting pressure from labor-sweating competitors is one of the central questions posed by research on contemporary economic restructuring. Scholars have fared much better at capturing this transformation in the aggregate than at the level of firms and business owners. For example, the turn toward cost-based competition and labor cost reductions in the food retail industry has been well documented (Davis et al. 2005). But the important question of how this transformation took place can be answered only inferentially. The employers interviewed for this book could not definitively state how they came by their workplace practices. For industry-standard labor law violations, such as paying overtime hours at the normal hourly rate, employers simply identified the practice as normal for the industry. Focusing on industry-level as opposed to economy-wide adaptations of degraded work practices helps to identify the important role played by the practice of scanning an industry for new ideas in market-making strategies and workplace practices. Especially when they operate in local-serving industries in which businesses compete block by block for market share, employers constantly monitor the competition. In food retail and residential construction, the pace at which employers churn through workers makes employees themselves a medium for transmitting ideas. Although some of the mechanisms for transferring ideas about workplace practice can be identified, the specific ways in which employers disaggregate, test, and evaluate particular technologies for degrading work and speeding the pace of production remains an important topic for future research.

## The Precarious Position of Undocumented Workers

By 2007 approximately twelve million unauthorized immigrants were present in the United States (Passel and Cohn 2011).[2] The overwhelming majority of these immigrants have come for the purpose of working, with most settling in urban areas, where they significantly impact the local labor market. In metropolitan Chicago, the area scrutinized in this book, undocumented immigrants constituted as much as 15 percent of the workforce by 2002 (Mehta et al. 2002).

Newspapers and popular academic accounts of immigration aggressively link documentation status to low-wage work and dangerous workplaces, and although undocumented workers disproportionately labor in degraded conditions, gaining legal work authorization would not eliminate their problems. From wage theft to absent safety equipment to last-minute changes to scheduled hours and pay, native-born workers also experience degraded working conditions and at a surprisingly high rate (Bernhardt et al. 2009). Thus, making sense of the role played by legal immigration status requires a careful analytical balance. Undocumented workers and the problems of degraded work are not synonymous, but these workers deserve extra attention for their uniquely precarious and vulnerable position in the labor market. Apart from the general legal indeterminacy that follows these laborers, three distinct aspects of working without legal authorization make undocumented workers especially susceptible to employer threats and unusually accommodating of work rule experimentation.

First, undocumented workers have a limited knowledge of U.S. labor laws. Owing to their formative work experience beyond the U.S. border, these immigrants typically possess limited knowledge of their legal rights in the workplace. Legal clinics, workers' organizations, and labor unions have found that workers remain unaware of basic legal prescriptions on the minimum wage, eligibility for overtime pay, and worker rights to vacation, sick time, and fair dismissal (Bernhardt et al. 2005; DeFilippis et al. 2007; Mehta, Theodore and Hincapié 2003). The employers of these workers can often break the law without their employees knowing it.[3]

Second, undocumented workers are loath to register complaints about workplace abuses for fear of their undocumented status coming to light. The fact that a worker's family members and friends frequently share her employer and stand to be disciplined in retaliation can intensify this reluctance (Waldinger and Lichter 2003). Employers often threaten to discipline or fire complaining workers directly—a threat that carries significant weight for individuals who owe large sums to the *coyotes* who escorted them across the border (Massey, Durand, and Malone 2003). Interest on *coyote* debt, secured by the worker's family and possessions in her country of origin, makes uninterrupted income streams a necessity for newly arrived workers. Given the choice of degraded work or mounting *coyote* debt, undocumented workers opt for degraded work. The need to pay off this interest also increases their susceptibility to employer reprisals in the form of retributive cutting of work hours or weekly pay.

These forms of reprisal against workers are slowly gaining an institutional footing as the result of legal changes reducing sanctions on lawbreaking employers and erecting barriers to employees qualifying for some workplace protections and benefits. Primary among these is the U.S.

Supreme Court's landmark ruling in *Hoffman Plastics Compounds v. NLRB,* which denies back pay to undocumented workers illegally dismissed by employers for union-organizing activities (National Employment Law Project 2003). Among notable state-level changes, a ruling by the Michigan Supreme Court denies undocumented workers the right to receive workers' compensation for on-the-job injuries (National Immigration Law Center 2004). Just as the legal patchwork created by state-level decisions on temporary employment provided a foothold for the expansion of the temporary help supply industry, these seemingly remote legal decisions increasingly formalize terms on which employers can legally discriminate against the undocumented workers they have knowingly, deliberately hired.

Third, a lack of certified employment skills, combined with limited English proficiency, slots workers into deskilled jobs. A large number of undocumented immigrants to the United States were rural laborers in their country of origin. Those immigrants who do have formal educational credentials often find that they translate poorly to U.S. labor markets, especially when their undocumented status is considered (Valenzuela Jr. et al. 2006; Valenzuela Jr. 2003). This lack of formal qualifications concentrates these workers in low-wage and cost-competitive segments of the labor market, creating areas of excess supply and substantially shifting the terms of labor market competition within particular industries and industry segments.

In these key ways undocumented status makes workers susceptible to employers' labor-degrading activities. But the form those degradations take is wide open. Far from flowing directly and simply from the fact of undocumented status, experimentation in the workplace depends on a score of other challenges, opportunities, and competitive threats employers face.

## Necessary but Not Sufficient: Unenforced Laws Lead to Uneven Workplace Outcomes

Undocumented immigrants come to the United States to work, and yet the work they do remains an afterthought in both media accounts and academic accounts of labor market change. In between the incompatible discourses on immigrant workers—that they takes jobs from Americans or, alternately, do jobs Americans won't do—lies the reality of employers who degrade work as part of a broader strategy for negotiating market insecurity and generating profits. Unfortunately, these strategies remain poorly understood, and the cost-minimizing employer suggested by most accounts of degraded work differs substantially from the specific businesses that workers, advocates, and public servants attempt to regulate.

At the level of industries, the firms degrading work in the United States share clear commonalities. With surprisingly few exceptions, they operate in local-serving industries—construction, retail, cleaning services, food services, hotels—insulated from international market competition. While insulation from competition with offshore rivals operating in nations with low factor costs should in theory mitigate tendencies to cost-based competition in locally oriented firms, other industry-level characteristics in fact intensify that competition. The most easily identifiable of these is the work itself. Degraded work arrangements are most prevalent in labor-intensive occupations, such as drywaller (but not electrician) in construction, hand packer (but not machine operator) in manufacturing, and janitorial and household worker in personal services. In some cases employers sweat labor as an alternative to making expensive capital investments, but in others the nature of the work being done restricts the capacity to substitute capital for labor. Residential construction work, for example, remains so bound up in the idiosyncrasies of individual buildings that few machines can substitute for the basic toil of demolishing walls, gutting bathrooms, and installing fixtures (Finkel 1997, 24). Similarly, capital technologies are unable to supplant the basic janitorial tasks of dusting and mopping or the hotel worker's core assignments of bed making and toilet scrubbing. Given limited capacity to substitute capital for labor, firms instead focus on limited labor costs and use capital investment primarily to reinforce control over workers (Braverman 1974).

The structure of the industries themselves likewise pushes firms toward cost-based competition. The locally oriented industries in which degraded work flourishes typically spread employment across a large number of small workplaces. The durable manufacturing industries of the Fordist-era economy, in which the current workplace regulatory apparatus was developed, were typically dominated by a small number of large firms that proved easy for regulators to visit and monitor. By contrast, degraded work practices are clustered in deconcentrated industries shaped by the absence of dominant firms and intense competition between a large number of competitors. Workplace inspectors and regulators struggle to cover an industry's numerous and geographically diffuse workplaces, and the number of organizing campaigns necessary to make collective bargaining the main mode of workplace governance within an industry outstrips the resources of every union.

Less noted but equally important, these smaller employers lack price-setting power and are more likely than manufacturers to compete based on cost. When market share is split between just a few key firms, products tend to be differentiated by quality as much as price, and interfirm competition revolves around branding, service, and name recognition. But as the number of participants in the markets grows, prices (rather than product differentiation or quality) become entrenched as the basis of competition (Hudson 2001). Beset by competition on product prices, deconcentrated industries typically demonstrate lower profit margins and a greater focus on restraining labor costs than do industries that readily provide other paths to profit. In addition to the labor intensiveness of the work and firms' minimal capacity for capital upgrading, this provides a strong incentive for employers to hold labor costs—not just wages but benefits, insurance payments, and all of the other costs of employment—as low as possible.

Industry dynamics can intensify this pressure to cut labor costs. Industries composed of smaller firms have lower barriers to entry in terms of start-up costs and fixed capital needs. As a result new establishments swiftly enter the market and begin competing for market share whenever there is obvious growth, particularly in industries such as residential construction, temporary help supply, and corner store food retail (Philips 2003; Peck and Theodore 2001; Ness 2005). Those new competitors often attempt to gain market share through price discounts, and the ensuing competition tends to keep the number of firms operating in an industry level relative to market share.[4] Such competitive dynamics reinforce the value of maintaining low labor costs as a means of realizing cost savings and building competitive advantage.

These competitive characteristics form an obvious barrier to efforts to improve working conditions; they place firms in positions where sweating work is an especially attractive option. But the repeated enumeration of these barriers—primarily in narratives about globalization but also in nationwide surveys designed to document the structural expansion of labor degradation—itself forms a significant barrier to the *conceptual* work community organizations, unions, and workers need to do in order to win change in the workplace. Simply put, focusing on labor-intensive work, cost-competitive industries, and small firm sizes suggests that employers in local-serving industries approximate the perfectly competitive employers that emerge from the Hobbesian stylizations of economics models. When condensed to a two-dimensional graph in a textbook, the real and complicated world of production and profit making becomes a cost-competitive abstraction in which it is nearly impossible to envision leverage for workers. But when considered in all their idiosyncratic detail, the firms degrading work appear entirely differently.

## Getting Local: How Workers' Organizations Translate Structural Employment Change into Local Organizing Strategies

Even when scholars draw attention to important distinctions between labor-sweating employers (Bernhardt, McGrath and DeFilippis 2008), the focus on *national-level* structural changes provides little guidance for the ad hoc assemblage of immigrant associations, worker centers, and local labor unions tasked with remedying the problem at the urban level (Fine 2006; Theodore and Martin 2007). Although these organizations increasingly are members of national networks engaged in policy maneuvers to mitigate the institutional sources of degraded work, their authority and reach are explicitly local: an immigrant worker's association in Los Angeles can protest individual employers and build relationships with county commissioners, but it cannot single-handedly double funding for OSHA and Department of Labor inspections. Though useful in the service of a (necessary) nationwide political agenda, framing degraded work as a systematic problem based on structural changes is fundamentally at odds with the delicate work of looking for leverage with particular employers, regulatory agencies, consumer bases, and state legislatures.

The most promising responses to degraded work—such as the local restaurant worker centers linked through the national Restaurant Opportunities Centers United network and community–labor campaigns based on the Justice for Janitors model—tailor their strategies in response to detailed research on local employers. Unfortunately, most organizing efforts operate with few dedicated staff, outside the domain of organized labor, and without access to national-level organizations that generalize knowledge of an industry's weaknesses and organizing opportunities. Just as often, they focus on industries that lack obvious organizing targets—as is almost always the case when the employers in question are construction contractors. The kind of expertise-driven research that fuels successful industry-focused campaigns lies beyond the reach of these hard-working but modestly endowed organizations (Milkman 2006).

The heterogeneous localized responses to degraded work need a conceptual framework through which to piece together ideas from other campaigns and to share and generalize their own responses to the problem. A crucial step in building this framework is to move past the stylized picture of employers as cost-competitive entities with few options for market success apart from shearing labor costs. This is not to say there is no truth to that perception. It accurately characterizes an essential part of what has happened to low-wage workplaces, especially when the firms in questions are subcontractors who operate outside the public view. But focusing on cost cutting without a broader focus on the industry, its regulations, and its unique market pressures means foregoing the opportunity to take advantage of the competitive asymmetries and weaknesses that allow workers' advocates to escape the increasingly unfavorable terrain of values-based organizing campaigns.

Many of the industries in which degraded work flourishes, including retail, residential construction, restaurants, building maintenance, and security, feature substantial interaction between customers and workers, allowing organizers to effectively use public pressure (Archer et al. 2010). In other industries—and often in those same industries—firms rely on spatially delimited markets and complex contracting processes, factors that insulate, mitigate, and complicate the drive toward cost-based competition (Bernhardt, McGrath, and DeFilippis 2008). Hotels need to locate near tourist districts, convention centers, and airports, a fact that UNITE HERE! union locals use to win concessions from employers seeking permits. Construction contractors need to assemble and reassemble teams of drywallers, framers, and general laborers every day, a need that makes street corner day labor shape-ups strategic sites for worker centers.

The competitive models and market pressures in these industries echo and diverge in ways that cannot be grasped without a framework that makes those dimensions of profit making explicit. The same theories of economic restructuring that motivated generalized community–labor response to deindustrialization a generation ago (see Giloth 1996) provide an ideal means for clarifying the industry-level specificity of degraded work pressures—and responses—today. In the 1980s opponents of leveraged buyouts and runaway manufacturing shops faced the same basic challenges that confront contemporary critics of employment inequality. In response to claims that deindustrialization was natural and inevitable, they seized on critical economic theories to identify distinct *limits* to the supposedly all-powerful hand of market discipline and the allegedly perfect mobility of manufacturing plants. This logic still applies. By seeking spatially delimited markets, targeting discreet subpopulations, retooling capital investment and bulk-purchasing strategies, and using organizational flexibility in creative ways, firms in local-serving industries chart distinct paths to limiting the persistent cost-based competition that threatens them. Identifying, naming, and testing the techniques that they use to do this yields an actionable map of potential organizing tactics and transferrable strategies that workers and their advocates can use to improve degraded work conditions.

## Identifying Limits to Cost-Based Competition and Opportunities to Reverse Degradation

The community organizer's instinct to focus on cost-based competition makes sense on its own terms. Virtually every scholar of economic development and economic restructuring agrees that the differences between price- and quality-competitive firms are crucial. The distinction between firms that compete through customized goods, skilled labor, and higher wages and cost-competitive firms that operate under conditions close to those of perfect competition remains one of the most essential and productive in the field. Among its other benefits, it foregrounds the importance of firm organization and strategy in industry analysis. Cost- and quality-based competitive strategies are seen to signal different sets of policy and community concerns and different strategies for encouraging employers to improve job quality. Just as important, considering a firm's strategy forces scholars to treat businesses as institutional actors responding to a bundle of concerns and opportunities—a remarkable improvement from the more economistic view that cost cutting drives all labor-related decisions.

Important though it is, the distinction between cost- and quality-based competitive strategies is often muddled at the industry level. Indeed, empirical work on firm strategies identifies clear ways that actually existing firms simultaneously compete on both low prices and product differentiation. As geographer Ray Hudson notes, the distinction tends to fall apart when one considers the reality that "a company can pursue several types of strategy simultaneously" (Hudson 2001, 144). The general concentration of labor-sweating practices in low-wage industries and higher-wage employment in firms stressing customization and product innovation cannot be ignored. But the relationship is fluid and dynamic. Hudson notes that many British manufacturers in the 1990s responded to competition from offshore producers by simultaneously investing in technology, pursuing customers with higher purchasing power, and *cutting wages* (Hudson 2001, 144). The conventional wisdom today says that sweatshop employees make interchangeable goods for which a retailer can command no price premium. But Saskia Sassen finds that many contemporary New York manufacturing sweatshops are devoted to the manufacture of custom clothing and furniture rather than to mass-produced textile work (Sassen 1998, 297). Rather than follow a fixed model, employers are often able to combine market and labor strategies that academic theories suggest are incompatible.

Why do some firms sweat labor when we expect them to reward work and vice versa? Analysts of restructuring emphasize that many factors besides the product at hand influence the production process. Andrew Sayer and Richard Walker's study of multinational manufacturers in flux found capital equipment investments to be a determining factor (Sayer and Walker 1992). Firms that invested multimillion-dollar sums in new technology rearranged their entire work processes around that technology in order to maximize their returns on investment. A firm could target equipment that either supported flexible production—and the highly skilled workers who went along with it—or low-cost production, the profits from which were most effectively realized by deskilled labor and cutting workers' pay.

But firms with limited investments in production equipment need not choose between approaches. From restaurants to residential construction contracting to neighborhood retail, the majority of the local-oriented industries degrading work fit this description. Far from having fewer strategic options available to them, as the conventional wisdom suggests, they have more. This insight is the major point of departure for identifying new organizing leverage in local industries that have long been thought to compete exclusively on cost. Low start-up costs and limited capital investment needs free firms to experiment with multiple competitive strategies. Without plant, property, and equipment automatically locking them into one strategy at the expense of others, firms can shift, combine, and recombine their competitive approaches, emphasizing different combinations of quality and cost in different situations.

Viewing service firms through this lens proposes a new set of key questions about conditions that mitigate what has previously been seen as an uncomplicated drive toward cost-based competition. Intuitively, we can think of several candidates: cases where consumers cannot identify or act on differentials in service cost (including cases of geographical isolation between firms, as is the case with many neighborhood retailers), cases where service quality is valued (such as high-end retailers or construction contractors of high repute), and cases where regulation can change competitive standards across an industry (living-wage ordinances come to mind). The empirical details in manufacturing industries differ, but the same conceptual categories—market segmentation, quality-based competition, regulatory restructuring—structure the conversation. What remains to be done is to formalize the theoretical translation, to spell out in clear terms how we can expect competition and employment terms in service sectors to change or resist change.

## Market-Making Power in Local-Serving Industries

Michael Storper and Richard Walker's formulation of strong and weak competitive strategies provides a useful vessel for this work. On the surface the strong/weak distinction directly maps onto the high-road/low-road distinction commonly used in the field of economic development (Storper and Walker 1989). Loosely speaking, strong forms of competition revolve around product quality and differentiation. These strategies carry tendencies toward the employment of skilled and well-paid workers, but exceptions to the general rule abound. Weak competition, like low-road competition, emphasizes low prices and cost cutting and suggests downward pressure on prices. Storper and Walker clarify the issue by suggesting that a firm's ability to pursue either one of these strategies rests on a series of internal and external factors absent in most industry analyses. To succeed with a strong strategy, a firm must be able to produce fragmented end markets—that is, it needs to identify or make distinctive specialty markets or submarkets that push most potential competitors out of the picture—and must be able to retool its production process in order to take advantage of market opportunities. Weak competition dominates when firms are price takers rather than price setters and when they cannot tailor products or services to take advantage of opportunities for differentiation (Storper and Walker 1989, 66–69).

Empirical support for this position comes from history and theory alike. Ann Markusen's *Profit Cycles, Oligopoly, and Regional Development* most clearly illustrates the trend (Markusen 1985). Following industries as they branch out from their historical homes over multiple business cycles, Markusen shows that the familiar descent from unionized high-wage manufacturing jobs to low-wage jobs in the U.S. South and offshore originates in a firm's diminishing ability to fragment markets and protect profit margins. When a firm launches a new technology or product, it has a distinct market advantage and can charge a sizable premium for its product. Historically, auto manufacturing in Detroit and aerospace in Seattle typify the phenomenon. But as competitors catch up and surplus production floods the initial consumer market, dominant firms can no longer command a price premium. This analysis reveals a footloose industry to be an industry in which firms settle for cutting labor costs after they have lost the ability to set prices. In exporting industries, capital mobility—the gradual relocation of General Motors from Michigan to the Upper Midwest and Canada, then the South, and then Mexico—provides evidence of diminished market-fragmenting power. Of course, we cannot use firm relocation patterns to identify competitive shifts in local nonexporting industries, but the underlying principles remain the same: firms with distinctive end markets and the ability to set rather than take prices have greater leeway to pay high wages. Despite the long-term theoretical neglect of local-serving industries, we can easily spot several key areas in which locally oriented firms have the ability to make markets.

As is the case with manufacturing firms, location provides the clearest information on a firm's market-making power. But the interpretation of this information differs. Firms in local-serving industries generally locate near their desired customer base (which can often be the same as their workforce base), and for sound reasons. Retailing has a limited catchment area; depending on the market and the size of the store, a retailer can expect competition to be limited to a few miles' radius (Reynolds and Wood 2010). Many of the industries cited in studies of low-wage work are mobile within local markets—think construction contractors, security contractors, or janitorial services firms. For these firms the crucial factor is where they perform their work rather than where they set up their business headquarters.

In the locally oriented industries in which degraded work strategies prevail, the locational component of strategy typically entails relocation into underserved urban neighborhoods and subregions, where the comparative lack of competition translates into expanded sales and increased rent-generating capacity. Significantly, the distinctive geographies of post-Fordist cities—characterized by highly differentiated pockets of wealth, poverty, immigration, disinvestment, and reinvestment—enhance a firm's ability to fragment markets by *offering increasingly fragmented consumers to target.* The proprietors of supermarkets, bodégas, and laundromats routinely scan the local market for areas of underservice, rising or falling income levels relative to the existing business mix, and pockets of new immigrant populations whose allegiance can be sewn up with appeals to coethnicity. In fact, a bustling business literature counsels would-be entrepreneurs on the opportunity to make a fortune in the minute geographies of ever-shifting urban consumer markets (See Faura 2004; McTaggart 2005).[5]

Supply chain dynamics often complicate this picture of market fragmentation. Industrial laundries, temp agencies, security contractors, and other firms providing business-to-business services appear to have little capacity to insulate themselves from cost-based competition (Bernhardt et al. 2005). They take the prices set by a highly competitive market, and the resultant pressure on wages and working conditions conforms with the popular view of these industries. But in other cases industries we would expect to be nakedly cost competitive show immunity from these pressures. As chapters 6 and 7 detail, residential construction contractors find that homeowners lack the skill to compare and evaluate bid prices, time, and material costs and a contractor's references. As a result the systematized bidding of residential contracting does not translate into the expected market pressure on firms. To the contrary, a contractor's ability to control the labor supply chain and to define the nature and scope of the necessary work places firms in a favorable position for setting prices.

Access to labor allows firms to convert market fragmentation into profit. No variable conveys more information about labor market strategies in local industries than does location. The business model of temp agencies rests, for example, on opening low-cost storefronts in high-unemployment and minority neighborhoods that provide easy access to the firm's product of low-cost labor power (Peck and Theodore 2001). Advocates of business-friendly inner-city reinvestment list access to a workforce in need of employment opportunities as a primary *benefit* of locating in low-income neighborhoods (Porter 1995). Firms access these workers through a variety of mechanisms, typically employing them as temps, contract workers, or day workers, or through some other form of contingent employment relationship.

Most analyses of low-wage industries emphasize the cost advantage of keeping employees at an arm's length and denying them both job security and nonwage benefits. But here, too, what on the surface appears to be a simple cost-minimization strategy in many cases doubles as a means of flexibilizing *production* and moving the firm into new markets (Bernhardt et al. 2005). Focusing on labor markets as an element of corporate strategy—rather than as a tool for minimizing labor costs—raises crucial new questions about how service firms operate. It suggests that the businesses we have viewed as *necessarily* low wage may instead pay poorly and degrade work out of convenience or opportunity.

## The Labor-Sweating City: Understanding Employers by Understanding Places

Remarkably, the income inequalities documented in minute detail by decades of scholarship understate the full extent of workplace inequality in the United States. Today's workplace realities appear to mimic en masse Peter Doeringer and Michael Piore's classic distinction between primary labor markets characterized by year-round, full-time work and upward mobility and secondary labor markets in which few institutional forces soften the blows of unmitigated and unregulated competition (Doeringer and Piore 1971). Originally developed to explain manufacturing, the concept of primary and secondary labor markets resonates as a broader analytical framework because it depicts separate labor markets with their own institutional arrangements rather than a single, undifferentiated market encompassing the entire U.S. labor force (interested readers should see Jamie Peck's *Work Place* for a genealogy of the concept).

The expansion of degraded work arrangements rests on a series of social, institutional, and political-economic rearrangements without which the decline of low-wage employment cannot adequately be accounted for. Far from functioning as marginal forces shifting supply-and-demand dynamics within a fundamentally stable labor market, contingent employment relationships, undocumented immigration, and weakened regulatory enforcement have changed the rules of employment themselves. Reckoning with this reorganization requires the rethinking of workplace analysis itself. The growth of degraded work arrangements is often invisible or obscured in aggregate analysis of the labor market, but it becomes extremely clear when the focus shifts to firms, industries, and, above all, workplaces. As the rules—formal and otherwise—governing the organization and conduct of work have been transformed employers have responded by reorganizing work, production, and their own strategies for profit making.

Like the growth of degraded work, the change in employer practices appears in much clearer form when analysis shifts to specific industries, industry segments, and firms. In local-serving industries the transformation in business strategy often shows up spatially as businesses target new neighborhoods, workforces, and subpopulations. The restructuring of the two industries scrutinized in this book becomes visible in this way. Food retail, long a one-size-fits-all industry, has pushed into previously underserved urban spaces through a business model built around access to vulnerable, immigrant workers and consumers. Similarly, the reorganization of residential construction manifests in day labor corners operating in neighborhoods where immigrants live and in the deployment of those workers to specific jobs in particular types of buildings and neighborhoods. Seen this way, degraded work arrangements need to be scrutinized in place. Focusing on a particular urban region facilitates the isolation of the distinctive demographic, economic, and institutional factors rearranging local labor markets. For this book that means grounding the study of industries in the study of Chicago. Combed through for research significance by generations of scholars, the city's economic landscape today differs from the recent past in subtle ways that reveal a great amount about employers and the jobs they offer.

# 3

# The City That Sweats Work

## *Growth and Inequality in Post-Fordist Chicago*

The taxi ride from Midway International Airport to the Chicago Loop speeds visitors through a century's worth of industrial history in the space of twenty minutes. Packed tightly against L tracks, rail yards, and the industrial waterways carved out of the South Branch of the Chicago River, the Stevenson Expressway offers an unsentimental view of the manufacturing past that moved the poet Carl Sandburg to label Chicago "the City of big shoulders"—a phrase as obsolescent as it is overused. Halfway through the journey downtown, visitors pass the belching smokestack of the Fisk power plant, a decidedly ugly landmark that stands in ever-sharper contrast to the increasingly opulent cityscape behind it. Even as the visitor to the city passes through an unpretty industrial space, the visual excess of Chicago's rebuilt downtown draws the eye.

Miles from the Loop, the shrinking landscape of Chicago's Fordist past begins to give way to physical markers of the city's much-discussed and little-understood rebound from a seemingly endless series of plant closings in the 1970s and the 1980s. Punctuated by the addition of sixty-, eighty-six-, and ninety-eight-story landmarks in the 2000s, the Loop's growing skyline draws the eye of visitors and residents alike. It is the most striking symbol of the new Chicago but not the most fitting. The city's transformation is more aptly epitomized at the margins of the celebrated downtown. The South Loop, home to little more than unused train tracks a few decades ago, now boasts miles of condos, townhouses, and residential towers to house the city's growing professional workforce. As the taxi exits the Stevenson Expressway for the Dan Ryan, this new minicity of condominiums shifts to the visitor's right. To her left lie 10,000 more units of newly upscaled housing in the formerly Mexican American working-class neighborhood of Pilsen and in the repurposed factories on the city's Near West Side. Decay in Chicago's "neighborhoods," the catch-all signifier for the inner ring of formerly middle-class areas devastated by deindustrialization, is now threatened by the seemingly unstoppable growth of the Loop and its professionals.

These visible symbols of polarization dominate narratives of inequality in Chicago and elsewhere for many reasons, including their obvious visual metaphors and the fact that the professionals who determine popular narratives of inequality (as well as those who consume them) spend a lot of time in and near central business districts. But the majority of Chicago's population has always lived in neighborhoods outside its storied center and the surrounding zone of transition, and the less-noted changes to those neighborhoods constitute a crucial piece of the story of contemporary economic restructuring. On the way to its rendezvous with architectural landmarks on the lakefront, the taxi from Midway skirts Brighton Park and Archer Heights, home to one of Chicago's multiple "Polish Broadways." Across the Chicago River, behind the Cook County Department of Corrections and freight tracks, lies La Villita (the Little Village), where the crush of consumer traffic to 26th Street's innumerable restaurants, supermarkets, and clothing stores brings the street to a standstill at all hours. Poorer than the professionalized lakefront neighborhoods on the North Side but higher in income than South and West Side ghettoes chronicled by generations of Hyde Park graduate students, these neighborhoods and their thriving low-wage businesses represent a critical but overlooked element in Chicago's ongoing experimentation with economic reconfiguration in the wake of deindustrialization.

Just as they focus on opulent downtowns, critical narratives of Chicago's white-collar rebirth and its attached economic inequalities focus on financial industries and the rarified analysts and deal makers whose spending on the job drives the skyline upward. The centralization of financial capital and the rise of financial command-and-control centers—Chicago's clusters around the merged Chicago Board of Trade and Chicago Mercantile Exchange—clearly lays the ground conditions for the workplace inequalities that define contemporary American cities (Harvey 1985). As the basic analytical formulations about global cities suggest, the well-heeled consumers employed in downtown skyscrapers play a crucial role as consumers of these services. But they are not the only consumers with income to spend, and businesses serving those professionals are not the only businesses to degrade work.

Understanding the production of low-wage jobs means finding the right industries to examine and the right place in which to examine them.

Residential construction and food retail provide revealing examples of the broad array of industries degrading work in Chicago and urban America. Both industries saw wages and working conditions deteriorate in the face of a formally strong economic boom. Residential construction was in many ways the signature boom industry of the dismal 2001–7 business cycle. Buoyed by Federal Reserve–backed speculation, the dollar value of residential construction in the United States expanded by more than 50 percent between 2000 and 2006. The success of food retail was less evident but perhaps more significant. Nationwide, food retailing chains continue to steer investment to suburban regions and to shutter stores in poorer and urban areas. But supermarkets have thrived in Chicago, reversing the national trend by aggressively moving into midincome areas. Significantly, these areas are defined by immigrant households, who made up nearly one-fifth of Chicago's population in the 2000s. Though immigrants and, especially, undocumented immigrants prominently appear in accounts of low-wage work, the stylized picture of downtown-driven inequality affords no opportunity to examine these households' important roles as consumers—an oversight that removes large segments of urban territory, population, and economies from analytical scrutiny.

Situating the residential construction and food retail industries within this complicated process of urban economic restructuring emphasizes their significance for popular theories on inequality. But the industries also resonate at the level of the macroeconomy. Their transformation during the mid-2000s mirrors the plight of nonprofessional workers writ large: both industries expanded rapidly, and both saw wages and working conditions deteriorate as profits grew. Nationwide, construction wages actually fell during a once-in-a-lifetime boom. The return of street corner day labor practices long thought to have been extinguished would have been momentous under any circumstances, much less during a record expansion. And the growth of food retail came at the cost of the mass downgrading of working standards in the industry. In the postwar era supermarkets were unique as service sector employers that offered wages and working conditions similar to those in unionized manufacturing. The disjuncture between rising output and diminishing working conditions in these industries raises a direct challenge to long-standing economic theories that treat growth as the essential condition for improvements in wages and working conditions. If record booms cannot trigger on-the-job improvements, then what possibly will?

The explanation for the mounting disjuncture between industry growth and employment outcomes lies in degraded work arrangements and the ways in which they have reconfigured the relationship between profit and working conditions. The severing of the once-fundamental relationship between growth and equity has long been noted at the national level (Freeman 2001). But responding to this problem at the urban and regional scale means understanding contextual specifics: specific places, specific industries, and specific end markets. The first step to mapping these details is to chart the sweeping transformations to the economy and the political economy of the city in which they occurred.

## Chicago's Ongoing Post-Fordist Transition

Chicago makes a uniquely revealing laboratory in which to examine the remaking of service industries, but not because it constitutes a representative case of U.S. urbanity. Since the rise of the Chicago school of sociology in the early twentieth century, scholars have treated it as paradigmatic of U.S. urbanism. The city's importance to urban studies derives not only from the Chicago school's hegemony but also from popular associations with the city itself. In the postwar era, Chicago was the nation's premier industrial metropolis, not just a Fordist city but a *maker* of Fordism itself (Doussard, Peck, and Theodore 2009). Along with its bustling factories, the city's informal status as capital of the Midwest—flat, plain, and all-American in the popular imagination—tacitly supported claims to paradigmatic status. Chicago was affectively normal, what Norman Mailer deemed "the great American City" after dismissing New York, Boston, and Philadelphia as too outward looking and too distanced from their immigrant pasts (Mailer 1968). Buttressed by these echoing associations, the long-standing tradition is to treat Chicago as representative of the United States and to broadly generalize from research conducted in low-income pockets of the city's South and West Sides (Bennett 2006).

If this paradigmatic Chicago ever actually existed, it amounted to little more than a stylized and unreliable memory by the mid-2000s. Manufacturing job losses began in earnest before 1970, even as scholars celebrated the city's importance as a manufacturer, and the process of deindustrialization itself is now more than forty years old (Berry et al. 1976). As is the case nationally, the process of *unmaking* Fordist Chicago has endured much longer than did postwar Fordism itself.

By 2005 manufacturing accounted for just 13 percent of the Chicago Metropolitan Statistical Area's employment base (U.S. Bureau of Labor Statistics 2006b). But as manufacturing waned, the familiar tale of inner-city hollowing out was stood on its head. Chicago's population grew in the 1990s, and the 2000s' housing boom brought waves of investment not just to the Loop and its environs but to Albany Park, Portage Park, South Lawndale, Rogers Park, and several other recently transitional and increasingly immigrant neighborhoods on the city's Southwest, Northwest, and Far North Sides. Immigration, always central to the identity of a city in which the surnames Vrdolyak and Blagojevich roll off the tongue with ease, had returned to levels unseen since the beginning of the twentieth century. Combined with four decades of income polarization and sometimes-jarring economic restructuring, these and other changes suggest that Fordism provides an increasingly inaccurate map to the ever-changing social and economic organization of Chicago. Nevertheless, scholars continue to bend received tropes about the city to fit the new realities of a postindustrial economy, ascendant finance, and mass immigration in lieu of evaluating such significant shifts in their own right (Koval 2006). In recent years researchers have undertaken the empirical task of charting the new Chicago, but owing to the messiness of the theoretical and ontological issues at hand, this scholarship has not fashioned—*cannot* fashion—a view of the city as neat and compact as the Fordist/paradigmatic ideal.

The economic ruptures and theoretical slippage induced by deindustrialization and the ascent of service sectors are prime concerns of this book. This makes the new Chicago an ideal research laboratory not because it is representative of the United States but because its long exit from Fordism has yielded an industry structure that remains balanced—less dominated by finance and low-wage services—when contrasted with New York and Los Angeles, the regions to which scholars instinctively compare Chicago (Abu-Lughod 2001; Bernhardt et al. 2009). Chicago's strong Finance, Insurance, and Real Estate (FIRE) sector, which comprised 8.3 percent of regional employment in 2007, was considerably smaller than New York's (10.9 percent over the same period) but proportionally larger than the FIRE sector in Los Angeles (7.4 percent of the local economy) and other large urban regions (U.S. Bureau of Labor Statistics 2006b). As a direct result, Chicago's wage inequalities are, though stark, less stark than those elsewhere. Compared with New York, the region had slower growth in extremely high-wage occupations, and a considerably larger portion of the workforce drew income from the middle of the wage distribution (Doussard, Peck, and Theodore 2009). The comparison with Los Angeles is very nearly the opposite. Low-wage industry-occupation clusters made up a disproportionate share of Los Angeles' job growth in recent business cycles, with the middle 60 percent of the wage distribution generating few net jobs. Distinctive for heavy industry in the Fordist era, Chicago in the 2000s stands out as a uniquely mixed economy in an era marked by extremes—more reliant on manufacturing than its peers on the coasts but more successful at capturing finance and advanced services than its industrial neighbors in the Midwest.

Lifting the mandate to view Chicago as an industrially paradigmatic city helps to clarify the analytical uses to which its distinguishing political-economic and institutional features can be put. Seen this way, the city's signature political-economic traits—the continued strength of organized labor compared with elsewhere, the Richard M. Daley (and later Rahm Emanuel) regime's singularly effective alliance with developers, the enduring impact of historical patterns of segregation on the contemporary organization of neighborhood economies and labor markets, and the seemingly antiquated coalition politics through which labor actions and community-organizing efforts are conducted—become crucial elements in the examination of workplace restructuring. What emerges is a specific, messy urbanity, not the highly stylized global city of the urban studies imagination.

## *Caught in the Middle: Chicago's Two-Tier Economy Reflects and Drives Income Polarization*

The most frequently cited narratives on global cities treat the economic and spatial polarization occurring within their borders as the by-product of the reorganization of the international economy. This is the familiar narrative of booming downtowns with high earners, disappearing manufacturing jobs, and buoyant growth in low-wage, deskilled services industries (Sassen 2001). The spatial dimension to these changes—the juxtaposition of the Upper East Side and Mott Haven in New York, of soaring property values next to mass disinvestment—makes them especially flummoxing and draws researchers toward the often overwhelming visual symbols of polarization (Mollenkopf and Castells 1991).

At the macrolevel this standard narrative describes Chicago very well. Between 1983—the beginning of Reagan-era economic expansion—and the mid-2000s, Chicago's rich grew richer, and its poor grew poorer. Households at the tenth percentile of income saw a 12 percent decrease in compensation over this time, whereas households in the ninetieth percentile saw a proportionally equal increase that translated into significant net wage growth (Doussard, Peck, and Theodore 2009).

The economic expansion of the 2000s extended the pattern of inequitable growth that first took hold nationally in the 1980s (Harrison and Bluestone 1988). Despite widespread growth in corporate profit rates and regional GDP, the typical household in Chicago grew poorer between 2000 and the end of the next business cycle (Table 1). The structure of employment undoubtedly played a key role. Manufacturing employment shrank by one-quarter during this business expansion, and the major growth industries were either high-wage sectors such as professional services or low-wage sectors such as arts and entertainment. Given this marked polarization of employment opportunities in such a short time period, it is easy to understand how household incomes fell and the poverty rate grew despite continued economic expansion.

This familiar picture of employment and income polarization in Chicago only hints at the degree to which the region has been transformed.

TABLE 1

**From Peak to Peak: Declining Incomes and Weak Job Growth during the 2001–7 Business Cycle, Chicago Metropolitan Statistical Area**

| | 2000 | 2007 |
|---|---|---|
| Median Household Income | $66,681 | $64,286 |
| Poverty Rate | 10.5% | 11.3% |
| Total Employment | 4,385,536 | 4,364,633 |
| Construction | 4.6% | 4.7% |
| Manufacturing | 14.4% | 11.0% |
| Trade, Transportation, and Utilities | 20.8% | 20.3% |
| Financial Activities | 7.1% | 7.3% |
| Professional and Business Services | 15.9% | 16.2% |
| Leisure and Hospitality | 8.0% | 9.2% |

All income figures are in 2011 dollars. *Sources:* row 2, 3, Ruggles et al. 2010; rows 4–10, U.S. Bureau of Labor Statistics 2006b.

Between 2000 and 2006 (the main years in which the research for this book was conducted), several historically poor areas on Chicago's South and West Sides saw median household income decline by more than $10,000. At the same time, income gains accelerated in the areas surrounding the central business district. As the Loop jumped its historical boundaries and pushed southward and westward, median household income levels in downtown Chicago and the Near West Side grew by more than $11,000. The speedily diverging fortunes of the Loop and the Pullman area on Chicago's Far South Side, where median household income fell by more than $14,000, provide one of many available measures of this shift. In just six years the gap in median household income between these rich and poor areas grew by a remarkable $25,000. Overall, the changes charted in Map 1 reinforce existing income divisions, with the historically more affluent North Side adding income (especially in the Lakefront areas), neighborhoods in the historically poor West Side witnessing drops in household income of more than $10,000, and every area of the South Side except for Hyde Park and gentrifying Bronzeville seeing its median household income fall by at least $5,000. Significantly, the divergence in income between the Loop and Chicago's poor neighborhoods was substantially greater during the economically optimistic 2000s than during the 1980s, heretofore the landmark moment in efforts to chart the polarizing impact of manufacturing job losses and downtown-oriented redevelopment (Rast 1999; Abu-Lughod 2001).

The striking geographic binarism of these changes belies the considerably more complex task of reckoning with the contingent, open-ended nature of Chicago's polarization. The visual metaphor of shuttered factories juxtaposed with an ascending downtown skyline suggests a fixity and semipermanence that the political-economic processes underlying Chicago's polarization lack. The Loop/neighborhoods binary implies that neighborhood-level income discrepancies in income are an *end point,* a geographically fixed resolution to the analytically prior restructuring of the U.S. economy at the national scale. In global cities theory and other top-down projections of national trends onto urban space, space matters not so much in its own right but as a means of measuring systematic urban-scale variations in the results of global corporate restructuring (Neil Brenner's commentary on the methodological confusions of the standard narrative of polarization provides a detailed analysis of this problem) (Brenner 2001). This treatment of space as a residual category entrenches the tendency to treat local-serving industries themselves as residual, uniform, and unchanging.

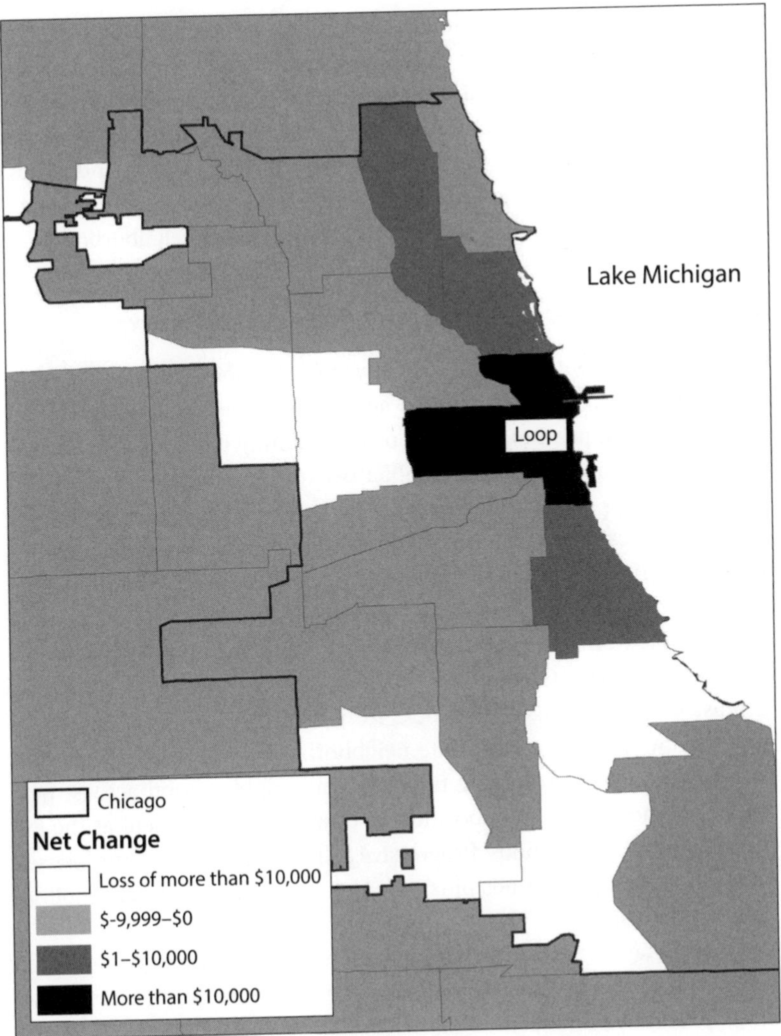


*Map 1. Median Household Income Change in Chicago Neighborhoods, 2000–6. All figures are reported in 2011 dollars.* Source: *Ruggles et al. 2010.*

But shifting focus to the internal lives of these rapidly changing neighborhoods identifies another perspective altogether. Behind the deepening of long-standing income divisions within Chicago lies a series of extensive changes to demographics and economies in neighborhoods caught between the push of deindustrialization and the pull of Chicago's expanding professional class. These neighborhoods in flux are not a footnote to economic restructuring but rather key sites through which the city's evolving economy is configured. Contra the received wisdom that downtowns are the ideal site in which to examine low-wage labor, these neighborhoods are distinctive sites of growth for low-wage work in local-serving industries. Degraded work in Chicago cannot be understood without a careful mapping of demographic and economic dynamics in those neighborhoods.

### *Polarization Reconfigures Local-Serving Industries along with Urban Space*

Recent demographic changes in Chicago's neighborhoods build on a long and defining tension between aggressive infrastructure investment (both public and private) in the Loop and declining investment in low-to-mid-income residential areas. Conflict between downtown interests and residential areas is a commonplace in the U.S. political economy, but the decades-long capture of Chicago's government by a developer-funded political machine makes the dichotomy especially stark (Royko 1971). The underlying focus of the Richard J. Daley regime's urban renewal projects was an effort to invest in and expand the Loop and to erect barriers (including the Cabrini-Green public housing projects and the University of Illinois's Circle Campus a few blocks from the Sears Tower) to encroachment by lower-income, nonwhite neighborhoods. Chicago's potent and famed community-organizing tradition and neighborhood activist networks cut their teeth on opposition to downtown investment at the expense of the neighborhoods. Progressive activism in Chicago thus focused on the Loop/neighborhoods binary and on a tangible, materialist politics of investment and jobs.

Harold Washington's brief but momentous reign as mayor from 1983 to 1987 reversed the longtime orientation of city politics around downtown development by literally installing activists in city hall (Clavel 2010). These activists and their allies in neighborhood organizations directly engaged the problems of deindustrialization by erecting industry task forces to identify policies for curtailing capital flight and by funding neighborhood activists to undertake aggressive economic development and job training activities (Clavel 2010). Jobs were the focal point of this nationally heralded progressive movement, and surprisingly, the Richard M. Daley administration, which took power two years after Washington's death of a heart attack in 1987, initially accommodated much of the jobs agenda. Belying his many similarities to his father, Daley Jr. initially slowed real estate development and embraced the Washington administration's Planned Manufacturing Districts, which insulated profitable firms from real estate speculation by restricting property owners' ability to quickly rezone and flip their properties for residential and commercial development (Rast 1999).

Jobs remained a central focus of community politics in Chicago throughout the 1990s and the 2000s, but the Daley administration ultimately steered investment toward the Loop with new vigor. By some estimates the city invested billions in Millennium Park, McCormick Place, Soldier Field, Navy Pier, and other lakefront attractions (Spirou 2006; Suchar 2006). This investment strategy heavily figures in the expansion of degraded work relationships in the city. Commercial construction jobs were governed by collective bargaining agreements and the Davis–Bacon Act; any comparison of their rewards with the skill levels involved aids the view that these were desirable jobs for the city's working class. But the labor exerted in those construction jobs built the physical infrastructure for tourist-oriented economic development, which generated significant growth in restaurants, hotels, and a variety of related leisure services industries known to degrade work.

The related construction of high-income residential properties in and near the Loop entailed a further downgrading of employment opportunities. As Saskia Sassen alertly notes in her research on global cities, residential construction for urban professionals typically entails the rehabilitation of older ("vintage") buildings for contemporary tastes. Where commercial construction work is capital intensive and requires high skill levels, residential rehabbing requires significant volumes of unskilled labor. Gutting old row houses and factories to be rewired and rearchitected is a brutal process in which workers can only rarely substitute technology and thought for muscle. Once these buildings have been gutted, the reconstruction process militates against aiding labor with capital equipment (working spaces are too small and idiosyncratic, and residential contractors are poorly capitalized), and the entire process is governed by an elaborate subcontracting system that nimbly pushes laborers' wages downward (Sassen 2001). Chapters 6 and 7 take up the residential construction industry in detail.

As the second Daley administration began to realize the growth machine's goal of bracketing the Loop with high-end residential real estate, this long-standing local redevelopment scheme was overwhelmed by the nationwide housing bubble that rapidly inflated in the early 2000s. With home sales experiencing annual double-digit gains and contractors taking out an ever-growing number of permits for new construction and residential rehabilitation, the low-wage residential construction industry became one of Chicago's chief growth industries. In the process the construction boom pushed out past the Loop and inner neighborhoods and into lower-income and immigrant-dominated neighborhoods distant from the central business district, particularly on the Northwest and Far North Sides.

Those neighborhoods—lower-income, ethnically identified, and adding residents by the thousand while Chicago's historically African American neighborhoods continue to shrink—represent an analytically crucial third pole in the heretofore bipolar narrative of urban inequality. The retail industries thriving in high-income Lakefront neighborhoods thrive in these neighborhoods, too—but they are organized and operated differently. The construction boom likewise pushed its way into the immigrant Northwest and Southwest Sides, but with different contractors, different workforces, and different end consumers. These neighborhoods are key to understanding the messiness and disorganization of Chicago's post-Fordist economic settlement and to clarifying the spatially and strategically contingent profit-making strategies of employers. The changes in local-serving industries and the potential for subsequent changes, both positive and negative, are starkly evident in these transitional spaces.

## Immigration Brings New Commercial Life to Chicago's Outer Neighborhoods

By the late 2000s more than 640,000 of Chicago's 2.82 million residents were born outside the United States. Echoing the city's status as a premier receiving destination for eastern Europeans in the early twentieth century, Chicago's contemporary immigrant population is relatively diverse. Nearly 20 percent of the foreign born originally are from Europe, and an additional 19 percent come from Asian countries. But in Chicago as elsewhere, immigration is primarily a story of Hispanic immigration (56 percent of the total) from the Americas (author's calculations from Ruggles et al. 2010). The city's immigrant population falls between the middle and the bottom of the income spectrum. In the late 2000s the city's main immigrant neighborhoods were neighborhoods that had been spared the sharpest income losses. In the Pilsen, Little Village, and Back of the Yards neighborhoods on the South Side, as well as in a majority of the Far Northwest Side, immigrants made up more than 35 percent of the population (Map 2).

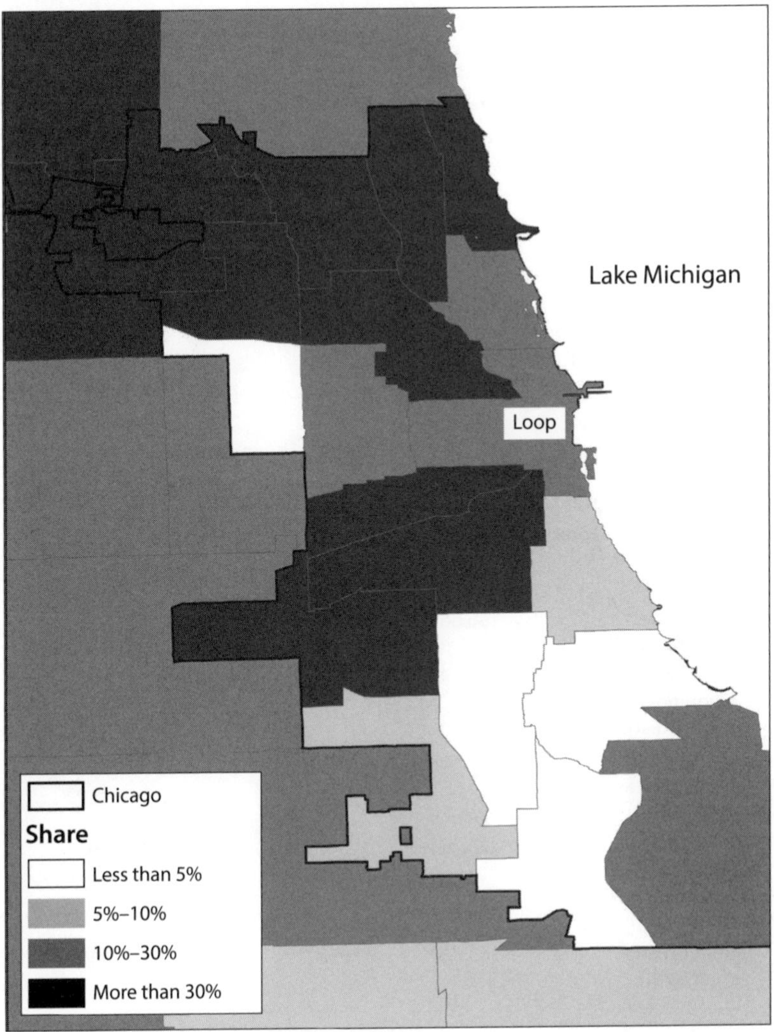


*Map 2. Immigrant Share of Population in Chicago Neighborhoods, 2006.* Source: *Ruggles et al. 2010.*

Although Chicago's immigrant-dominated neighborhoods were generally lower-income areas, they were not marginal by most economic accounts. In fact, six of the nine neighborhood groups with an immigrant population of 30 percent or more had median household incomes above the citywide median (Table 2). Although the story of immigration

TABLE 2

**Foreign-Born Population and Household Income in Select Chicago Neighborhoods, 2006**

| NEIGHBORHOOD GROUP | POPULATION | % FOREIGN-BORN POPULATION | INCOME CHANGE (% FROM 2000) | INCOME RANK AMONG 19 CHICAGO NEIGHBORHOOD GROUPS |
|---|---|---|---|---|
| Portage Park–Montclare–Belmont Cragin (Northwest) | 160,254 | 44.2% | -13.4% | 7 |
| Pilsen–West Side (Near South) | 110,871 | 42.3% | -15.9% | 16 |
| McKinley Park–Back of the Yards–Bridgeport (South) | 168,672 | 40.8% | -16.1% | 13 |
| Jefferson Park–Forest Glen–North Park (Northwest) | 150,687 | 39.6% | -0.9% | 6 |
| West Rogers Park (Far North) | 136,663 | 35.9% | 10.3% | 5 |
| Norwood Park–Dunning–O'Hare (Northwest) | 139,282 | 35.8% | -11.3% | 3 |
| Little Village–Southwest Side (Southwest) | 212,608 | 32.1% | -12.1% | 8 |
| West Town–Humboldt Park–Logan Square (Near Northwest) | 226,244 | 31.5% | -0.3% | 9 |
| Rogers Park (Far North) | 168,804 | 31.2% | -0.3% | 11 |

*Sources:* author's calculations from Summary File 3 of U.S. Census 2000 and the U.S. Census Bureau's 2006 American Community Survey. Both are available online.

to Chicago is undisputedly an economic story, the economic impact and residences of the new migrants defy simple explanations that suggest immigrant households start at the bottom of the economic ladder.

The higher-than-average median household incomes in these immigrant-dominated community areas do not reflect higher hourly wages. Nationwide, the typical foreign-born worker employed in a full-time job earns $8,600 per year less than the typical domestic-born worker ($33,000 versus $41,600).[1] But owing to larger family sizes, greater labor-force participation, and the large number of hours worked for immigrant households, the gap in median household income between households headed by native- and foreign-born individuals is proportionately smaller, $46,800 versus $50,700.[2] In other words, Chicago's immigrant-receiving neighborhoods are simultaneously *low wage* and *middle income.* Analyses of economic polarization (including this one) typically focus on the low wages paid to inner-city workers. Using this sound logic, past analyses of Chicago's postindustrial economic growth have pointed to low wages in South Side and West Side neighborhoods as evidence of limited capacity for business growth and profit—if the residents of these impoverished areas were going to earn a paycheck, they were going to do it in the Loop or in one of the region's many growing suburban employment centers (McMillen and Lester 2003).

This continues to be the case in Chicago's African American neighborhoods, where labor force participation rates, wages, household income, and neighborhood employment opportunities remain low. The intention here is not to continue giving these problems short shrift but rather to situate them within the overall restructuring of Chicago's economy. Here, it is important to note that the city's African American population declined by more than 170,000 during the 2000s, whereas the Hispanic and immigrant populations expanded rapidly. Given Chicago's persistent ethnic and racial segregation, these changes play out as neighborhood changes. Hispanic and immigrant neighborhoods represent a growing portion of the Chicago economy, and these neighborhoods are in several key ways distinct from what Bob Beauregard has termed "the stylized Urban Ghetto" of the popular imagination (Beauregard 1993).

To begin with, they are areas of population growth. A seemingly unbreakable process of cumulative causation marked the hollowing out of inner-city neighborhoods in Chicago and elsewhere during the 1970s and 1980s. As job losses in primary industries mounted, household incomes fell. This in turn weakened neighborhood purchasing power, feeding further economic and employment losses. Population outmigration sealed the pattern by further thinning demand for goods and services and sending housing prices downward. Steady population growth in Chicago's immigrant-receiving neighborhoods has reversed the process, resulting in the renewed economic expansion of significant clusters of neighborhoods on the city's Southwest and Northwest Sides (Koval and Fidel 2006).

This population growth has fed the expansion of neighborhood commerce and services. Even as Chicago's policy elites turned their focus to the threat of a spatial mismatch between Chicago's job-seeking population and suburbanizing employment base, these new ethnic enclaves were generating substantial employment in *locally oriented* businesses: ethnic retailers and wholesalers, importers, legal and professional services, immigration services, and construction. On foot or behind the wheel, the contrast between the deserted Roosevelt Road commercial strip on the city's African American West Side and the thriving immigrant enclaves to the immediate south is impossible to miss. Traffic on 26th Street, the heart of the Hispanic Little Village, moves slowly. Dozens of supermarkets, remittance agencies, and service providers compete—with neon signs, music broadcast in the street, and street vendors peddling foods and goods on seemingly every corner—to absorb the neighborhood's growing Hispanic income (Wilson 2011).[3] The effect is the same in Mexican Pilsen to the northeast, Polish Jackowo on the Northwest Side, the Paseo Boricua in Humboldt Park, Devon Avenue's Indian enclave on the Far North Side, and dozens of smaller commercial districts scattered throughout the city (Paral 2006; Rangaswamy 2006; Erdmans 2006). In a very tangible way, the global economic and population dislocations that produced Chicago's bustling downtown have fed the growth of new local industries with distinctive products and market segments and buoyant consumer demand. Rather than reading off the traits of these businesses from the stylized template of the one-size-fits-all low-wage service industry, it is important to evaluate these businesses in their own right.

A sharper focus on these locally oriented businesses suggests a particular fit between Chicago's expanding degraded work practices and employers' strategies for making markets and extracting profits. Many of these businesses hire immigrants at low and subminimum wages while selling their goods and services to the neighborhood population—effectively selling to their own worker base. The overlap between worker and consumer populations suggests a spatially delineated, contemporary variant of early Fordism as practiced by its namesake employer in Detroit. Yet as contemporary observers have suggested, the observed pattern more closely resembles Fordism in reverse: in their efforts to target low-wage populations, employers achieve price reductions by slashing labor costs, further reducing the income levels of their consumers.

In many areas these employer–consumer relationships manifest as a neat picture of coethnic exploitation. Remittances and high-interest loans comprise an alarmingly high share of many neighborhood economies (Wilson 2011). Employers in the Southwest Side's Hispanic enclave rarely make anything in the conventional sense of the term. Instead, they compete to absorb consumer spending. At a neighborhood level there are obvious continuities between contemporary ethnic enclaves and the older extraction economy of the U.S. urban ghetto (Schaffer 1973). But at the level of the individual firm, the ability to segment and make markets stands out. The intricacies of marketing to a coethnic consumer base, combined with the distant geographical remove of potential rival retailers and service providers, suggest that these firms' low labor costs are not necessarily linked to end prices and market transitions. This point is engaged in more detail in chapter 4.

Immigration is just one part of the complex story of ongoing economic restructuring in Chicago, but it is an important part. As the existing body of research on the topic demonstrates, the problem of degraded work spans industries and geographies and cannot be reduced to a problem of immigration. Yet Chicago's burgeoning immigrant enclaves call attention to a number of specific ways in which the stylized picture of undifferentiated low-wage industries does not hold. Employers in these neighborhood submarkets target distinctive populations and income groups that effectively bound their end markets and restrict competition. Far from being generic, the competitive models these firms pursue are highly specific and often varied—understanding them on their own terms is crucial to mapping the workings of service industries, especially in large urban areas in which foreign-born households make up one-quarter or more of the total population.

## The Local State Abdicates: Unions and Community Organizations Jump Scales to Confront Degradation

The withdrawal of the state from its previous commitment to enforcing New Deal labor laws provides a basic condition of possibility for the growth of degraded work. Here, as with basic social services, labor unions and community-based organizations have stepped into the domains formerly policed by defunded regulatory agencies. In the aggregate, scholars label this phenomenon the formation of a *shadow state* constituted from increasingly strained not-for-profit organizations (Wolch 1990). That term inaccurately characterizes the growing cohort of not-for-profits engaged in the problems of low-wage labor markets. Rather than simply attempting to *replace* vanished state services, these organizations undertake activities the state never pursued: they organize workers, and they systematically work at multiple regulatory scales in an attempt to equalize the increasingly asymmetrical power relationship between capital and labor in the workplace.

In Chicago these organizations—worker centers but also local labor unions, neighborhood associations, fellowship societies, and others—form the main response to the immiseration of low-wage work. That they do so in a city whose rigid and highly effective political machine unilaterally dismisses appeals on the behalf of low-wage workers suggests clear lines along which to situate Chicago's low-wage labor market within the broader United States. Because Chicago's worker centers and other worker advocacy organizations lack significant access to powerful local institutions, they are forced to look either down to narrowly defined and politically isolated acts of advocacy on the behalf of particular workers and neighborhoods or up to state and national officials who entertain proposals that the Daley and Emanuel administrations—and their extensive allies among elected officials *and* many neighborhood organizations—reject.

The Chicago machine's strong and effective opposition to measures aimed at the bottom of the labor market—at one point, the Daley regime closed access to a public property that had been designated the site for a worker-regulated day labor shape-up—places the city's labor advocates in a somewhat exaggerated version of the basic tension most organizing campaigns face. Nationally, worker centers build their ranks by providing basic services that draw workers together to form a cohort of grassroots activists. But as Janice Fine notes in her analysis of the worker center form, the most effective worker centers win their successes by mobilizing relationships with elite officials and institutions, usually at the local scale (Fine 2006). Strong institutional opposition in Chicago and Cook County (whose political institutions overlap with the city's in both formal and informal ways) leave workers' organizations to move back and forth between *individualized* advocacy campaigns targeted at specific businesses and *state-level legal reforms* built through access to officials insulated from Chicago's parochial politics.

The absence of an urban-scale focus (as opposed to neighborhood or state-level activities) extends beyond engagement with elected officials. Following a long-standing local practice of narrow, neighborhood-level identification among progressive community organizations, Chicago's worker centers and their allies route their advocacy through neighborhood-level identification and institutions. A representative list of these organizations includes the Albany Park Worker Center, named for a Northwest

Side neighborhood with immigrants from dozens of nations; the Centro Comunitario Juan Diego, rooted in the geographically isolated South Chicago neighborhood on the Southeast Side; the Latino Organization of the Southwest Side; and the Logan Square Neighborhood Association. Other organizations, such as the San Lucas Worker Center and Mexico Solidarity Network, took extensive efforts to move beyond the neighborhood model of organization, but perhaps inevitably, they were interpolated by other organizations on the basis of geography, rather than their designated foci. Rare among these organizations, the Interfaith Worker Center, located on the Far North Side, has successfully moved beyond a neighborhood focus, but that success arises in part from its affiliation with the national Interfaith Worker Justice network, in whose headquarters its offices lie.

The entrenched conduct of Chicago's worker advocacy activities through neighborhood networks limits the ability of advocacy organizations to work in collaboration, a point that emerges in detail in my studies of the food retail and residential construction industries. Community–labor organizing in Chicago proceeds through a deal-making institutional framework in which negotiations echo the formal deal making of the famed Chicago political machine.[4] This stands in sharp contrast to the flexibility and institutionally inventive organization of the Los Angeles–based community–labor coalitions at the forefront of several successful organizing campaigns (Milkman 2006). Indeed, Chicago's worker centers, in contrast with those in Los Angeles and elsewhere, are weakly networked (Fine 2006). That observation applies more broadly to the city's progressive neighborhood organizations writ large. After coming together to form a landmark rainbow coalition that swept Harold Washington to office in 1983, the capacity of Chicago's neighborhood organizations to jointly push citywide reform has atrophied. In 2006 many of the organizations that appear in this book were involved in a fierce campaign to pass a citywide minimum wage for big-box retailers (known locally as the Big-Box Bill). Then-mayor Richard M. Daley persuaded several original supporters of the law to vote against overriding his veto—and he did it by expertly splitting African American–focused community organizations from their onetime allies through claims that the law would steer retail jobs away from Chicago's poorest areas (Sites 2007). Unable to find common cause on a broad workplace pay law with clear benefits for low-wage workers, Chicago's fabled network of community activists has provided limited support to worker centers and community organizations engaged in smaller, neighborhood-identified campaigns. These long-standing tensions had the unfortunate effect of intensifying the foundational focus of worker centers and other advocates on individual projects rather than on systemic advocacy and reform.

## Degraded Work in Food Retail and Residential Construction

Among the many problematic sectors Chicago's community–labor organizations engaged in the 2000s, food retail and residential construction stand out as businesses that promise to illuminate the broader restructuring of local-serving industries. In terms of their end markets and goods, each is a quintessential local industry of the type typically overlooked in even the most thorough accounts of economic restructuring. Yet during the mid-2000s, each industry was rapidly remade by strong demand growth, targeted neighborhood-level investment, and the continuing in-migration to Chicago of willing laborers with little to no ability to contest conditions in the workplace. The world of work and production is too complex and varied for any sector or set of industries to meaningfully represent the whole. But these industries highlight key dimensions of the remaking of local economies, and their direct linkages to downtown investment and the consumption needs of a populace with shrinking household incomes make them important in policy terms.

Yet the two industries "make" different types of things, do so in substantially different ways, and—crucially—provide employers different tools with which to insulate themselves from market pressures. The food retail industry, with its small profit margins and cost-based competition, is more likely to force employers to degrade work as a matter of competitive necessity. Residential construction, by contrast, offers greater opportunities for niche-based competitive strategies and labor market practices that feed high value-added, quality-based competition. The following sections outline key differences between these industries, particularly in terms of the strategic dimensions traced in chapter 2 and in this chapter's discussion of Chicago: their ability to fragment end markets, the impact of the production process itself, and employers' strategies for accessing labor.

### *The Food Retail Industry Fragments along with Chicago's Urban Landscape*

Buoyed by the potent metaphor of the food desert, activists and scholars have in recent years turned their attention to long-term disinvestment in urban food retail (Pothukuchi and Kaufman 2000). The population density models, market segmentation models, and real estate investment patterns that drove the food retail industry's flight from city to suburbs were intricately tied to the familiar urban problems of falling incomes, population loss, and infrastructure disinvestment (Pothukuchi 2005). Economic development entrepreneurs as distinguished as Michael Porter began to identify inner-city food retail markets as sites of significant competitive opportunity as early as the mid-1990s (Porter 2005; Ferguson and Abell 1998). In this case, the private sector closely followed in scholars' footsteps. By the time the food desert issue was popularized, retailers already were returning in significant numbers to lower-income, inner-city locations (Mari Gallagher Research and Consulting Group 2006).

Buoyed by the entrepreneurial research of Mari Gallagher, a local consultant, food deserts became a major policy concern in Chicago in the late 2000s. The timing was in many ways ironic. As the *Chicago Tribune* began to publish its first pieces on the issue, Walmart was already engaged in a high-profile negotiation with the city council to gain planning approval for four retail grocery supercenters to be located in the city's low-income South and West Sides (see Sites 2007).[5] Nationwide, Walmart and other big-box retailers had long employed a distinctive competitive model, premised on the combination of low wages and economies-of-scale purchasing power, to move into higher-cost inner-ring suburbs and inner cities (Zook and Graham 2006). Market saturation—throughout the United States and, increasingly, in Chicago's collar counties and suburban Cook County—and rising population density in many Chicago neighborhoods had led the retailer to target the longtime labor stronghold of Chicago as one of the most desirable remaining markets for expansion in North America (Mehta, Baiman, and Persky 2004). Although big-box firms such as Walmart and Target were the most visible investors in inner-city food retail, they were late joiners to the trend. In the previous decade national chains featuring smaller establishment sizes (such as Save-A-Lot and Food 4 Less) had targeted expansion efforts toward Chicago's burgeoning Hispanic and immigrant neighborhoods. Less easily measured but more significant than big-box retailers in terms of market share was the rise of midsize independent grocery stores that paid near the legal minimum wage and frequently violated wage-and-hour, workplace safety, and collective bargaining laws.

These midsize grocers are the primary site of labor degradation within the food retail industry in Chicago. They operate in predominantly immigrant neighborhoods and occupy a distinct niche in a segment of the consumer market that both national chain supermarkets and big-box retailers have effectively ceded. Their average floor space of 20,000 square feet was the industry standard twenty years ago but today places them at about half the size of new chain supermarkets (Pothukuchi 2005). In fact, many of these stores operate in old facilities that Chicago's two major chains, Jewel and Dominick's, have abandoned within the past fifteen years. As most analyses of retailing predict, employers in this industry segment emphasize low prices. Cut-rate produce and meat surround the entrance to virtually every store, and consumers develop buying allegiances based on the quality and cost of fresh food. Yet low prices comprise only the most visible part of these firms' competitive strategies. These thriving midsize retailers successfully effect ethnic solidarity with their customers—using music, displays, and holiday foods fitted to the multicontinental mix of immigrants who account for a large part of consumer purchasing power in the city's outer neighborhoods—and take advantage of Chicago's open-air markets and thriving wholesaling industry to tap niche products neglected by international retailing chains with limited sensitivity to neighborhood idiosyncrasies (Faura 2004). Far from functioning as simple cost cutters, firms in this dynamic market segment combine the ability to fragment and differentiate markets with cut-rate labor costs and high worker productivity.

The traditional view on retailing does not accommodate this reality, and yet this combination of product quality and cost cutting lies at the center of a potent competitive strategy. In the midsize industry segment, low prices are accompanied by widespread employer efforts to hold down labor costs. Unionization is rare or nonexistent, and employers freely admit to hiring undocumented workers and paying the minimum wage or less (King, Leibtag, and Behl 2004). But central though low pay is in this industry segment, getting the most out of employees extends beyond holding the line on wages. Workers report long hours, unstable pay, threats of violence against prounion activity, constant threats of job termination, and a general workplace atmosphere in which the threat of retribution against unsatisfactory behavior always looms (Ness 2005; Bernhardt et al. 2005).

The mass deskilling of occupations within the industry plays a central role in this price-based competition (Davis et al. 2005). Employment tasks in supermarkets are either heavily routinized (e.g., inventory, checkout) or labor intensive and easily taught (e.g., meat cutting, produce stocking). Employers have much to gain from holding down labor costs and receive limited returns from employing highly skilled labor. Thus, maintaining low labor costs is one sure path to profit in an industry that offers few. The nature of food retailing—which like the idealized industries of economics textbooks offers consumers the opportunity to make exact price-based comparisons between interchangeable products—leaves firms with relatively few opportunities to expand profits through price increases. Instead, most retailers seek to expand aggregate profit—but not profit margins—by generating additional sales volume. Opportunities to pad profit margins are rarer. Firms can attempt to cut either overhead and supply costs through consolidation and economy-of-scale bulk purchases or, more commonly, labor costs for a given level of sales.

This overview of the industry supports both a simple economic analysis emphasizing the links between labor costs and price cutting and a more expansive inquiry instead focused on the cultural construction of the wildly heterogeneous and segmented end markets in a city undergoing rapid ethnic, income, and neighborhood changes. The task for organizers and regulators interested in improving working conditions in the industry is to conceptually sever the labor-sweating tactics of these firms from the sophisticated market-making techniques that implicitly and falsely suggest a predisposition toward higher-wage employment.

### *Big Contracts and Cheap Workers: The Residential Construction Boom*

In terms of output, the residential construction industry was one of the great economic successes of the otherwise feeble 2001–7 business cycle. Nationwide, the total dollar value of housing construction rose by more than 50 percent (U.S. Census Bureau 2000c, 2001, 2002, 2003b, 2004b, 2005c, 2006b). But as was the case for the economy writ large, these output and profit gains yielded minimal benefits for workers. Nationally, pay rates for residential construction held steady despite a white-hot labor market. In Cook County pay rates actually fell, and working conditions worsened significantly.

In Chicago the dramatic changes in industry employment practices were most evident in the booming day labor street corners at which contractors hired workers throughout the boom. The working conditions of day laborers offer a glimpse into what the U.S. workplace might look like had the New Deal never happened. At the end of a grueling work day, day laborers often walk away without pay or with lower wages than expected thanks to their employers docking them for lost contracts or inadequate work. (Sometimes, employers simply leave without paying at all.) On-the-job injuries are common to the point that it is impossible to ignore the limited dexterity of many workers' hands. Even when they avoid wage theft and observable on-the-job injuries, workers pay a physical price for their efforts. Working without formal training and often with minimal safety equipment, many day laborers quickly develop enduring back and wrist injuries and suffer from heavy exertion and exposure to heat and dust (Buchanan 2004).

As is the case for any degraded work arrangement, the brutality of these working conditions implies that labor cost cutting is indispensable to construction contractors. And indeed, the cost-saving benefits of hiring day laborers (manifest in the unheard-of phenomenon of industry wages falling during a record employment boom) are clear. As in food retail, labor costs are one of the primary expenses for contractors, and hiring contingent day laborers—who daily bid down their own wages in a spot market and have little power to negotiate favorable working conditions—has a clear and direct impact on the bottom line. Evidence of contractors' preference for undocumented workers (a group to which the overwhelming majority of day laborers belongs) can be seen in the remarkable fact that as construction work began to disappear in late 2006 and early 2007 formally reported construction employment remained level (Pew Hispanic Center 2007). This finding confirms what other studies of construction and day labor have reported: that a substantial portion of the residential construction workforce is employed informally (Center to Protect Workers' Rights 2002).

Yet despite this focus on cost cutting, the residential construction industry does not otherwise bear the characteristics of a sector in which unmitigated interfirm competition and price cutting reign. Though significant portions of the work are fully deskilled, others—ranging from drywalling to framing doors to basic carpentry—entail a far higher formal skill level than is found in a typical industrial laundry or hotel, or in neighborhood retailers. And the organization of the industry itself suggests substantial variation in contractor practices. The volume of construction work is highly variable—not just from season to season but within and across business cycles and quite often over the course of an individual job. In order to complete a small rehabilitation project, a contractor typically brings in a number of trade specialists, including drywallers, carpenters, and pipe fitters, to undertake specialized tasks. The sheer difficulty of hiring and coordinating these specialists places contractors at persistent risk of cost overruns and idle work time (Finkel 1997; Philips 2003).

In addition to providing general contractors with functional flexibility and the ability to avoid paying idled workers, the subcontracting system formalizes cost-based bidding throughout the construction process. As they install a new bathroom or gut a century-old three-flat construction contractors will formally and informally solicit bids for general laborers, electrical contractors, pipe fitters, and other specialists and general laborers. This repeated bidding process holds down labor costs, yet the relationship between labor costs and end prices in residential construction is weak. Even in the best of cases, homeowners and fledgling developers (new entrepreneurs who made up much of the residential market in Chicago in the early 2000s) are ill equipped to understand the construction process and to evaluate bids from contractors. In other words, the bidding process functions much less transparently between homeowners and contractors than it does between contractors and subcontractors. Surprisingly, the information asymmetries of the process leave general contractors considerable ability to fragment end markets and control the price-setting process. This market-making power was especially potent late in the 2000–6 housing boom, when demand for remodeling and equity loan–driven home improvement significantly outstripped the supply of available contractors.

This discrepancy between cut-rate day labor and high bid prices fueled by the boom raises a provocative question central to any effort by organizers, regulators, or academics to identify responses to degraded work: did contractors capitalize their ever-lower labor costs into bids, or were they able to pocket low labor costs as extra profit?

## Researching Local Industries: Creative Data Sources and Creative Methods

Local-serving industries such as residential construction and food retail remain underresearched in part because they are difficult to study. The standard data and methodological tools used in industry studies have limited purchase when market share is diffuse and individual business establishments are small. The problem begins with the extremely limited information provided by commonly used Census and Bureau of Labor Statistics data sources. Standardized industry codes provide finely grained detail on manufacturing industries, distinguishing Hosiery and Sock Mills, for example, from Sheer Hosiery Mills. But these same classifications lump all supermarkets—big-box, limited assortment, meat and produce, specialty—into a single industry category. The problem is more severe with residential construction. Though the North American Industrial Classification System provides a handful of classifications for general contractors, it provides no way to distinguish whether specialty contractors work in the labor-intensive residential construction industry segment or in the capital-intensive and often unionized commercial construction segment.

A better set of industry codes would solve only a small share of the research problems, especially in residential construction. To the never-ending frustration of low-wage construction workers, the contractors and trade specialists who build housing additions, install vanities, remodel kitchens, and divide rooms rarely maintain fixed business addresses. The typical contractor I encountered in my research provided a business card with a cell phone number only—no land line, no address, and no licensing information. When I back-checked the contractor names against incorporation records filed with the Illinois secretary of state or the City of Chicago's registry of known business aliases, I found an official record no more than one time out of ten. Invisible even to the workers they hire, these construction contractors are clearly omitted from federal data sets, with the result that typical industry-study methods would fail to reach the very employers of interest in questions of workplace downgrading.

A typical response to these shortcomings is to rely on secondary data sources, an approach I embraced. Trade journals, industry association reports, and special reports from the Bureau of the Census and the Department of Labor (especially the Economic Census and the Census Bureau's Nonemployer Statistics, which captures information on sole-proprietorship businesses through tax filings) provide information on firm-level expenditures, labor costs, and other industry characteristics that help researchers to stitch together a comprehensive picture of industry change. Starting with this limited information, I developed a research model that interrogated the expansion, contraction, and restructuring of different industry segments. Focusing on the changing boundaries of industry segments considerably clarified the research task. By narrowing the field in which employer strategy was to be examined to particular industry subsegments, I was able to simultaneously narrow the list of research questions and research subjects. My plan for data collection and analysis was to triangulate heavily (Fielding and Fielding 1986). By tacking back and forth between lines of questioning, types of data, and types of research subjects—and consistently comparing the findings from every source as the investigation progressed—I was able to corroborate core conclusions and isolate with confidence significant findings on employer strategy and its variabilities.

I studied Chicago's food retail and residential construction sectors between 2005 and 2009, focusing my efforts on understanding *where* the profit created by degrading work went and *how* access to vulnerable workers changed competition and employer strategy in the industry. A slight majority of the data in this book was retrieved during a sustained one-year engagement during the 2006 calendar year.

My primary research tools were interviews and participant observation. Interviews established and went far toward answering the main questions at issue in each industry. I conducted a total of fifty-six food retail interviews—twenty-two with employers, seventeen with employees, and nineteen with other industry participants—between March 2005 and July 2009. The sampling frame from which I drew these interviews was surprisingly easy to define. It consisted of the owners of midsize independent supermarkets (10,000 to 40,000 square feet with a median size below 20,000 square feet), workers in those same supermarkets, and officials in labor unions and community-based organizations operating in the industry and the neighborhoods where they thrived.

I began by interviewing a subset of employers stratified to represent different sizes of firms and then expanded the interviews to cover workers and other industry participants. The easy accessibility of business owners and the forthright way in which they discussed sensitive employment questions made the strategy of beginning with firms, as opposed to workers, especially productive. The food retail employers I interviewed owned a total of forty-seven establishments at the time; as a group they represented approximately 8 percent of the nonchain food retail market in Chicago.[6] Accessible through repeated on-site visits to their stores, these employers made themselves available for interviews lasting an average of one and one-half hours. No employer formally declined an interview, although some simply could not be reached.

The findings and conclusions from a first wave of employer interviews anchored my subsequent conversations with workers, most of whom were recruited into the study through labor unions and community-based organizations. With tentative maps of industry structure and profit-making models in hand, I used these worker interviews not just to document degraded working conditions (many of which the employers themselves had mapped) but also to understand day-to-day workplace practices and the reasons why workers persisted in working amid routine labor law violations. Complementing these worker interviews with interview data from other industry participants, I launched a second round of employer interviews designed to probe and validate my revised findings. I stopped seeking additional interviews when the responses from employers began to echo one another.

Because the residential remodeling subsegment of construction was considerably harder to identify than were midsize supermarkets, I took the opposite approach in that industry, beginning with workers rather than employers. Day laborers work for a broad range of residential contractors (e.g., framing, drywalling, demolition, remodeling), a fact that places them in an ideal position to provide an overview of the types of contracts and jobs in which degraded work flourish. I conducted a total of eighty residential construction interviews—fifty-four with workers, sixteen with employers, and ten with other industry participants—primarily in 2006 and 2007. The sampling frame contained general contractors and specialty subcontractors, day laborers, other laborers employed by these contractors, and a set of other industry participants consisting primarily of construction labor unions and not-for-profit agencies serving the day labor workforce.

I recruited workers from the day labor corner in Albany Park on the Northwest Side; from the Albany Park Worker Center and the Latino Union, the organization that ran it; from San Lucas Worker Center, a community-based organization supporting workers who sometimes worked as construction day laborers; and from Mexico Solidarity Network, a not-for-profit organization whose Chicago branch worked closely with many immigrant workers and day laborers. The interviews were primarily conducted in Spanish and ranged in duration from fifteen minutes (the longest amount of time I could secure talking to a worker waiting for a contractor at the shape-up) to two hours or more, as sometimes happened during slow days when few contractors visited the Albany Park Worker Center to offer work.

Knowing that access to contractors would be fleeting, I used these worker interviews to map the scope, conditions, and prevalence of degraded work in the industry. In particular, I asked workers to describe the types of contractors and types of properties on which they worked. Spread out over fifty-four interviews, these questions established that day laborers worked primarily for residential remodeling contractors and for small specialty subcontractors who competed on cost. The interviews also established the geography of this work (primarily the North Side and the near northern suburbs), the relationship of the contractors hiring day laborers to other contractors, and the general finances of contractors. Before starting the contractor interviews, I tested and deepened the conclusions from worker interviews by conducting an extensive review of the available secondary materials. With these data in hand, I began the contractor interviews. Interviews lasted on average one hour and fifteen minutes and ranged from half an hour to two and one-half hours in length.

### *The Importance of Observing Employers and Workplace Conflicts Directly*

In both industries, but especially in residential construction, these interviews went hand in hand with participant observation. In residential construction, helping day laborers negotiate pay disputes, rent problems, and everyday relationships with contractors were the essential methods through which I built the trust to obtain interviews. For one year between mid-2006 and mid-2007, I spent the equivalent of a full work day per week working with and for day laborers. For most of this period, I served as an occasional coordinator at the Albany Park Worker Center on Chicago's Northwest Side. In this role I met many contractors and became familiar with the surprisingly haphazard process through which contractors assembled the materials, work plans, and workers to fulfill five-figure bids. During this period I also was a part of the center's Wage Theft (Robo de Salarios) Task Force. This put me in the position of tracking down contractors who had failed to pay day laborers as promised, a common occurrence in the industry. Following wage disputes up the subcontracting chain—from unpaid day laborers to the labor subcontractors who had refused to pay them to the homeowner or general contractor who had begun the process by withholding pay from everybody else—provided rich data on the ways in which contingent employment relationships regulate the industry's ever-present risk and pay disputes.

My relationship with these workers eventually led me to perform a number of employment-related favors outside the auspices of the worker center. In particular, I negotiated disputes with landlords and spent many afternoons helping workers to file claims at Cook County's small claims court. These experiences were invaluable in highlighting the overall contingency of day laborers' lives: most of the day laborers I met shuffled jobs and apartments so constantly that they were rarely able to make scheduled appointments to visit a contractor, a landlord, or a judge at small claims court.

My participation with food retail workers consisted of a small number of employer protests, handbilling in a few establishments, and dozens of hours spent walking through the supermarkets themselves to observe butchers, produce packers, and foremen at work, as well as low-income families as they shopped. These methods helped to illuminate the rapid pace and serious demeanor of work, as well as the importance of fresh produce and meat to the supermarkets' competitive model, in a way that interviews alone would not have.

In each industry I repeatedly moved back and forth between the complex primary data and a broad range of secondary information that could clarify, confirm, and challenge the findings I had made. In food retail this secondary data primarily consisted of trade publications, especially the journal *Progressive Grocer,* and various reports from the Food Market Institute; a burgeoning entrepreneur's literature for new supermarkets attempting to profit from "ethnic" populations (see especially Faura 2004 and Perkins 2004); select industry data from scholars, particularly King, Leibtag, and Behl's "Supermarket Characteristics and Operating Costs in Low-Income Areas" (2004), a report for the U.S. Department of Agriculture; and the marketing firms TradeDimensions and InfoUSA, who provided market-share data and a list of establishment addresses from which to build my sampling frame, respectively.

The secondary data sources available for residential construction were considerably more limited, although they could be used more straightforwardly. The Census Bureau's Nonemployer Tax Statistics provided highly aggregated but useful data on the finances of residential remodeling contractors. For a broader picture of the basic segmentation of the residential construction industry and its composition in Cook County, I relied on the Census of Construction. For wage and compensation data, I used the Bureau of Labor Statistics' Quarterly Census of Employment and Wages (ES-202) data and the Current Population Survey. Although these data did not speak directly to the issue of degraded work, they helped to establish a consistent picture of falling establishment size and increasing subcontracting in the industry and cohere with other sources of evidence. Still, the data provided few clear clues by themselves. It was only through the *relational* work of linking workers to contractors, contractors to general contractors, and general contractors to particular submarkets within Chicago that I was able to build a testable model of profit making and labor degradation in residential construction.

These methodological details form an important plank of the book's core argument. Degraded work remains an elusive problem, nearly invisible to policy makers, in substantial part because it is so difficult to see. Degraded work practices are concentrated in particular industry segments and occupational niches, in subsets of employers that cannot readily be identified from industry employment and payroll totals, and in firms whose changing strategies and workplace practices cannot be understood without close study of their business models, labor practices, and market niches. Mapping, understanding, and responding to degraded work means supplanting industry analysis conducted at a distance with detailed mixed-methods work whose content, sequence, and validation must be continually reassessed and adjusted.

### *From the Globe to the Firm: Charting Degradation at the Scale of Neighborhoods and Workplaces*

Urban research faces the often unnoted challenge of adapting ideas developed to explain national and international developments to fit urban-scale economic and political-economic realities, realities that cannot be deduced from the bigger picture. Some of the resulting slippages are obvious. Moving from globalization-derived concepts that stress the multiregional remaking of urban economies *in the aggregate* to investigations of particular cases of urban restructuring entails a necessary shift from the abstract to the particular and from a globe-encompassing model to the sometimes dissonant specifics of individual economies. Critics of the conceptual and methodological shortcomings that follow often characterize the problem as one of top-down, overdetermined analysis (Smith 2001; Sellers 2002). This critique is useful but incomplete. The problem is not just the direction of the analysis but also the measurement error that results from applying global categories locally.

The presumed antidote is to examine urban economic reorganization from the ground up, to move from the particular to the general instead of vice versa. But these efforts, though helpful, run into similar obstacles if they use conceptual categories inherited from work on global economic structure. In particular, the binary quality of common descriptions of inequality—evident in Mollenkopf and Castells's dual city formulation and in the common metaphor of polarization—collapses enormous volumes of complex economic restructuring into the flattened analytical category of a disappearing middle. Often treated as an end point, polarization can be productively thought of as a process, one in which disappearing middle classes and midincome neighborhoods adapt, change, and restructure as professionals and entry-level workers pull further apart. A dual economic structure looms as the logical conclusion of Chicago's ongoing economic changes, but in the meantime, local-serving industries are growing, contracting, and remaking themselves in ways that cannot be deduced from the broader pattern of economic reorganization.

Adopting this process-based view of local economic restructuring in particular helps to clarify the actions of employers in industries uniquely sensitive to local changes. Whereas changes in employment at automotive assembly plans, investment banks, and law firms reflect changes in the distant markets with which those industries interact, the restructuring of employment in retail, construction, and other local–serving industries modulates in accordance with the strategies firms pursue in order to take advantage of the complex and localized shifts in population and income that follow deindustrialization. Understanding these industries on their own terms helps to flesh out incomplete conceptualizations of economic reorganization. It does something more tangible, besides. The necessarily localized picture of industry transformation in the following chapters provides a detailed competitive map in response to which organizing and legal strategies for improving employment can be tailored.

The benefits to this approach emerge in the close study of Chicago's local-serving industries. Viewed from afar, residential construction and food retail appear to provide limited potential, if any, for firms to upgrade wages and working conditions without sacrificing their competitive position in the market. But a localized analysis reveals clear and structured areas of surplus profit, built from operating, locational, and contracting practices that insulate firms from intensive price-based competition. At present the path to taking advantage of this analytical step forward—to building a fuller accounting of urban economic change or crafting strategies for upgrading wages and working conditions—remains unclear. But the opportunity to treat these industries as dynamic and capable of workplace change exists. The opportunities emerge clearly in the food retail sector, where new entrepreneurs are flourishing amid a little-documented industry boom.

# 4

# Oases in the Midst of Deserts

## *How Food Retailers Thrive in Disinvested Neighborhoods*

After decades of disinvestment by international chains, food deserts—neighborhoods whose typically low-income residents lack access to fresh and affordable food—strain the budgets and bodies of tens of thousands of households on Chicago's historically African American South and West Sides (Cotterill and Franklin 1985). But the spread of food deserts has been reversed in the city's expanding immigrant neighborhoods, where the news that many Chicago residents lack access to fresh food seems like a bulletin from another world. Bright, bustling supermarkets crowd the major thoroughfares of the Little Village, Pilsen, Portage Park, Rogers Park, and Belmont-Cragin. They celebrate fresh food, lining the entrance and, sometimes, the parking lot with bins of fresh produce at prices that would be unthinkable in a chain supermarket: tomatoes, $0.49 per pound; lemons, four for a dollar; red peppers, $0.99 per pound.

Inside, these neighborhood markets bustle with tightly packed shoppers and workers. Accordion-laden *norteño* music saturates the air in La Villita and the Hispanic neighborhoods on the Northwest Side, but this being Chicago, the visitor can hear pop from Bosnia, India, Bulgaria, and points in between. The bright colors, ebullient music, and forced cheer almost mask the tightness of the space. At less than 20,000 square feet on the average, Chicago's bustling neighborhood supermarkets are less than half the size of the typical new supermarket built today. Because their delivery bays are few and their aisles are narrow, these businesses reverse the long-term industry trend by substituting labor for capital. Workers—usually Hispanic and immigrant—drive vans to the Chicago International Produce Market every morning to pick up the day's produce. Butchers staff cut-to-order meat counters of the type that disappeared from chain supermarkets long ago. In a simple but exhausting response to the difficulty of fitting forklifts into cramped spaces, workers carry box after box of produce and dry goods to the shelves, effectively substituting sweat for technology.

The layout of these growing retailers betrays their essential business model. The cereal boxes, frozen dinners, and packaged goods that take up the bulk of the space in chain supermarkets are typically confined to just a few aisles. To reach a bag of rice, shoppers have to pass through a maze of fresh fruits and vegetables—some establishments go so far as to build hairpin turns into their voluminous produce sections—and then a long butcher's counter ringed by shoppers patiently waiting to request the cut of their choosing. As the cashiers staffing the few available registers work their way through long lines of penny-pinching customers they enter hundreds of produce item numbers from memory. Every store has bar code scanners, but they do relatively little of the work, considering that fresh foods make up a majority of purchases.

Once the product of isolated cases of entrepreneurial wizardry, these burgeoning midsize supermarkets—significantly larger than corner stores but constrained by small and outmoded facilities—are now the result of a highly successful, easily reproduced business model that diverts considerably more business from Chicago's unionized supermarkets than do either Walmart or Target. In the eyes of many advocates, this model confirms an optimistic trend in urban economic development. Since the mid-1990s, business school ambassadors for the inner city's competitive advantage have touted the high unemployment rates, low-wage households, and underserved markets of poor urban neighborhoods as the raw materials of a highly profitable strain of urban redevelopment (Porter 1995). A decade ago, these advocates hailed food retail as an archetypical industry for rebuilding neighborhood economies, a view that now dovetails with the mounting concern over food access among urban planners (Initiative for a Competitive Inner City 2002; Dunkley, Helling, and Sawicki 2004; Mari Gallagher Research & Consulting Group 2006). At their best, Chicago's midsize supermarkets promise a unique competitive elixir that provides jobs for the jobless and fresh, affordable food for neighborhoods recently blighted by commercial disinvestment.

But the downside of these booming supermarkets seems likely to cancel their benefits. Since the 1950s, food retail has been the rare service industry in the United States that reliably offers above-poverty wages and stable jobs to less skilled workers (Davis et al. 2005). As recently as 2003, workers in the industry's dominant segment of unionized chain employers typically earned wages of eleven dollars per hour or more and received full employment benefits, including health care (Grudin 2004). Walmart and the discount food retailers currently pushing their way into large U.S. cities buck this (comparatively) high-wage model in favor of pay rates at or near the minimum wage and a free hand in scheduling workers and setting rules and job tasks in the workplace. Those same low-wage practices only begin to describe employment conditions in Chicago's midsize supermarkets, which accounted for four times as much market share as Walmart and its big box peers in the 2000s. Although wage levels in these supermarkets often surpass the legal minimum, a variety of degraded work practices characterize the day-to-day business of the industry. Workers earn subminimum "tipped" wages, but without tips. Employers fine their employees for taking bathroom breaks, lunch breaks, and vacation days. The emerging problem of just-in-time scheduling—in which employers expand or contract a worker's scheduled hours on the spot to match labor costs with retail volume on an unexpectedly busy Tuesday afternoon or a surprisingly quiet Saturday morning—frustrates workers' efforts to align their primary jobs with secondary jobs and child care. Most strikingly, workers who seek union representation to remedy these problems are dismissed, harassed, and denied wages, all in clear violation of federal law.

These low wages and poor working conditions undeniably reflect simple opportunism on the part of employers with access to vulnerable populations of undocumented workers. But the way those employers meld that opportunism with classic strategies for fragmenting and making markets is distinctive. The expansion of food retail into lower-income Chicago neighborhoods is not a haphazard process but rather the outcome of a fully realized competitive strategy based more on access to niche suppliers and low-income consumers than on access to a workforce whose conditions of employment could be degraded at will.

The complexity of this strategy suggests an alternate path to reregulating what was once a family wage service industry. Standard analyses of industry structure and restructuring suggest that these supermarkets face a stark choice between competing on food quality and variety or on low costs. Given the low-income neighborhoods they target, this would not be much of a choice at all. But in reality these labor-sweating employers do both: they sell highly specialized foodstuffs national supermarkets cannot stock and high-quality meat and produce at low prices that chains cannot approach. Unpacking the various components of this strategy and clarifying the extent to which labor-sweating represents opportunism rather than competitive necessity suggests new approaches for organizing workers and crafting public policy interventions to reverse the slide in job quality.

## Fordist Supermarkets: From Corner Retailers to International Industry

The success of the new midsize supermarkets flourishing in large cities builds from the historic underserving of lower-income urban neighborhoods by large supermarket chains, and it does so in a straightforward way. These retailers have carved out market share by moving into neighborhoods—and often facilities—long abandoned by the chains. Yet behind this seemingly straightforward story of disinvestment, opportunism, and reinvestment lie deep structural changes within the food retail industry itself. As it has followed the long-run cycle of urban disinvestment and latter-day gentrification, the industry has shifted from a small-scale local industry to a Fordist industry complete with vertical integration and internal labor markets to a quintessentially post-Fordist industry struggling with market saturation and increasing cost competitiveness. Accordingly, evaluating the growth of midsize retailers in low-income neighborhoods means understanding the industry-level trends leading to the historical rise and current decline of chain supermarkets.

Chain grocery stores emerged in the mid-1950s, most frequently from independent businesses that expanded by building new facilities or acquiring other locally owned independent supermarkets (Burns 1982). These growing chains sought increased profits through continued growth, and given the rapid growth of suburbs, it is not surprising that they quickly moved beyond the city limits. Suburbs didn't just offer the potential for growth—they offered the potential for growth on terms immensely favorable to the high-volume, low-margins grocery business (Pothukuchi 1985). Whereas the size and, hence, profit-making potential of grocery stores had been historically constrained by the high cost of central-city land and the difficulty of developing suitable retail sites in tightly packed neighborhoods, suburbs presented chain groceries with inexpensive land and the potential for large, state-of-the-art buildings with ample room for parking (Dunkley, Helling, and Sawicki 2004). The drive to suburban expansion was intensified by the fact that many of the residents populating these new suburbs had relocated from the cities in which grocery chains began, thus reducing consumer density. Impelled by the stick of thinning urban neighborhoods and drawn by the carrot of easy development, the major grocery chains continue to the present day to shutter old sites and concentrate capital reinvestment in the growing urban periphery.

The organization and profit-making models of the industry also changed as a part of this push out of the urban core. The easy comparability of prices on food items makes the industry come remarkably close to textbook conditions of perfect competition. As national chains bought up regional chains they intensified this cost competitiveness by instituting price wars with large competitors upon moving into new markets (Pongracz, n.d.). As a result of both the nature of the products and the institutionalized drive to cost-based competition, pretax profit margins in the industry typically hover under 1 percent (Food Marketing Institute 2007). With cost cutting established as a basic order of business for both firms and consumers, grocery chains primarily build profits by adding sales volume. The volume-based sales strategy is evident in the physical organization of the modern grocery store, which has steadily grown larger as supermarket chains have added nongrocery revenue sources (e.g., prepared-food counters, banking facilities, and restaurants). The median square footage of grocery stores in higher-income suburban areas is nearing 40,000 square feet. By contrast, the median square footage of the stores that chains have ceded to independent grocers in poorer urban neighborhoods is just 17,000 square feet (King, Leibtag, and Behl 2004).

Beyond the construction of larger stores, the drive to add total revenues is most evident in the structure of the industry. Partially as a means of realizing economies-of-scale discounts from suppliers, partially as a matter of industry maturation, and partially as a means of adding to total sales volumes, grocery chains themselves have consolidated. The industry's first wave of consolidation almost directly coincided with the first period of urban retail disinvestment. From 1955 to 1964, large grocery chains acquired dozens of subsidiary chains and hundreds of stores each year. This burst was halted not by the chains themselves but by regulators. Fearing that the brisk pace of acquisitions would lead to an oligopolistic and noncompetitive industry, the Federal Trade Commission began in 1965 to issue judgments prohibiting larger grocery chains from acquiring any company with sales of more than $500 million. When these ten-year judgments expired in the late 1970s, large grocery chains vigorously renewed their acquisition activity (Burns 1982). This kicked off a merger-and-acquisition period that has continued to the present. In the mid-2000s approximately

80 percent of the grocery stores in higher-income areas were owned by chains of 10 or more stores; more than half were owned by chains of more than 50 stores; and more than one-third were owned by chains of 750 stores or more. In observing these changes, labor unions representing industry employees increasingly talk about the globalization of the supermarket industry and the attendant cost-cutting pressure that falls on local supermarket chains as they are incorporated into national chains such as Safeway and Supervalu.

Given these particulars of industry organization—the drive to market expansion, industry domination by a handful of large firms, and cost-based competition—it is not a stretch to conceive of the contemporary food retail business as Fordist. Taking advantage of their size—in every sense of the word—grocery chains seek economies-of-scale cost reductions from purchasing discounts, spread shared overhead costs over an ever-increasing number of stores, and pursue capital-equipment improvements and technological innovations enabled by the growing size of supermarket facilities. And like Fordist manufacturing industries, they do so with a large portion of their workers under union contract.

## Fragmented Incomes and Populations Challenge the Fordist Retailing Model

Like Fordist modes of production in manufacturing, the Fordist strategy in food retail has inherent shortcomings. Foremost among these is the limitation of growth as a means of generating profit. After expanding regionally and nationally, the major grocery chains in the United States have effectively saturated suburban markets and run out of new opportunities for regional growth. Additionally, the consumer landscape in which retailers operate has changed dramatically. Where Fordist manufacturers have restructured to incorporate flexible production techniques and tailor output to increasingly fragmented consumers markets, food retailers increasingly must reckon with cultural and income fragmentations in their previously homogenous customer base (Harvey 1989). For a number of reasons, both the large chains and their main competitors have been unable to do so.

First, urban locations pose physical challenges to profit-making strategies predicated on large business establishments. Population density, small lot sizes, and high land costs in large cities make the assembly of the large facilities on which the Fordist retailing model depends both logistically difficult and financially risky (Turock 2005; Initiative for a Competitive

Inner City 2002). At a basic level space is a prerequisite for profit making. But by and large, it is a luxury unaffordable to new entrants into the retail grocery business in densely populated cities such as Chicago. To begin with, opening an urban supermarket often entails high up-front capital outlays in the form of site-acquisition costs related to the logistical and legal complications of purchasing and receiving planning approvals for the multiple lots needed to house a grocery store. For these reasons many of Chicago's recent entrants into the midsize supermarket industry made the decision to enter the business only *after* a suitably large property requiring minimal capital investment became available (Boston Consulting Group 1998; Dunkley, Helling, and Sawicky 2004).

But the real physical constraints of operating an urban supermarket become clear after the site has been obtained. The considerable effort and capital cost involved in site acquisition produce supermarkets that are often half the size or less of suburban supermarkets. The smaller square footage immediately removes a number of competitive options—such as a warehousing format or profit-padding sales in clothing, electronics, and housewares—from consideration.[1] Smaller overall square footage and older buildings also increase operating costs. For example, small delivery spaces and antiquated loading facilities increase the expenses—labor and otherwise—involved with shipping and receiving and restrict the overall pace at which merchandise can be circulated and sold (King, Leibtag, and Behl 2004). With fewer overall products to choose from, urban consumers tend to make a larger number of grocery shopping trips. As a result, urban supermarkets spend more than others on labor costs, particularly for cashiers and shelf stockers (King, Leibtag, and Behl 2004). This is where persistent price-based competition exerts a clear impact on industry structure and profitability. Urban supermarkets, like others, have a limited ability to compensate for increased operating costs by raising prices. Accordingly, their owners generally accept diminished profit margins, find new means for cutting operating costs, or open new establishments only when especially high population density, household spending, or geographical isolation from competitors can compensate for diminished margin potential.

The viability of Fordist production models in manufacturing industries depended on firms' ability to sustain the virtuous circle of rising wages and rising production by expanding gross output, identifying new end markets, and insulating themselves from competition (Amin 1994). These conditions are coming undone in the food retail industry just as surely as they have in manufacturing. As a mature industry with limited capacity for expansion and stiff competition on the horizon, the large-chain segment of food retail faces a number of distinct threats. The first, familiar from news coverage of Walmart's contested efforts to enter Los Angeles, Chicago, and New York, is increasing competition from new sources. The conditions of limited competition are waning as dollar stores, drug stores, specialty foods stores, and warehouse retailers make inroads on the sale of food items that were once the sole province of supermarkets (Davis et al. 2005). Walmart's 1,400-plus supercenters, which combine discount grocery stores with the company's standard discount retail outlets, attack chain grocery market share through both price reductions and convenience and constitute a particularly acute threat to industry market share. Because profit seeking in the industry depends in large part on isolation from competition—in terms of physical distance, prices, product mix, or services—the proliferation of these alternative sources of groceries strains the ability of large chains to generate profits against the high-overhead, union-labor structure they have developed.

The majority of these new competitors place cost cutting at the center of their business models. With a handful of exceptions, new competitors employ nonunion workforces whose total compensation costs are substantially lower than those of the large chains (Davis et al. 2005). This is especially true in the case of Walmart and Target, whose supply-chain pricing power yields deep cuts in the cost of retail goods, allowing them to undercut the large chains—sometimes dramatically. In response to the low-cost workforces of these competitors, employment restructuring and other efforts to slash labor costs are now routine in the major chains, as are two-tier wage agreements, in which new union hires accept substantially lower starting wages, as well as lower overall pay and benefits ceilings, than previously hired workers (Tarnowski 2006; Progressive Grocer 2006).

The major chains' commitment to cutting wages and benefits became evident in the Southern California grocery lockout of 2003 and 2004, in which local chains owned by Safeway and Supervalu absorbed hundreds of millions of dollars in lost revenue in order to secure diminished wage and benefits scales for new union enrollees (Grudin 2004). The lockout strategy worked in large part because of the options that store acquisition and geographical expansion offer to the large chains. In the days of smaller, regionally concentrated chains, the strike was an effective weapon because it could easily cut off a substantial portion of a conglomerate's revenue. But the size of larger, geographically extensive chains insulates them against this strategy. With a base of hundreds or thousands of stores to generate sales, they can wait out a strike with minimal risk. Industry consolidation amounts to a straightforward demonstration of the aphorism that capital doesn't have to eat, but labor does.

Cost aside, chain supermarkets are suffering from widespread consumer fragmentation and the growing mismatch between diverse consumer populations and the one-size-fits-all product offerings and store formats that have long been the industry standard. Fordist supermarkets developed in a context of limited competition, growth in the middle class, and comparative ethnic homogeneity. National product lines and standardized retailing formats fit this population with a modicum of ease. But today, they struggle to adapt to increasing consumer fragmentation. These changes have led chain grocers to lose market share to new, independent competitors more keenly tuned to the needs and wants of immigrant and ethnic populations.

## The Rise of Midsize Independent Supermarkets and Degraded Work

The growth of midsize independent supermarkets catering to immigrant populations—often referred to as *supermercados* in Chicago, although that label does not fit the dozens of establishments catering to other populations—in large cities is part of an urban reinvestment trend far more complicated than existing research on urban food retail suggests. Across multiple cities food retailers are moving into central-city neighborhoods whose long-term abandonment by retailers has been a point of contention among community-based organizations and lower-income consumers (Pothukuchi 2005). In the broadest sense food retail growth in central cities depends on the increasing heterogeneity of cities, at least in market terms (Pongracz 2006). Income polarization, immigration, changing ethnic makeup, and the widening gulf between well-off and low-income neighborhoods all provide the basis for competitive strategies in which food retailers target narrow population segments that fall outside the purview of national retailing chains who pursue one-size-fits-all business models (Eisenhauer 2001).

Because it is a point-of-entry city for immigrants and home to a large financial services industry, fragmentation has been dramatic in Chicago. From 1990 to 2006, the Hispanic share of the population grew by nearly

50 percent; the foreign-born population rose to nearly 22 percent of the city's total; and the share of high-income households earning more than $100,000 per year more than doubled, from 8 to 17 percent (Table 3). The growth of these population segments—particularly the Hispanic and foreign-born populations—has sped the development of new industry segments in food retail. The most readily visible, albeit most limited, industry segment belongs to chain and niche retailers targeting high-income neighborhoods. Gentrification and employment polarization in U.S. cities have produced ever-growing residential pockets of high-income earners, especially in large cities plugged into global financial networks. These populations are easily targeted by large chain supermarkets, whose sales models have favored high-income consumers for decades. They have also provided fertile ground for niche and specialty food retailers (such as Whole Foods and Trader Joe's) that emphasize unique and/or high-quality products. Despite the press they receive, the market share of these niche retailers is quite low. Together, they accounted for less than 1 percent of the total food retail market in the Chicago metropolitan area at the time of my research.[2]

On the other end of the spectrum, the persistent—and in many cases growing—poverty of inner city neighborhoods has provided new expansion opportunities for discount-driven retailers such as Walmart, Target, and Food 4 Less, whose cumulative market share in Chicago rose from 1.9 to 3.3 percent between 2001 and 2005.[3] These warehouse discounters draw on (mostly) nonunion workforces and economies-of-scale purchasing power to provide large cost discounts. Despite the attention this industry segment has received, it is actually slower growing and smaller in terms of market share than the industry niche occupied by discounters who provide cut-rate prices on a small selection of goods. Led by Aldi and Save-A-Lot, these retailers, known in the industry as limited-assortment stores, keep costs down by acquiring cheap land, offering few frills in terms of store layout and service, and offering a limited set of products and product sizes.[4] Although typically limited to less than 10,000 square feet, these stores have grown steadily, particularly in Chicago's lower-income and African American neighborhoods.[5] From 2001 to 2005, the market share of limited-assortment retailers in Chicago rose from 2.2 to 3.9 percent. The limited-assortment format constrains, however, the long-run growth potential of these stores, which typically feature bare-minimum quantities of fresh meat and produce and which cannot easily accommodate the niche-shopping needs of increasingly diverse urban populations.

TABLE 3

**Population and Income Fragmentation in Chicago, 1990–2006**

| | 1990 | 2000 | 2006 |
|---|---|---|---|
| Population | 2,783,726 | 2,895,964 | 2,749,283 |
| Race | | | |
| White | 45.5% | 42.0% | 36.5% |
| Black | 39.0% | 36.6% | 35.3% |
| Asian | 3.7% | 4.2% | 4.9% |
| Hispanic | 19.2% | 26.0% | 28.2% |
| Foreign-Born Population | 17.2% | 21.7% | 21.8% |
| Income | | | |
| Share of Households Earning $100,000 or More | 8% | 15% | 17% |
| Share of Households Earning Less Than $50,000 | 30% | 27% | 31% |
| Share of Households Earning Less Than $25,000 | 53% | 51% | 56% |

Income thresholds are in 2006 dollars. *Sources:* author's calculations from Summary File 3 of U.S. Census 2000 and the U.S. Census Bureau's 2006 American Community Survey. Both are available online.

Together, these high- and low-income neighborhoods will be familiar to most readers as the core stylized facts about urban economic restructuring in the 2000s. Yet the majority of new competitors in food retail operate outside such obviously polarized spaces, targeting instead the transitioning immigrant neighborhoods on Chicago's Southwest, Northwest, and Far North Sides. In fact, supermarkets that serve immigrant populations are the signature success story of urban food retail reinvestment (Initiative for a Competitive Inner City 2002). The typical supermarket in these neighborhoods is full service and offers dozens or hundreds of ethnic and specialty foods unavailable in large chains.

Yet despite the scale of their offerings, these firms are financially lean. To begin with, they are modest in size (10,000 to 20,000 square feet, compared with the 35,000-square-feet average of chain supermarkets) (King, Leibtag, and Behl 2004). They also employ a nonunion workforce and use more labor per unit sold than any other industry segment (selling $101 per

TABLE 4

**Supermarket Establishments and Market Share by Store Format, Chicago Metropolitan Statistical Area**

| MARKET SEGMENT | | 2001 | 2003 | 2005 |
|---|---|---|---|---|
| National Chains | Establishments | 282 | 281 | 269 |
| | Market Share (%) | 62.7 | 56.3 | 58.8 |
| Big Box | Establishments | 10 | 13 | 14 |
| | Market Share (%) | 1.9 | 2.0 | 3.0 |
| Limited Assortment | Establishments | 29 | 57 | 109 |
| | Market Share (%) | 2.2 | 2.7 | 3.9 |
| Midsize Independents | Establishments | 257 | 285 | 325 |
| | Market Share (%) | 9.5 | 10.8 | 12.2 |
| Other | Market Share (%) | 23.7 | 28.2 | 22.1 |

Store formats were determined by size of ownership group, use of independent supplier networks, and research on individual firms. *Sources:* author's calculations are from TradeDimensions 2002; 2004; 2006.

hour of labor versus $133 in the large chains). By staying small and flexible, these retailers exploit not only the underservice of the lower-income neighborhoods in which many immigrants live but also the inability of large chains to press their bulk purchase pricing advantages into service on culturally specific ethnic foods and fresh meat and produce (Pongracz 2006; Faura 2004). In Chicago these midsize independently operated supermarkets account for a significantly larger share of the market than do either the big-box discounters or limited-access retailers (Table 4).

Employers in each of these four industry segments—large chains, warehouses, limited-assortment stores, and midsize independents—pursue distinct operating strategies. Walmart-style warehouse discounters compete on cut-rate prices but not on produce and meat. Limited-assortment stores offer cut-rate prices to the exclusion of selection. Midsize independent supermarkets stand out because they combine multiple competitive strategies at use in other industry segments. Like warehouses and limited-selection retailers, they substantially undercut chain supermarket prices. And like Whole Foods and other niche retailers, they offer highly specialized goods that most food retailers do not.

The midsize industry segment is most potent in large cities with substantial immigrant populations, including Boston, New York, Chicago, Atlanta, Los Angeles, and Oakland (Boston Consulting Group 1998). The viability of these locations as sites for profitable food retail investment suggests that a driving force in the growth of urban food retailing is the emergence of identifiable (and presumably lower-income) immigrant groups. Yet few accounts of the industry's transformation explicitly knowledge the tacit focus of these business models on new immigrant populations.

As a result, the distinctive competitive challenges facing these retailers go unnoted. Existing research on midsize supermarkets generally ignores their cost-cutting practices or, remarkably, attempts to explain their ability to thrive despite the inaccurate assumption of *higher* overall food costs (Bolen and Hecht 2003). This raises the question, if low food costs depend on economies-of-scale bulk purchase discounts, then how do immigrant-serving supermarkets sell at costs well below the industry norm?

A review of degraded work strategies across industries suggests that low labor costs are the answer. As cataloged in chapter 2, food retail stands, behind construction, as the industry in which labor law violations have been most extensively documented. Unlike day labor work in construction, which tethers labor law violations to the extreme contingent employment status of workers, the degradations of low-end food retail work—denial of overtime pay, increasing weekly hours without increasing pay, and constant employer retribution against workers—are fully intertwined with an otherwise standard full-time employment relationship.

The relationship between low-cost food and low-cost labor potentially puts urban planners and community organizations in the uncomfortable position of choosing between affordable and readily available food, on the one hand, and jobs that pay a living wage, on the other. Yet as the elements of business operation in this industry segment—specialty goods, low prices, expansion into previously disinvested areas—suggest, the growth of urban food retailers cannot be simply read off from broader cycles of disinvestment and urban demographic change. Answering the question of why and how these retailers succeed means dissecting their business model and making sense of the necessary and opportunistic factors underpinning the segment's growth. An in-depth examination of competitive strategy can answer the bottom-line question of whether degraded work is a necessary component of reinvestment in city neighborhoods. The results have the power to declare false the supposed trade-off between reinvestment and good jobs.

## Midsize Supermarkets Exploit Holes in the Fordist Model

Where Walmart undercuts the chains on costs and upscale retailers outflank them on product specialization, immigrant food retailers take advantage of each of the main weaknesses in the Fordist competitive model: they are cheaper; they offer customized products the chains cannot; and as smaller stores with lower overhead costs, they operate profitability on parcels of land and in neighborhood markets that are too small for larger stores. Table 5 summarizes the main differences between midsize independent retailers and the chain supermarkets that have vacated cities.

The limitations of small size and old facilities predispose these retailers to compete on terms substantially different from those of the large chains. At 17,000 square feet the median small urban supermarket is less than half as large as its full-size competitors. These smaller supermarkets operate in facilities that are substantially older (a median age of thirty-seven years versus seventeen years for the large chains) and on average belong to chains containing just five total stores, as opposed to 140 for full-size supermarkets. Because they lack the facilities and bulk-purchasing power to drive economies-of-scale purchasing discounts and capital-intensive operational

TABLE 5

**Nationwide Characteristics of Midsize Urban Food Retailers, 2002**

| BASIC CHARACTERISTICS | MIDSIZE INDEPENDENTS | LARGE CHAINS |
|---|---|---|
| Median Square Footage | 17,000 | 34,000 |
| Median Store Age (Years) | 37 | 17 |
| Median # of Checkout Lanes | 5 | 10 |
| Median # Stores in Ownership Group | 5 | 140 |
| Neighborhood Population Density (Persons per Square Mile) | 1,587 | 1,453 |
| % Sales from Food Stamps | 13.3 | 3.0 |
| Median Household Income (2004 Dollars) | $41,600 | $59,600 |
| % White Population of Surrounding Area | 63 | 85 |

Statistics for midsize independents are drawn from the fifth of urban supermarkets serving the lowest-income populations. Figures for large chains correspond to supermarkets serving percentiles 60 through 80 of income. *Source:* adapted by the author from King, Leibtag, and Behl 2004.

efficiencies, it is not surprising that small retailers target a different segment of the consumer market. On the average, 13 percent of the food in these stores is purchased with food stamps, compared with just 3 percent in large supermarkets. They also operate in neighborhoods in which the median household income ($52,000 in 2002) is below the U.S. median of $55,900 (author's calculations from Ruggles et al. 2010; all figures are in 2011 dollars).

Research on community food systems and food safety suggests that these smaller retailers will charge more than large supermarkets because their purchasing costs are significantly higher (Short, Guthman, and Raskin 2007). Yet midsize supermarkets are able to offset a good portion of their higher purchase costs through substantially lower labor costs. Large supermarket chains are Fordist not just in their mass-production buying practices but also in their accommodation of union labor. In the mid-2000s nearly half of the large urban supermarkets in the United States employed a union workforce, as opposed to just 16 percent of small independents. As a result of their nonunion status and other factors, hourly wages in small supermarkets are about one-third lower—a figure that likely understates the labor cost differential given the expensive employee health plans in operation in most unionized workplaces. These lower costs in turn lead to a different organization of employment within the workplace. As efficiency-wage theories of the labor market would predict, employee turnover rates at the lower-wage stores are nearly double those in the higher-paying union stores (Katz 1986). In other words, small supermarkets cope with their pricing disadvantage not just through different pay rates but also through different employment practices.

Drawing on a substantially cheaper labor force, small urban supermarkets augment product sales with basic services and invest minimally in technology (Table 6). They are more labor intensive and employ far more workers per $100 of sales yet, owing to their lower per-hour labor costs, pay considerably *less* in total wages (8.5 percent of sales versus 10.5 percent in large chains). These low labor costs, combined with the constraints of operating in smaller, older facilities, also help to explain other aspects of the midsize supermarket operating model. Most striking, these businesses derive 31 percent of their sales revenues from labor-intensive meat and produce, compared with 21 percent in the large chains. These raw numbers understate the difference. Because their produce and meat prices are often 40 to 50 percent lower than those in the large chains, a better estimate is that midsize supermarkets sell nearly twice as much of these items.

TABLE 6

**Sales, Payroll, and Services in Urban Supermarkets**

| | MIDSIZE INDEPENDENTS | LARGE CHAINS |
|---|---|---|
| Sales and Payroll | | |
| Median Sales per Square Foot | $7.50 | $9.33 |
| Labor Hours per $100 in Sales | 0.99 | 0.75 |
| Payroll as % of Sales | 8.50 | 10.50 |
| Median % Sales from Produce | 31 | 21 |
| % of Establishments Offering Specific Products and Services | | |
| Carry-Out Food | 50 | 88 |
| In-Store Bakery | 48 | 80 |
| Internet Ordering | 7 | 30 |
| In-Store Banking | 16 | 28 |
| In-Store Pharmacy | 12 | 58 |

Statistics for midsize independents are drawn from the fifth of urban supermarkets serving the lowest-income populations. Figures for large chains correspond to supermarkets serving percentiles 60 through 80 of income. *Source:* adapted by author from King, Leibtag, and Behl 2004.

Far from merely rejecting the mass-ownership, economies-of-scale competitive model embraced by the major chains, midsize supermarkets have instead adopted a fully coherent countermodel that deliberately exploits the gaps in chain supermarkets' strategies. It is important to understand these businesses in their own right because just as the chain grocery competitive model is overtly Fordist, they embrace a clearly post-Fordist competitive strategy—one that substantially changes the rewards workers can expect from employment.

### *Placing Chicago's Growing Independent Supermarkets within the National Picture*

As a onetime manufacturing center that has taken on its own distinct mode of post-deindustrialization growth, Chicago makes a revealing location in which to examine the restructuring of the food retail industry. During the 1960s and 1970s, Chicago's food retail industry consolidated and fled from what was in many ways the paradigmatic city of U.S. Fordism (Abu-Lughod

2001). The city's deep racial segregation, its frequently booming economy, and its strong union presence all positioned it at the forefront of the socioeconomic trends that supported the industry's transformation. Chicago's size likewise amplifies industry trends. The extremes of large cities, from big populations to larger numbers (and often shares) of high- and low-earning households, allow the development of larger retail facilities capable of exerting stronger leverage on the large chains' basic economies-of-scale advantages (Donohue 1997, 106). Thus, chain grocery stores in Chicago are larger and attempt to carve out more physical market space than do their peers in Milwaukee, Minneapolis, or other smaller cities.

At the same time, Chicago's experiences with economic restructuring, immigration, and post-Fordist growth position it at the forefront of the trends underscoring the current restructuring of food retail. Hispanics, many of them undocumented and shunted into low-wage segments of the labor market, comprised 28 percent of the city's population by 2006; even by the Census Bureau's conservative estimate, approximately 22 percent of Chicago's population was foreign born during the same period (author's calculations from Ruggles et al. 2010). These immigrant job seekers struggle for employment in an increasingly polarized labor market. Although Chicago has in principle recovered from deindustrialization and the massive job losses of the 1980s, poverty and unstable low-wage employment are growing. The upsurge in low-wage employment leaves the major grocery chains open to competition based on price as consumers seek cost reductions as a means of compensating for falling real wages. In turn, the impact of the city's increasingly uneven income distribution is magnified by Chicago's historic and enduring patterns of racial segregation.

## The Ethnic and Material Basis of Reinvestment

The flight from low-income neighborhoods and the restructuring of Chicago's food retailers conform neatly to known geographies of the retail grocery sector and the industry's changing economics. Driven partly by industry trends toward consolidation and greater store size and partly by declining population density and the arrival of minority and often poor consumers, Chicago's major grocery chains, Jewel and Dominick's, began in the early 1960s to replace old stores with newer, larger facilities and to close stores in poorer neighborhoods altogether (Gallagher 2005). Given the city's persistent residential and employment segregation, grocery flight took on distinct racial overtones (Abu-Lughod 1999). The shuttering of supermarkets in the city's poorer and predominantly minority neighborhoods continued through the 1980s and the 1990s, resulting in substantial underservice of African American neighborhoods (Mari Gallagher Research and Consulting Group 2006). By the mid-2000s only eleven of the seventy-one Chicago supermarkets (15 percent) operated by major grocery chains lay within predominantly African American neighborhoods. Given that African Americans account for nearly one-third of the city's population, this marks a pattern of deep underservice.

The story of full-size supermarket withdrawal is much the same in the city's predominantly Hispanic neighborhoods, but with one important difference: a substantial number of midsize independent supermarkets have opened their doors in the past decade. Hispanic neighborhoods in Chicago are now crowded with supermarkets able to extract substantial profits from selling to customers whom large chains have abandoned (Map 3). The expansion of this industry segment is so rapid that it is nearly impossible to chart its numbers. By the most conservative estimate, eighty-two midsize independent supermarkets matching the industry-minimum definition of $2 million or more in annual sales did business within the city limits of Chicago in the mid-2000s.[6]

Even these cautious estimates suggest the importance of this market segment. Industry insiders agree that midsize independents account for 12 to 13 percent of total market share in Chicago (Figure 2). By comparison, Walmart and Target, the big-box retailers whose cost-cutting approach has spurred wholesale labor cost retrenchment within the industry, accounted for just 3.3 percent of total Chicago metro area market share (TradeDimensions 2006). In Chicago the sheer number of these stores, their geographical concentration in immigrant-heavy neighborhoods on the city's Northwest and Southwest Sides, and their high cumulative annual sales position them as a large and growing segment of the food retail industry. The basic profile of these upstart firms—small, independent, nonunion, and immigrant serving—suggests a competitive strategy in which low-cost goods and highly differentiated product offerings serve as the basis for building market share.

## How Independent Supermarkets Compete

By pulling out of minority and immigrant neighborhoods, major grocery chains have ceded substantial portions of the Chicago market to potential

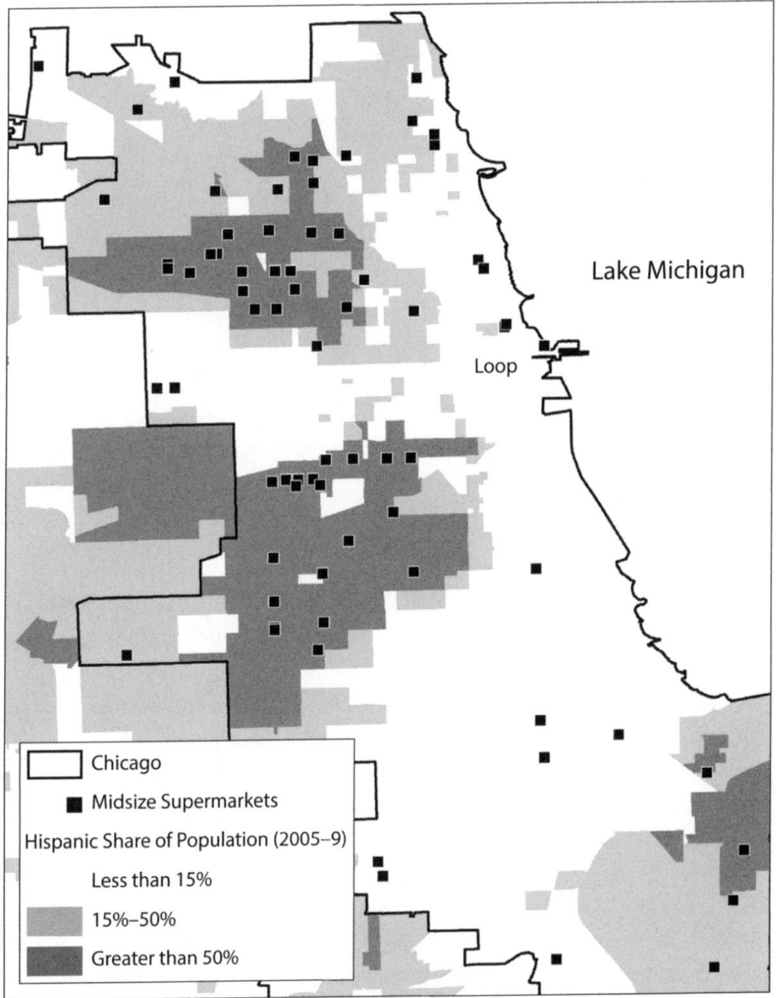


*Map 3. Location of Midsize Supermarkets and Hispanic Population.* Sources: *InfoUSA 2005; Ruggles et al. 2010.*

competitors, and the chains' one-size-fits-all model of grocery offerings have expanded this opportunity. Their emphasis on private label (i.e., store brand) and mass-market products maximizes their economy-of-scale advantages but leaves little room for them to stock the wide range of ethnic goods—distinct cuts of meat, spices, types of produce, and packaged goods—sought by residents in these underserved neighborhoods. Midsize

| **Individual Stores** | |
|---|---|
| Number | 82 |
| Median Square Footage | 17,000 |
| Median Annual Sales | $2.5 million |
| Median Employment | 18 |
| **Market Segment** | |
| Total Square Footage | 1.23 million |
| Total Sales | $250 million |
| Total Market Share | 12–13% |
| Total Employment | 2,000 |

*Figure 2. Floor Space, Employment, and Market Share of Chicago's Independent Supermarkets. Owing to differences in geographic coverage, these data do not precisely align with Table 4.* Source: *author's estimates are from 2005 InfoUSA data.*

independent supermarkets have exploited both of these competitive opportunities, first through trial-and-error growth but increasingly as a matter of instrumental and deliberate strategy.

The composition of the physical facilities of midsize supermarkets often underlines just how different they are from the large chains. Although midsize stores contain on the average less than half the square footage of the large chains, they often devote a greater area of their floor space—not just proportionally but in net terms—to produce and meat. This physical detail, combined with the shared ethnicity of shoppers and workers, identifies the basic aspects of the competitive mode: target underserved populations, provide goods the large chains don't stock, and leverage low labor costs into cut-rate prices on labor-intensive goods.

### *Targeting Neighborhoods and Populations That Chain Supermarkets Ignore*

Chicago's midsize supermarket industry segment, as currently composed, was born out of the modest experiments of ethnic entrepreneurs who spotted the obvious failure of large chains to target immigrant populations. One of the industry's earliest entrepreneurs echoes a common sentiment in explaining the lived experiences through which he identified the market demand his supermarkets eventually filled:

> About forty years ago . . . you had [the major chains] trying to sell to Mexicans by having tortillas [and little more]. . . . But they did it from a buying-power point of view, which is a mistake, because personal contact is key to this business. . . . So we opened a little grocery in the neighborhood, just selling basic stuff you couldn't get at the big stores.

The entrepreneur's family eventually expanded the chain to six establishments, which were sold in the mid-1990s. The founders of two other growing supermarket chains tell similar stories. Observing large chain supermarkets' ineffective efforts to add a wide range of ethnic items to their products, they used modest capital investments to open small stores in Hispanic neighborhoods. When these stores were quickly overwhelmed by customers, they opened successive—and successively larger—branches. Today, these three chains together total more than twenty stores.

In the process of converting their businesses from modest corner stores to full-fledged regional chains, the owners of these businesses gradually replaced their initial neighborhood-level experiments with well-honed and highly deliberate expansion strategies. Today, they describe a site location process that echoes the cold calculations of volume and competition major chains use to site new stores. The owner of a successful chain explains, "We open for two reasons. One, we look at the percent of Latinos to see if it is enough to open a store. . . . Two, we look for a space with at least 20,000 square feet [of selling space] and parking space. . . . And anywhere a big store goes out, we go in." He is echoed by an entrepreneur who was recently enticed to enter the industry owing to its simple business model: "We go where the Hispanics are. We don't really compete with anybody else."

Because many new entrants into the industry also base their decisions on this basic calculus, a pattern of disinvestment-cum-reinvestment is clear in Chicago's immigrant neighborhoods. The successful chain owner elaborates on his comment with a succinct description of the pattern, "Anywhere you see a big chain move out, you see three or four new smaller stores."

### *Protecting Markets by Constructing Ethnic Identity*

As they push out beyond the midsize industry segment's historical base in Hispanic neighborhoods, new businesses in the industry apply this same logic in a broader and cruder form. Consider the site location criteria used by a North Side entrepreneur who operates a handful of small and profitable supermarkets. He explains, "We look for population density and strong ethnic population. . . . I want an ethnic population, any ethnic population. I don't care which one it is. . . . Give me a strong ethnic presence [in the neighborhood], and we'll figure out the rest."

Locating near ethnic populations—tacitly defined by grocers as non-African American minorities, immigrants, and non-Anglophones—provides these businesses with a captive consumer population that cannot be easily picked off by the chain supermarkets. The competitive advantage begins with the typically high population density and frequently diminished transportation access of Chicago's nonwhite and immigrant neighborhoods. The owners of midsize supermarkets use ethnic population as a proxy for the base factors—population density, limited consumer access to competitors—essential to profit making in a low-margin, high-volume business. Within specific ethnic populations they target recent isolated arrivals to the United States who seek foodstuffs and shopping environments similar to those in their countries of origin (Tarnowski 2006). In this way seeking out ethnic populations simultaneously identifies sites underserved by major chains and a customer base whose loyalty can be easily earned.

Thus, midsize supermarkets go to great lengths to incorporate ethnicity—as constructed through product offerings and a store's identification with certain types of goods in the eyes of customers—into their day-to-day operations. In fact, many attribute the continued viability of their businesses to this understanding and marketing of a constructed ethnicity. For the owner of a struggling business in an African American neighborhood, African American ethnicity provides an increasingly flimsy shield against chain stores' encroachment into his market share. Whereas the large chains struggle to stock the preferred cuts of meat, produce, and imported products of new immigrant populations and to communicate to non-Anglophones, they can target African American neighborhoods effectively when they choose to do so:

> I'm sure that if you'd study the Hispanic stores, with all the language barriers and the cultural barriers, they're probably going to survive a whole lot better than a lot of midsized stores are going to survive. . . . So for me, there's less "hold" on the customer [than there is for Hispanic-service stores]. . . . But still there are cultural differences [that keep African Americans shopping here]; there is

> still that sense of community; there is still that sense of pride in seeing a business owned by someone who looks like you, seeing a business run by someone who looks like you surviving.

Music and bilingual staff are import components of ethnic food retail, but adopting the measures that gird an ethnic shopping experience requires a more situational understanding of neighborhoods and immigration. Virtually every establishment offers money-wiring services and check-cashing counters. When space allows, these supermarkets also offer legal advice on immigration matters. Other touches are even more customized to the historical experience of customers. As an extreme example, consider the first-wave entrepreneur discussed in the previous section. He illegally imports—and quietly sells to long-term customers—low-cost pharmaceuticals otherwise available in the United States only by prescription and only at a high price. These drugs are available over the counter in Mexico, and for midsize supermarkets seeking an ethnic identity, offering them at cheap prices is a valuable means of making the supermarket seem familiar to recent immigrants. It is one of the numerous means of creating an ethnic shopping experience that remain unavailable to the big chains.

The personal attentions of employees, from the supermarket's owner to butchers and cashiers, enhance this appeal. The same employer casually lists a number of simple touches that convey authenticity and command loyalty from customers:

> You can walk into a [big chain store], and probably, it's a little cheaper for a Coke, for a Campbell's soup. But you come into my store, and you're "Mr. Gonzales," and the girls call you by your name. The smells are familiar. The music is in Spanish. The colors and piñatas are all there. It's your heritage that's hitting you. . . . We are more than just a grocery store. We're an event. We have people coming in to meet with me. I'm a legal advisor. I'm an accountant advisor for them. I'm a liaison.

Supermarket owners seek workers whose appearance and first language clearly mark them as coethnics for the store's customers; in some cases this means managing the hiring process to ensure that a relatively small workforce (of thirty or so employees on the average) is divided along multiple ethnic lines (see Valdes 2000). Coethnicity in the workforce matters because of the emphasis business owners place on personal connections and service within the store.[7] For workers, learning customers' names and memorizing family details and relatives' names is one of the job's most basic requirements, a foundational rule preached by the owners of the region's many expanding independent supermarket chains. Here, the ethnic components of competitive strategy merge with the flexible-production components. With larger clienteles, language barriers, and employee handbooks written to emphasize throughput rather than highly individualized interactions between workers and customers, large chains are not designed to craft this type of detailed connection with consumers.

Establishing an ethnic competitive niche requires the successful navigation of dozens of decisions about product lines, product placement, pricing, workforce strategy, store layout, and all the other minute details that draw consumers away from the big chains and establish loyalty to new supermarkets. The wrong food or music, the failure to embrace a key holiday, or the absence of a certain staple can signify inauthenticity and drive customers elsewhere (Perkins 2004). As a common means of creating an ethnic atmosphere and the ensuing customer loyalties with a minimum of time and error, many newly ensconced businesses turn to the importers and suppliers of ethnic goods for both products and advice on the day-to-day operation of the store (Lewis 1998). The newer entrepreneur who operates a handful of small supermarkets on the North Side explains the unexpected evolution of his business practices:

> Let's say we're going into a neighborhood that's all German. I know nothing about Germans; I know nothing about German food in general. If I'm in the neighborhood and opening a store, I have to find the major supplier of German products, and that's what starts the ball rolling. Once you have one supplier come in, then the suppliers find you. They'll tell you need this product, you need that product. . . . The first year, you'll make a lot of mistakes. By the third year, [business] is normal.

Nationally, independent grocers seek out the importers and the distributors of ethnic products as experts who provide free and effective counsel on establishing a store's service to particular populations (Lewis 1998).

This strategy is particularly potent and easy to pursue in Chicago. Owing to the Chicago region's historical role as the warehousing and distribution center of the Midwest, its strong international shipping connections, and the presence of a large and diversified immigrant population, it is a center for importers and distributors of ethnic foods. As of 2005 the Chicago-area food wholesaling sector had more than 1,400 establishments and an establishment location quotient of 1.3 (author's calculations from U.S. Census Bureau 2007), indicating a large share of import and distribution activity relative to the area's overall employment.

The power of such customization has not escaped industry analysts and the large chains. In recent years the food retail industry has nurtured a booming literature counseling large chains and prospective entrepreneurs on ways to make grocery shopping an irreplaceable ethnic experience (Perkins 2004; McTaggart 2005). The recommended tactics for creating ethnic identification range from the prosaic (emphasizing Spanish-language music, cleanliness, and bilingual signage) to the specific (hiring at the neighborhood level and seeking out custom ethnic suppliers). With these measures, however perfunctory they may seem, large supermarket chains and the marketing and research institutions that support them attempt to chip away at midsize supermarkets' hold on immigrant consumers.

But to date, midsize supermarkets have felt little pressure from these tactics. As Scott (1997) argues, the abstract rationality of modernist enterprises such as the corporation by nature misconstrues and ignores the intricacies of local knowledge, economies, and lived experience. At a fundamental level the owners of these establishments remain convinced that the chains simply will not be able to make the necessary customizations in store layout, employment, goods, and pricing no matter how hard they try. As a high-ranking officer of the independent, privately held Texas chain H. E. Butt explains in a trade publication:

> You really have to understand, almost neighborhood by neighborhood, where people come from and how they like to shop. . . . We don't have a cookie-cutter model in terms of new store development. Each store is built in a custom way that responds to the individual needs of the neighborhood—everything from paint colors to what's stocked on shelves. If you launch a particular line of products or design one format for Hispanics, it oversimplifies what's a more complex opportunity. (McTaggart 2005, 28)

## The Best of Both Worlds: Employers Combine Customized Retail with Cut-Rate Prices

These carefully pitched and coded ethnic appeals form a crucial component of competitive strategies designed to target immigrant consumers. Invisible in employment statistics and measures of market share, midsize businesses' strategies show a clear fit between the continuing fragmentation of Chicago along neighborhood and ethnic lines and the resulting opportunity for entrepreneurs to carve out new market niches in a local-serving industry whose internal mechanics are typically excluded from broader narratives of economic restructuring.

The prevalence of specialized selection and appeals to coethnicity in the industry constitute significant curbs to the naked cost-based competition that prevails in many kinds of retail. Yet cost-based competition remains a significant ingredient in the industry's transformation. Because immigration status is strongly tied to income, family structure, purchasing habits, and other factors crucial to the design of profit-making models in retail, the ethnic segmentation these midsize supermarkets adeptly mine doubles as *income* segmentation. Chicago's immigrant consumers shop from a position of deep material need. Saddled with low incomes, unstable jobs, the burden of supporting family abroad, and, often, border crossing debts, immigrant consumers turn to upstart supermarkets for the simple reason that these firms offer deep discounts (Perkins 2004; Faura 2004).

Here, the quality- and differentiation-based components of the midsize model merge with a more fundamental appeal to cost cutting. Freed from the capital investment requirements that force most businesses to choose between strategies based on economies of scale and cost cutting, on the one hand, and product differentiation, on the other, the entrepreneurs building this market segment combine niche marketing of the type nationally organized chains cannot pursue with cut-rate prices those chains cannot provide.

As they charted their plan for responding to the industry's growing workplace abuses, the community and labor organizations engaged with Chicago's food retail workers designed organizing campaigns that called into question the authenticity and neighborhood insider status of these businesses. The varying successes and failures of the campaigns that followed depended less on the intangible trait of authenticity than on the real and material needs that bound low-income consumers to businesses whose maltreatment of workers was an open secret.

# 5

# "They're Happy to Have a Job"

## *Midsize Supermarkets and Degraded Work*

Orthodox economic analysis insists that undocumented workers earn low wages due to the risk employers take in hiring them. Because U.S. law forbids hiring foreign nationals who do not possess visas and other required paperwork, employers cut their wage payments in order to set aside funds for potential fines, or so the story goes.[1] The employers themselves know better. During the 2000s, high-profile Immigration and Customs Enforcement raids on employers such as Perdue were the rare exception to the reality of nonenforcement in industries dominated by small workplaces. Rather than shrink from hiring undocumented workers owing to their precarious status, these firms race to employ them precisely *because* of their precarious legal status and the power that precariousness confers upon employers.

The typical owner of a midsize supermarket in Chicago speaks freely and eagerly about his enthusiasm for undocumented workers, and with good reason. The basic workplace laws regulating wages, safety conditions, the pace of work, and employees' remedies for dangerous and abusive working conditions are irregularly enforced at best for undocumented workers. Fast working and flexible, these employees deliver high output levels in exchange for low pay, with employers maintaining an unusually free hand to fire nonfavored workers, speed up the pace of work, cancel scheduled rest periods, intimidate employees into working while sick, and ignore safety standards.

Two legal developments during the 2000s removed any doubt that the benefits of hiring undocumented workers exceeded the small penalties leveled on the few who were caught. The 2002 Supreme Court decision *Hoffman Plastics Compounds Inc. v. NLRB*, mentioned previously, rules that employers owe no compensation to undocumented workers illegally dismissed in retaliation against union-organizing activities, even in cases when the employer knows the worker is undocumented (National Employment Law Project 2003). In effect, the ruling allows workers to exempt themselves from compliance with key portions of the National Labor Relations Act by hiring undocumented workers—a distinct advantage to firms eager to avoid unionization.

Around the same time, the Social Security Administration further systematized this selective application of the law by initiating a policy of sending no-match letters advising employers that no recorded person matched the Social Security number provided by certain employees. The letters required no action by employers, most of whom were well aware of the problem. But they fashioned an easy pretext for dismissing workers involved in community or union organizing or who lodged complaints about wages, wage theft, and working conditions. Although no-match letters were halted by litigation in 2007 (and later resumed in 2011), they were a constant feature of workplaces during my research.

The story of vulnerable workers and opportunistic employers unfortunately is a commonplace in research on low-wage labor markets (Milkman 2006). This fact makes the intersection of these familiar labor-sweating practices and other competitive strategies very important analytically. While comparatively low wages represent an essential element of the midsize supermarket's competitive model, those low wages are rarely contested, even by workers seeking union representation. Instead, organizing campaigns in the industry focus on problems with working conditions. Those working conditions, the owners of these businesses make clear, play a significantly smaller role in competitive strategy than does the need to signal ethnic solidarity with the immigrant populations who account for the majority of the consumer market.

Two embedded case studies of community–labor organizing efforts at competing employers illustrate the importance of appeals to ethnic solidarity and the impact those appeals have on worker-organizing campaigns built around familiar appeals to justice and fairness. Together, these embedded cases suggest that the segmentation of the low-wage labor market is the primary obstacle to community–labor organizing strategies, both in terms of employment practices and in terms of the cost-saving needs of the consumers who frequent midsize supermarkets.

## How Supermarkets Target Low-Income Populations

The construction of a cultural identity supports retail entrepreneurs' ability to appeal to immigrant households. Many of the elements of this identity are economic and speak as much to consumers' status as households eking out a living at the bottom of the labor market as they do to their national origin. The standard cultural customizations in Chicago's midsize supermarkets include not just music and hard-to-find cuts of meat but also check-cashing services, money wiring, and low-cost pharmaceutical remedies. The material need underpinning these services becomes particularly clear when the prevalence of tabs for customers short on cash is considered. Though not a critical element of success, several employers, including the previously mentioned successful chain owner, provide credit to longtime customers as a means of showing respect and earning loyalty.

> We endear ourselves to the general public. They can come to you and say, "I didn't get my check this week. I'm going to take the groceries, and I'll come and pay you Monday morning." You can't say no to them, because they come to you every week. You can't do that. . . . This is something that big stores can never imitate.

For the recent immigrants who meet their basic subsistence needs with purchases from these businesses, immigration status and continued identification with their countries of origin are bound up with the very factors—low social status, poor labor market position, remittances needed by family members abroad—that impose daily conditions of material need. These conditions of material need underpin the location of midsize supermarkets almost as surely as do the microgeographies of the immigrant and Hispanic populations. Across Chicago midsize supermarkets are readily found in lower-income neighborhoods (Map 4).

Map 4 demonstrates the specialized geographic niche these supermarkets occupy. Though they target lower-income neighborhoods—typically those with a poverty rate between 10 and 30 percent—they typically avoid Chicago's lowest-income neighborhoods. In doing so, the owners of midsize supermarkets set up their businesses to target consumers who are cost

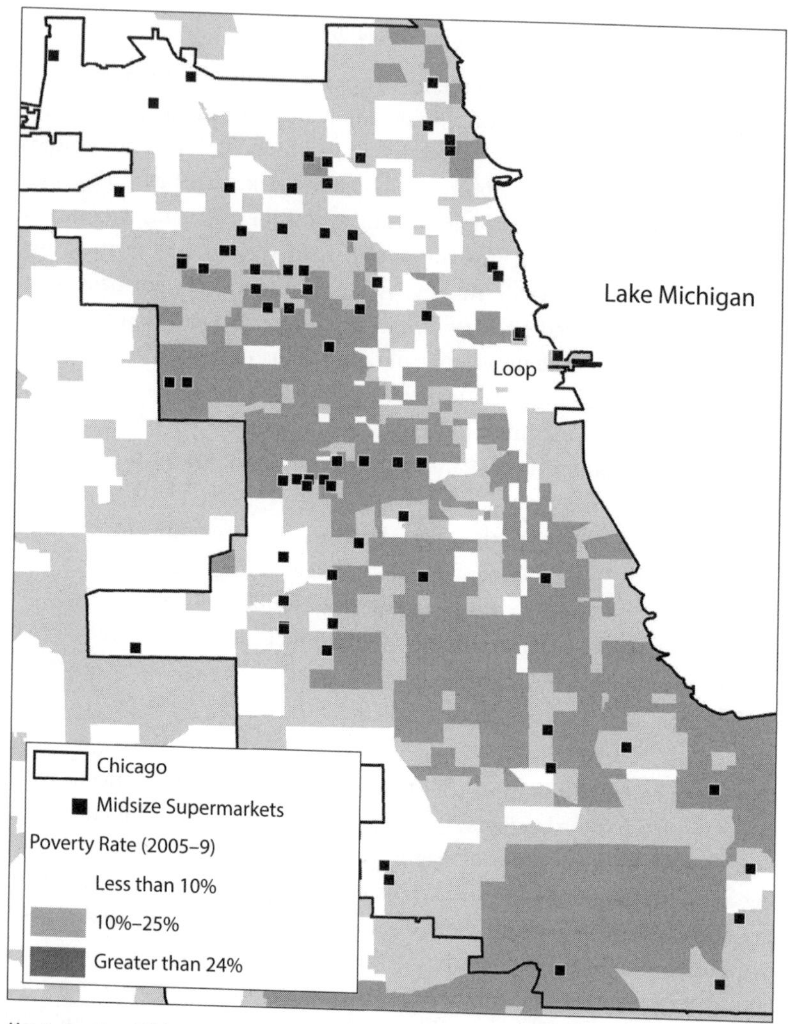


*Map 4. Location of Midsize Supermarkets and Poverty Rate.* Sources: *2005 InfoUSA data; Ruggles et al. 2010.*

conscious—and thus responsive to cost cutting—but whose cumulative expenditures can total large sums, due to household size and population density. With low incomes at the base of their location strategy, exploiting the rigidity of the Fordist food retailing model means exploiting the chains' high overhead and labor costs.

### *Building Market Share with Cut-Rate Meat and Produce*

Without exception the owners of midsize supermarkets emphasize that the low per-capita incomes of immigrant and ethnic households make cut-rate prices a clear and easily pursued path to profit. In this way, material need provides them with an enduring competitive advantage that full-size supermarkets cannot co-opt. As one new market entrant succinctly puts the issue: "This is a real straightforward business.... What we do is easy. Our customers won't shop at [the big supermarkets]. Their prices are too high."[2]

Price, as much as the ethnic strategy, is the bottom-line reason why the owners of midsize establishments feel immune to competition from large chains. A longtime owner explains the extent of his price advantage as follows: "I can undercut big chains—I don't worry about them. I'd worry about another independent. I don't care if Cub Foods or Walmart moves in next to me. It don't make no difference."

That deep price advantage emboldened the North Side entrepreneur operating a small handful of midsize supermarkets to seek direct competition with a unionized chain. "We opened our first store right next to [a chain]. It didn't matter. We undersell them fifty cents on the dollar on meat." The processed foods that take up the bulk of the space in large-chain supermarkets fit nicely with their volume-based purchasing strategy and appeal to the consumers those stores serve. But compared with predominantly white, higher-income households, minority, immigrant, and ethnic populations spend a substantially larger portion of their grocery budgets on meat and produce (Table 7).[3]

As Table 7 shows, Hispanic households have significantly lower aggregate income levels. But they prepare more food at home, thus spending more than other households on groceries ($4,140 versus $3,500 annually) and substantially more on meat and produce ($2,000 versus $1,475 annually). Business owners understand the structure of household demand and place meat and produce at the center of their operations. The successful entrepreneur who recently entered the industry explains with clarity the basic layout of Chicago's midsize supermarkets: "I make sure to put the produce right in the front of the store. We try to have something really good and cheap right up front so people come in and see the prices. That's what matters to them."

The owner of a chain of Latino-focused supermarkets concurs, emphasizing the importance of meat purchases to customers who were rarely

TABLE 7

**Annual Grocery Spending by Household Type**

| | HISPANIC | | NON-HISPANIC | |
|---|---|---|---|---|
| Median Household Income (2006) | $44,389 | | $58,903 | |
| United States | $43,763 | | $58,087 | |
| Chicago City | $44,282 | | $64,954 | |
| Grocery Spending (2004) | | | | |
| Produce | $827 | (18%) | $630 | (17%) |
| Meat | $1,366 | (30%) | $981 | (26%) |
| Other | $2,320 | (51%) | $2,202 | (58%) |
| Total | $4,514 | (100%) | $3,814 | (100%) |

All figures are in 2011 dollars. *Sources:* rows 1–2, Ruggles et al. 2010; rows 3–7, U.S. Bureau of Labor Statistics 2006a.

able to afford it in their countries of origin: "Even when we were just running a small store the size of a corner store, we had a big meat counter." A competitor echoes his words, noting the central role of meat purchases in consumer spending: "Meat is our biggest seller. Almost all purchases have meat. And purchases over twenty dollars always have meat."

Offering ample amounts of meat and produce at low prices is a competitive necessity and the most powerful way to draw limited-income households to the store. On mass-manufactured products, midsize supermarkets, particularly in urban areas, operate at a pricing disadvantage owing to the costly operating environment and their limited ability to secure bulk purchase discounts. But they operate from a profound cost advantage on fresh meat and produce. Forming relationships with the city's numerous wholesale markets and distributors allows these businesses to acquire high-quality goods at relatively low prices. An employer on the Northwest Side explains:

> The reason why an independent can do well is the ease of distribution. There are so many wholesalers that you can choose from to buy import groceries. That's number one. Number two, the ease of buying produce in Chicago. From your largest independent to your smallest independent, having the Chicago market [an open-air

> wholesale market on the city's Near West Side] makes it easy for anyone to go get himself a small van, go get his purchases, bring his produce to the store.

But even more fundamental, midsize supermarkets can hold down prices on these goods thanks to the simple fact that the same neighborhoods that guarantee them price-conscious consumers with strong loyalties also provide a low-cost workforce willing to handle these labor-intensive goods for wages that are a fraction of the major chains'.

### *Linking Labor Costs to Product Prices*

The owners of midsize supermarkets identify their ability to hold down labor costs as the primary means for cutting prices on the produce and meat that are essential to their competitive edge. Hourly wage-and-benefits costs in Chicago's unionized chain supermarkets ran between thirteen and seventeen dollars per hour in the mid-2000s (United Food and Commercial Workers 2007).[4] By contrast the standard hourly wage in midsize supermarkets hovered around eight dollars per hour (in 2006 dollars), and employment benefits are provided infrequently, if ever. As the longtime owner explains, entrepreneurs in the industry see collective bargaining agreements as the main obstacle facing the major grocery chains: "We don't have no unions. Our wages are not as high as theirs [the big chains']. We can actually sell stuff cheaper than they can. [That's why] I can undercut big chains."

The North Side entrepreneur operating a handful of small stores draws a direct line between wage levels and prices on meat, one of the most labor-intensive goods in any store:

> We cannot be unionized, cost-wise. It's impossible. It's prohibitive. The union-minimum salary per department is not conducive to a small business. . . . [The big chains] make the wage differential up in prices. When you go to a big chain and buy a skirt steak, it's $5 per pound. I sell it at $2.50 per pound. That extra $2.50 all goes into [labor] costs at the big stores.

A cursory look at the operating fundamentals of the food retail industry supports this perspective. As the means to expanding profit under the Fordist model have exhausted themselves, chain grocers' profit margins have stagnated; industry analysts read the increased consolidation of large food retailing chains as an attempt to add in profit volume what individual chains can no longer add in margins (Yerak 2006). Beyond the problem of competition from Walmart and warehouse stores, the large chains have launched new attacks on their long-unionized workforces as a means of rebuilding profit margins by lowering labor costs. Although some specialty stores and niche markets such as Whole Foods have succeeded in carving out market space and profits through means other than cost-based competition, supermarkets in general enjoy few opportunities to increase profit margins by any means other than holding down labor costs and tapping economies of scale that have long since exhausted their potential to improve the bottom line. For midsized supermarkets this makes low prices on labor-intensive meat and produce a central pillar of their business strategy; nonunion status thus approaches competitive necessity.

The often bleak economies of the surrounding neighborhoods buttress employers' ability to cut labor costs by ensuring an ample and willing labor supply. According to the owner of a single-site supermarket on the North Side, turning away the excess of job seekers can be more time consuming and difficult than finding qualified workers: "Do we place help-wanted ads? Are you kidding me? We get four or five of these [waves a stack of walk-in job applications] every day. It costs us a lot in paper." The previously mentioned longtime owner answers the question with similar bluntness: "We don't find workers. They find us. I haven't placed a help-wanted ad since 1980."

By locating in lower-income neighborhoods, midsize supermarkets satisfy two basic requirements of their competitive strategy: they gain access to cost-conscious consumers on the consumption side and access to labor markets with an excess of job seekers on the production side. The underlying employment–consumption relationship functions something like Fordism in reverse. Whereas the family-supporting wages of the mid-twentieth century begat swelling consumer demand that fueled subsequent growth in high-wage jobs, the low wages and employment instability of the lowest tier of the labor market today compel workers to limit their expenditures. This in turn amplifies the benefits to employers of cutting product costs and holding the line on wages.

Employers' claims about their price reductions are not empty. Table 8 charts the cost of a representative basket of food for Hispanic households at twenty different Chicago supermarkets. Employee compensation costs

TABLE 8

**Comparisons of Employee Compensation Rates and Food Prices**

| CHAIN | HOURLY COMPENSATION* | COST OF REPRESENTATIVE FOOD BASKET | | | |
|---|---|---|---|---|---|
| | | MEAT | PRODUCE | OTHER & DRY GOODS | TOTAL BILL |
| Chiapas | $7.00–$8.00 | 5.97 | 3.10 | 12.86 | 21.93 |
| Food Basket | $7.00–$8.00 | 5.86 | 2.22 | 14.06 | 22.14 |
| Juan's | $8.00 | 6.27 | 2.36 | 14.36 | 22.99 |
| Tommy's | $8.00 | 5.87 | 2.70 | 14.95 | 23.52 |
| Joe's Fruits | $8.00 | 5.87 | 1.88 | 16.66 | 24.41 |
| Chicago Foods Inc. | $7.00–$8.00 | 5.97 | 3.30 | 15.26 | 24.53 |
| Bountiful Harvest | $8.00–$9.00 | 5.97 | 2.96 | 15.66 | 24.59 |
| The Produce Place | $6.50–$8.00 | 5.97 | 2.90 | 16.06 | 24.93 |
| Supermercado Diaz | $7.00–$8.00 | 5.46 | 4.76 | 14.75 | 24.97 |
| Grocery Baron | $8.00–$9.00 | 5.87 | 3.20 | 16.16 | 25.23 |
| Lindo Chicago | $7.00–$8.00 | 5.77 | 3.82 | 15.86 | 25.45 |
| Supermercado Nogales | $7.00–$8.00 | 6.27 | 3.57 | 16.26 | 26.10 |
| Illinois Foods | $6.50–$8.00 | 6.87 | 3.06 | 16.66 | 26.59 |
| Zach's | $6.50–$7.50 | 5.97 | 3.66 | 17.26 | 26.89 |
| National Markets† | $16.50 | 10.27 | 5.87 | 11.26 | 27.40 |
| American Markets† | $15.35 | 12.97 | 7.46 | 14.27 | 34.70 |

*Includes benefits
†National chains

*Sources:* Price survey of Chicago food retailers performed by the author, May 22–25, 2007. Food basket contents were developed following U.S. Department of Agriculture outlines and matched to purchasing patterns of low-income households as documented by the U.S. Bureau of Labor Statistics 2006a. Hourly wages were estimated by asking owners, managers, and workers to supply a range of typical hourly pay rates.

appear in the left-hand column.[5] The right-hand columns display prices for a representative market basket containing twenty-some widely available types of produce, meat, and packaged goods, weighted to match the actual spending patterns of Hispanic households as recorded by the Department of Labor's Consumer Expenditure Survey. The far-right column weights these prices in order to present an estimated food bill for a standardized selection of frequently consumed goods at each store.

As predicted, these supermarkets have limited power to secure bulk purchase discounts, reflected in the comparatively high costs they charge on the brand name packaged goods. But they compensate for these higher prices on packaged foods with large discounts on labor-intensive meat and produce.

Business owners identify the low-wage/low-price combination as the lynchpin of their strategy for serving cash-strapped Hispanic and immigrant households. Meat and produce sales drive independent supermarkets' competitive advantage. Several of the day laborers who appear in this book confirm this account. Tasked with stretching their uneven and often low earnings to cover both the cost of living and remittances to family abroad, these workers avoid chain supermarkets for the stated reason that they cannot afford them.

### *Labor Intensification, Chain Consolidation, and Other Elements of the Midsize Competitive Model*

The direct relationship between low wages and deep price cuts on the products that account for half of immigrants' food budgets suggests an element of competitive necessity: if wages were raised, midsize supermarkets might lose their price-setting power and see their competitive edge over the chains diminish. This implies that raising wages and improving working conditions might undermine the competitive advantages that allow workers to be employed in the first place.

Yet low wages and nonunion workforces are not the only ways in which these employers compete. Although lower than the large chains' pay rates, wages in this industry segment are often $1.50 or more per hour above the Illinois minimum wage of $6.50 (at the time of this research). They also show considerable variance, ranging from subminimum wages in many establishments to nine dollars per hour or more in some of the emergent independent chains. Each and every employer reports healthy business, and seventeen out of twenty plan to expand their operations. Although lower wages (in comparison with the large chains) are an indispensable component of the midsize competitive model, they are not the only one.

## Evaluating Midsize Supermarkets' Expansionary Goals

Nationally, smaller supermarkets often make up for their pricing disadvantage through family ownership and holding overhead costs to a minimum. Many elements of this lean management style facilitate the ability of these supermarkets to customize themselves to small market niches. First and foremost among these is meat-and-produce purchasing. The large union chains typically centralize purchasing at the national level, cut meat at regional distribution centers, and ship the prepackaged final product to stores (American Meat Institute 2003). For midsize supermarkets the meat-and-produce delivery system simply consists of a few vans and a handful of drivers who begin each morning with a trip to the open-air produce markets and meat wholesalers on Chicago's Near West Side.

A second point of difference in overhead structure is the absence of corporate offices. Without exception the owners of Chicago's midsize supermarkets participate in the day-to-day management of the stores. Eight out of the fourteen local firms and chains priced in Table 8 also involve family members in day-to-day operations. As these lean supermarkets have grown, Chicago's large chains have taken on new overhead costs as part of their purchase by international conglomerates. Officials in the region's labor unions characterize the changes as part of the globalization of the food retail industry. Whereas the chains once sought out purchasing bargains from local suppliers, they now draw on the international supply networks of their parent companies. This overhead, like union labor costs, increases operating costs for the chains and at least partially offsets the pricing advantages of their economies-of-scale purchasing power.

As Chicago's midsize supermarket industry segment consolidates and comes under the control of a handful of ambitious and growing chains, some aspects of the chain model have surfaced. Several emerging chains now number five to ten stores and have the sales volume to generate bulk-purchasing power on dry goods and packaged items. Although their prices on dry goods still fall short of those at the large chains (which average $11.76 for a representative bundle versus $15.49 in midsize supermarkets), the larger midsize supermarket chains have pushed down their dry goods costs to near the same range (Table 9). The relationship between the cost of dry/packaged goods and chain size is straightforward. With the exception of two especially low-cost supermarkets, labeled here by the pseudonyms Chiapas and Food Basket, the large chain supermarkets that dominate the Chicago food retail sector provide lower costs on packaged goods. As the size of the retailer falls, the prices of these items, which cannot be driven down through low labor costs, rise. Single-store food retailers and smaller chains (of two to five stores) have dry goods costs that are generally

TABLE 9

**Labor Costs and Prices on Labor-Intensive Goods**

| EMPLOYER | NUMBER OF ESTABLISHMENTS | HOURLY WAGE | MEAT AND PRODUCE COSTS† | |
|---|---|---|---|---|
| | | | BILL | RANK |
| Supermercado Nogales | 5–10 | $7.00–$8.00 | $5.77 | 1 |
| Illinois Foods | 2–5 | $8.00–$9.00 | $5.87 | 2 |
| Joe's Fruits | 2–5 | $6.50–$7.50 | $5.97 | 3 |
| Food Basket | 1 | $7.00–$8.00 | $6.27 | 4 |
| Tommy's | 2–5 | $6.50–$8.00 | $6.87 | 5 |
| Juan's | 1 | $8.00 | $7.75 | 6 |
| The Produce Place | 5–10 | $7.00–$8.00 | $8.08 | 7 |
| Bountiful Harvest | 5–10 | $8.00 | $8.57 | 8 |
| Chiapas | 10+ | $8.00 | $8.63 | 9 |
| Chicago Foods Inc. | 1 | $6.50–$8.00 | $8.87 | 10 |
| Supermercado Diaz | 2–5 | $8.00–$9.00 | $8.93 | 11 |
| Supermercado Nogales | 5–10 | $7.00–$8.00 | $9.07 | 12 |
| Illinois Foods | 5–10 | $7.00–$8.00 | $9.27 | 13 |
| Joe's Fruits | 1 | $6.50–$7.50 | $10.22 | 14 |

†From price survey (see Table 8).

*Sources:* Price survey of Chicago food retailers performed by the author, May 22–25, 2007. Food basket contents were developed following U.S. Department of Agriculture outlines and matched to purchasing patterns of low-income households as documented by the U.S. Bureau of Labor Statistics 2006a. Hourly wages were estimated by asking owners, managers, and workers to supply a range of typical hourly pay rates.

one-third higher than those in the larger midsize chains. This variance in costs provides employers a means of expanding sales and adding to profits apart from squeezing labor costs.

## Labor Intensification and Workplace Control

Just as wages and prices vary among Chicago's midsize supermarkets, so do working conditions. Through measures as diverse as nonpayment of overtime, illegal dismissal of workers, and punitive cuts to wages and hours, employers in Chicago's midsize supermarket sector extract high-effort labor and rapid work rates. At the same time, these labor-intensification measures and the broader institutionalization of workplace insecurity of which they are a part provide employers a degree of workplace authority and control that although difficult to measure, changes the strategic options available to them.

Labor intensification provides employers with the same bottom-line benefit as low pay: more labor output per dollar spent. Employers are well aware of this benefit and emphasize its importance to the day-to-day operations of the business—and to winning customers. In the shorthand calculus of the industry, undocumented workers are the workers of choice because they are eager to prove themselves and willing to work at rapid rates without complaint. The first-wave entrepreneur who built his business by observing the underservice of Mexican American neighborhoods explains the benefits of exploiting coethnics with a candor that is commonplace in the industry:

> About half of my workers are undocumented. The honest truth is that they are honest and hard working. Because they know you take a risk. . . . And in return you get people that are giving 120 percent. . . . And they're very honest. They will not take anything, because they're afraid of losing their jobs. They're afraid that somebody might retaliate and do harm to them because their undocumented situation makes them very frail. . . . They're punctual. It can be 120 degrees [in the stockroom], and you'll actually have to tell them to stop working, to say, "Come on, go home."

The successful entrepreneur who recently entered the industry draws a line from undocumented status to the industry's emphasis on customer service: "A lot of my people have *coyote* debt—$3,000 or $4,000. . . . They care about getting their hours. They care about getting a check at the end of the week. Service and my name are the most important parts of what we do, and you get really good service from them."

Undocumented status gives employers a freer hand in the workplace and is the prime enabling factor behind a host of employment practices that maximize profitability by either intensifying the pace of work or effectively cutting hourly pay. As I show, undocumented status makes workers loath to contest labor law violations that might bring their immigration history to light, identifies workers as financially needy and susceptible to threats of job loss or reduced pay and paid hours, and marks them as unfamiliar with basic workplace laws to begin with. Employers with a large number of undocumented workers on their payroll maintain great flexibility over wages, working conditions, and the organization of work and extract maximum effort from their employees.

Despite the popularization of political discourses emphasizing border security, the legal will supporting prosecution of employers with undocumented workers remains weak. Enforcement is particularly ineffective in local-consumption and service industries, whose comparatively small establishments move them to the bottom of the list of federal enforcement priorities. Even when enforcement is strict, the small per-worker fines levied on noncompliant employers provide little deterrent to hiring employees whose low wages and high work rates save their employers in labor costs. The North Side entrepreneur who operates a handful of small supermarkets explains the strategic indifference toward work eligibility documentation: "My best butcher is an undocumented guy who's been here about twenty years. A lot of the guys, they give you papers, and they don't look quite right. But hey, I'm not an immigration inspector."

The single-site operator who expressed frustration with the large number of employment applications he receives is more blunt. More so than his words, his exasperated tone and sharp sarcasm convey the sentiment that only outsiders to the industry would expect employers to follow immigration laws. "[My workers] all give me documentation. Look, I'm not going to take it if it's printed on a Bazooka [bubble gum] wrapper. But I don't know if it's real or if it's fake. I had one girl for a while who what she presented me, it wasn't good enough. I told her to go get it fixed, and she did."

Owing to their limited knowledge of U.S. labor laws, their fear of coming to federal authorities' attention, border crossing debts, and the absence of higher-grade employment options, undocumented immigrants labor in workplaces shaped by the presumption of near-complete employer power over terms of compensation, working conditions, and employment status. As employers explain it, workers' eagerness to stay employed at all costs transforms the terms on which work tasks and work rates are negotiated. In the case of the first-wave entrepreneur who built his business to respond to his childhood experience of underservice, labor sweating is shrouded in protectiveness toward recent immigrants. "I've had guys who just got here from Mexico show up at store," he explains. "It's cold out. They don't have a place to live. I give them some work and connect them with a place to live. They're really grateful after that."

The successful chain owner explains the same dynamic more matter-of-factly: "People will come to work here and not know how good it is to work here. Then, they quit to work somewhere else. But when they see how bad [the jobs and pay are] out there, they come back here to ask for another chance."

Grateful or just desperate to maintain a steady income, employees in Chicago's midsize supermarkets work in environments where even the most basic components of U.S. labor law and employer behavior may be disregarded at any time. Department managers systematically heap high-volume verbal abuse—often racially inflected—on workers. Although employees frequently work more than forty hours per week, overtime pay premiums are rare; even when employers promise to pay time and a half for overtime, the extra pay appears only episodically. Most vexing to employees, paid work hours vary without notice, oscillating back and forth between long stretches of steady employment and individual weeks and days in which the agreed-upon hours do not materialize.

These individual employment abuses are embedded within a broader pattern of employer retribution. Workers know that if they request overtime, take allotted lunch breaks, or request vacation time to which they are officially entitled, they may be furloughed, dismissed, or reassigned within the workplace. Having assisted workers with the reclamation of wages and hours owed at more than a dozen Chicago-area supermarkets, the head of a workers' rights organization characterizes the workplace environment as follows: "It's like an hacienda. The managers routinely shout at the workers, and the workers get in line. There's a lot of favoritism. Some workers are just exempted for whatever reason. Others seem to easily fall into the role of getting bossed around."

The director of a neighborhood-focused organization that has supported *supermercado* employees invokes the same image: "It was like an hacienda. Everyone could see that the workers were treated poorly. The foremen would stand there with their arms crossed and stare at the workers, who'd work as fast as possible. Anyone could see they were unhappy, but the employer did it."

## Charting the Full Extent of Degraded Work Practices

Day to day, neighborhood-based community-based organizations (CBOs) and other workers' organizations field complaints about basic violations of the Fair Labor Standards Act, most typically nonpayment of overtime, subminimum wage pay, misclassification of employees as contract workers, and smaller-than-promised paychecks. These rote labor law violations remain routine in substantial part because of a second, more elusive type of violation: consistent employer retribution against workers who push for their basic rights to be enforced. Workers, union organizers, and CBO officials alike reserve their strongest complaints for the widespread employer practice of cutting the hours of and dismissing or otherwise reprimanding workers who push to receive promised vacation time, breaks, and pay rates. Figure 3, compiled from interviews with employers, workers, labor union officials, and community-based organizations, catalogs labor law violations and conditions of work intensification for eleven low-wage employers, listed by the same pseudonyms used previously.

Chronic employer violations of basic wage-and-hour laws shape the workplace in the midsize supermarket sector. At a minimum employees show up for work knowing that they will be ineligible for legally guaranteed overtime pay or that their flat weekly pay rates will sometimes average out to hourly rates below the federal minimum wage. Problematic though they are legally, these endemic and rote violations are lesser irritants to workers than are other conditions of the job. In fact, employers routinely describe the nonpayment of overtime as a competitive *advantage* in luring workers. The employer on the Northwest Side explains:

> At the chains they make let's say $9 per hour, but they only get twenty hours. That's $180 a week. Over here, let's say they're making $7 or $7.50, close to the minimum wage. . . . But here they get fifty hours a week because I don't pay time and a half, and they don't have to go get that second job now they're getting their forty hours regular. Add it up. So even though it's not a job that's paying extremely well, for people who are working hard, who's trying to get a start, they appreciate that.

A prominent workers' rights advocate explains the problem from an organizer's perspective: "It's a problem we run into a lot with the workers. They just care about how much they get paid, and they don't care about the hours."

As the Northwest Side employer suggests, low wages per se are less of a problem for most workers than are unpredictable schedules and paycheck totals.[6] Consider the representative case of a longtime butcher whose hours and pay were cut after his involvement in a union-organizing campaign

| Employer | Hourly Wage | Wage-and-Hour Conditions | Intensification Conditions |
|---|---|---|---|
| 5–10 ESTABLISHMENTS | | | |
| Chiapas | $8.00–$9.00 | Wage docking; clock manipulation | Punitive hour cuts; punishment for union involvement; pay increases based on demerits; verbal abuse; unannounced layoffs during slow spells |
| Food Basket | $6.50–$7.50 | Minimum wage starting pay; overtime is paid | Verbal abuse; punitive dismissal; all pay raises conditional on pace of work |
| Juan's | $8.00 | Total pay does not vary with hours worked | Pay raises based on pace of work |
| Tommy's | $8.00 | Nonpayment of overtime; discrepancies between hours worked and hours paid | Access to increased work hours based on favoritism, ongoing assessment of pace of work |
| 2–5 ESTABLISHMENTS | | | |
| Bountiful Harvest | $8.00–$9.00 | Nonpayment of overtime | Recruitment of young workers to minimize pressure for health insurance |
| Grocery Baron | $8.00–$9.00 | Hours increases conditional on waiving overtime pay rates | — |
| Illinois Foods | $6.50–$8.00 | Subminimum wages; hours paid do not match hours worked; flat pay rates mixed with long hours | Punitive wage cuts and assignment of labor-intensive jobs; verbal abuse, including threats to family and property; employee dismissal; curtailing of hours |
| Islas Bonitas | $6.50–$7.50 | Hourly pay capped at $7.50 with the understanding that worker tenure is short | Pay capped at $7.50; informal and in-kind benefits for senior and preferred workers only; mandatory trial period upon hiring |
| Neighborhood Food Basket | $8.00–$9.00 | Hours paid do not match hours worked | Workers dismissed for organizing and during slow periods; extra work tasks shifted to existing employees without pay increase; all workers limited to fifteen weekly hours to minimize organizing capacity |
| SINGLE SITE | | | |
| International Grocery Corp. | $8.00–$9.00 | Hours paid do not match hours worked; unpaid overtime; pay cuts and late checks during slow spells | Frequent verbal abuse of workers; dismissal of workers during slow periods and reassignment of their tasks to others without increased compensation |
| The Produce Place | $6.50–$8.00 | Illegal nonpayment of overtime | All workers limited to fifteen weekly hours to minimize organizing capacity |
| Supermercado Diaz | $6.50–$7.50 | Subminimum wages | Hours, schedule flexibility, and continued employment based on ongoing assessment of worker effort |

*Figure 3. Degraded Work Practices in Chicago Food Retailers.* Source: *employer and worker interviews.*

was discovered. Despite illegal reductions and despite the verbal abuse, poor safety equipment, and routine degradations (including the denial of bathroom breaks), he remains committed to keeping his job for the simple reason that it is steady.

> I stay at this job because I can get a lot of hours. The bad stuff is the same everywhere. . . . . Where else am I going to work? I can go to *la parada* [the day labor shape-up] or *las agéncias* [temporary labor agencies] or work part time in a restaurant kitchen. But here, I know how much I make per hour, and I know I'll get enough hours at the end of the week.

For low-wage supermarket workers, employment in a supermarket presents a respite from the constant search for stable employment at the bottom of the labor market. But by adding and subtracting hours worked and changing pay rates, midsize supermarkets re-create the very labor market instability that their workers seek to escape with full-time employment. This day in, day out renegotiation of wages, hours, and total pay can be better understood as the foundational component in a broader employer program of labor intensification, charted in the far right-hand column of Figure 3. Although most employees of midsize supermarkets are employed de jure as full-time salaried workers, their de facto employment status is closer to that of the temporary workers: hours, pay rates, job responsibilities, and employment status can be changed at any time and without notice.

Taken as a whole, this institutionalization of insecurity within the workplace speeds up the pace of work and secures higher work rates than those the large chains receive. These intensification measures magnify the cost saving employers obtain as a result of hiring low-wage undocumented workers. Even without straying into the murky economic waters of productivity, the equation is simple: workers in *supermercados* perform substantially more work per hour than do workers in the large chains, and they do it for about half the cost.

## The Value of Degraded Work to Employers

Although employers in the midsize supermarket industry segment call low wages and their control over working conditions necessary elements of competition within their market niche, the evidence demonstrates the lack of a clear relationship among wages, labor, conditions, and product prices. The lowest-wage employers within the industry fall everywhere on the cost spectrum. For example, they are the third-, tenth-, and fourteenth-cheapest sellers of meat and produce (Figure 3). This broad variance in the relationship between labor costs and product prices underscores the degree to which success as a midsize supermarket rests more on underselling the large chains than on underselling other *supermercados.*

Put another way, employers need not cut product costs to the minimum in order to benefit from degraded work practices. Once the store's ability to undersell the chains by a broad margin on meat and produce has been established, per-pound prices on meat and produce in midsize supermarkets fluctuate—and they do not fluctuate in lockstep with wages and labor practices. Methodologically, it is impossible to determine the precise relationship between degraded work and competitive necessity without an employer agreeing to share detailed and confidential financial records. But other aspects of the operations of these workplaces suggest the multiple uses of degraded work. The example of Chiapas, a rapidly expanding midsize chain that successfully defeated a union-organizing drive, illustrates the other advantages to employers of degraded work.

### *Pushing Down Risk, Expanding Market Share: The Example of Chiapas Markets*

A midsize chain with aspirations to displace Chicago's major chain supermarkets in many neighborhoods, Chiapas capitalizes on low-cost labor, high work rates, large sales spaces, and growing economies-of-scale buying power to offer the selection and scope of a chain supermarket at considerably lower prices ($21.93 versus $27.80 for the standard basket of goods charted in Table 8). The day-to-day operations of Chiapas differ, however, from the typical model of the low-wage, low-cost supermarket.

To begin with, labor-intensive goods constitute a relatively small component of Chiapas's price advantage. Its per-pound prices on meat and produce are nearly the highest among the midsize supermarkets surveyed. Instead, Chiapas derives its cost advantages from modern capital-intensive facilities and its growing power to command bulk purchase discounts. Among midsize supermarkets it also is a relatively high-wage employer. Hourly pay for butchers and produce workers in 2006 started above eight dollars and reached ten dollars or more after standard semiannual raises of twenty-five cents took effect. Workers receive modest vacation and sick time as part of their employment, and other aspects of the employment relationship often left to chance in other midsize supermarkets—including scheduled rest periods and meal times—are written into Chiapas's formal employment policies. On paper, employment at Chiapas looks similar to unionized employment at the large chains, minus health care coverage. Yet despite its comparatively high prices on labor-intensive goods, work at Chiapas is characterized by a complicated system of work-intensification and employee-monitoring measures that speed the pace of work and give the employer nearly complete control over the workforce and its own plans for expansion.

Workers at a North Side Chiapas establishment filed with the National Labor Relations Board (NLRB) for a union election in the early 2000s, hoping that a collective bargaining agreement would improve their ability to take advantage of the benefits the employer technically offered. Employee complaints scarcely touched on wages. But hours worked were another matter. Department managers regularly cut and rearranged workers' hours for two reasons. The first can be termed numerical flexibility (see Harrison 1994). During busy weeks workers would near forty hours of paid work after just a few days on the job. To avoid paying overtime, managers often cancelled scheduled weekend shifts without notice, as one of the store's butchers explains:

> If you normally work Sunday through Thursday and the first of the month [when business picks up owing to refreshed balances on food stamp cards] falls on a Friday, you work Friday. But then your hours will be shortened on Sunday to make sure they don't have to pay overtime. . . . . Or let's say you're working second shift [from 2:00 p.m. to 10:00 p.m.] on a slow day. At seven your boss will say, "OK, you're done working now; go home. But be here tomorrow at 11:00 instead of 2:00."[7]

A second set of wage-and-hour problems more properly falls under the heading of employer retribution and efforts to intensify the pace of work. Although workers at Chiapas were formally entitled to safety equipment and measures such as paid holidays, sick time, lunch breaks, and bathroom breaks, workers who asked to take them frequently had their paid employment hours cut in response. As a result, workplace terms that seemed favorable to workers on paper in reality looked little different from those in other midsize supermarkets. Another butcher, employed by the firm for many years, explains some of his common experiences:

> If you call in sick to work, they come and tell you the next week, "You're only working two days this week." . . . Another worker just asked about his vacation time, and they put a check by his name on the log, and he worked fewer hours the next week. . . . No matter what you do, if they don't like you, you get a check.

Department managers at Chiapas maintained a list of checks (functioning as recorded demerits) next to each worker's name. The managers then used a three-strike system in evaluating performance and granting raises. Depending on the manager and on a worker's status within the workplace, virtually any on-the-job action other than hard, fast work could merit a strike. The first butcher quoted elaborates:

> If they enforced the three-strike rule evenly, everyone would be fired within a day. Show up late for work, that's a strike. Have a client complain, that's a strike. Go to the bathroom for too long, that's a strike. I had so little time to go to the bathroom that I couldn't take off my butcher's apron before leaving the counter. Then, I got a strike for wearing my butcher's apron in the front of the store. . . . Complain that you're not being allowed to take vacation time, that's a strike. Make a bad cut [to a piece of meat], that's a strike. . . . When you get breaks, they watch you closely. And they always count the minutes faster than you do.

With the threat of these strikes always looming, workers rarely asked questions and rarely complained. Butchers received little workplace training and no safety equipment for the job—itself performed in a chilled area without coats or other clothing to protect workers from the temperatures—and did not ask for any. The entire 20,000-square-feet store had just one forklift to move palates of food; workers were often asked to carry sixty-pound palates of produce and meat themselves to compensate for the shortage. Across occupations workers were constantly monitored and often asked to perform dangerous or unscheduled work activities.

At the time that employees at Chiapas filed with the NLRB for a union election, more than 70 percent of workers supported unionization. Through a combination of dismissals, cuts to paid hours, and employee intimidation, worker support for collective bargaining fell below 50 percent in the final election. In the run-up to the election, Chiapas slashed the hours of prounion workers—to the point that several quit the store in order to be able to find a more stable paycheck. Others were furloughed through unscheduled *descansos*—rests at the manager's discretion. Some prounion butchers were reassigned to work in the new position of *pollero* [chicken butcher], a deliberately deskilled position whose primary purpose was to discipline. These punitive measures were accompanied by selective enticements. Several workers were given raises and promised future pay increases if they voted against union representation. Even these inducements were coupled, however, with retribution. After receiving their small pay bumps (from fifty cents to one dollar per hour), the favored workers were asked to do the work of the dismissed prounion workers, effectively increasing their workloads by one-third.

The coda to the failed union election at Chiapas is perhaps the most revealing aspect of this case. Three years after the initial union election failed, one of the lead prounion workers had begun to round up worker support for a new NLRB election. Given that the odds of improving working conditions at Chiapas seemed so low, the longtime butcher was asked, why bother? His response underscores the extent to which the deep segmentation of the low-wage labor market and the lack of higher wages and stable jobs for undocumented workers undermines their bargaining power: "Why do I stay here? This is a good job. It's not much better anywhere else, and here, at least, I can get a lot of hours. Unless I can learn English and get a car and move to the suburbs . . . or get work at a union store . . . this is my best option." Threats of dismissal and employer retribution were potent at Chiapas for the fundamental reason that workers lacked other viable labor market options. When forced to choose between marginally improving their job and the risk of losing it, they opted for security.

The unsuccessful union election at Chiapas illustrates the importance of the nonwaged aspects of degraded work among Chicago's midsize food retailers. Chiapas has rapidly grown with meat and produce prices that although lower than those of the large chains, are not cost competitive with those of its peers in the midsize market segment. Instead, it benefits from degraded work practices in other ways: through the ability to vary employees' hours at will, the ability to defeat collective bargaining votes that may change its cost structure down the road, and a degree of control over workers and the day-to-day operations of the store that large supermarkets lack. Although doubtlessly important to the underlying business model at Chiapas, degraded work is not an essential part of the cost-cutting measures fundamental to competition in this market segment.

The particulars of Chiapas's ambitions and workplace practices make it an ideal example for illustrating the weak links among degraded work, cost cutting, and the multiple ends to which employers use degraded work. Several other examples from my research make these points, as well. Workers at International Grocery Corp. sought union representation after the employer's misreading of the Chicago Hispanic market resulted in low sales volumes, abrupt employee dismissals, and incomplete paychecks. For International Grocery Corp., which (illegally) shut its doors after workers won a union election, degraded work shifted the risk inherent in bad business decisions from employer to worker. A similar story can be told at Neighborhood Food Basket, where degraded work allowed the firm to recoup some of its financial losses after it misread the Chicago market in terms of products and prices. And degraded work practices have allowed Tommy's supermarkets to quickly move into new neighborhoods with a minimum of research, safe in the knowledge that the firm's basic cost structure is low. After conveying the size of the gap between their prices and prices at the large chains, the owners of midsize supermarkets emphasize that degraded work improves their business options in ways that extend far beyond mere cost cutting.

## A Natural Experiment in Workplace Organizing: Illinois Foods and Neighborhood Food Basket

The phenomenon of degraded work raises three key questions: Why do employers degrade labor? Why do workers remain in these jobs? And what can workers, community organizations, and other planning actors do to improve wages and working conditions? The first question has been addressed. To the end of undercutting the large chains, employers pursue degraded work because they must competition-wise. Lower overall labor costs are the only way these small firms can generate price discounts on labor-intensive goods. But the capitalization of labor-cost savings into price cuts is not absolute. Among midsize supermarkets, wages, the intensity of degraded work practices, and overall prices on labor-intensive goods vary unsystematically: some labor-intensive workplaces have high product prices; some high-wage workplaces have low prices; and many others fall in between.

The excess of supply reported in neighborhood labor markets, along with the persistent fear of workers at Chiapas and elsewhere of losing their jobs, suggests an answer to the second question: the deep segmentation of the low-wage labor market results in the de facto inability of workers to find better jobs. Much more remains to be said about this fear of job loss and the ways in which it conditions employer strategy and workplace operations. As the growth of this industry segment and its poor workplace practices have become clear labor unions, community-based organizations, and neighborhood organizations in Chicago have intervened in an effort to pressure employers into changing the terms of work.

Almost without exception, these strategies have failed. The parallel organizing efforts at Illinois Foods and Neighborhood Food Basket, two employers that came under fire from labor unions and community organizations in the early 2000s, provide an opportunity to examine why. Although similar in many ways—both targeted Mexican immigrants; both claimed territory in a historically underserved neighborhood; and both emphasized cheap meat and produce—the two retailers were differently attached to the community. Illinois Foods opened its doors at a time when the neighborhood had long been underserved. Neighborhood Food Basket was, by contrast, a newcomer, an experimental ethnic-format supermarket run by a national chain whose arrival had been supported by high-profile assistance from the City of Chicago. Illinois Foods' constructed status as a community insider ultimately allowed it to survive the organizing campaign, despite the high public profile of its unfavorable labor practices. By contrast Neighborhood Food Basket quickly succumbed to the pressure of the organizers, in part because it was viewed as a community outsider and in part because it had badly misread competitive standards in the industry.

### *Low Pay, Dangerous Working Conditions, and Employer Intimidation at Illinois Foods*

The pseudonymously named Illinois Foods came under community pressure in the early 2000s for subminimum wages, systematic employment abuses, and illegal retaliation against workers who had participated in a union-organizing campaign. The strongest complaints came from workers who had been employed at the store for many years and, after their frustrations mounted, filed with the NLRB to hold a union election. In the ensuing months the owners of Illinois Foods dismissed several prounion workers and cut the hours and engaged in on-the-job harassment of others, ultimately shrinking the store's once-overwhelming union support to the point that less than one-fifth of eligible workers ultimately voted for union representation.[8]

Workers' support for union representation was above all based on basic violations of wage-and-hour laws. Throughout the 1990s many workers were employed for as little as $2.80 per hour. Workers also routinely worked more than forty hours per week but did not receive time-and-a-half pay for the extra hours, as the Fair Labor Standards Act stipulates. These violations in overtime pay were embedded within a broader pattern of mismatches between hours worked and pay received: paychecks frequently did not match the hours for which workers had punched the clock.

Workers' leverage in resolving these pay issues was compromised by both their immigration status and the presence of a number of work-intensification measures within the workplace. Virtually all of Illinois Foods' employees were undocumented immigrants. This limited their bargaining ability in three primary ways. First, many of the workers were uncertain of the labor laws governing their employment. Even when recounting their employment at Illinois Foods years after the fact, they misquoted the minimum wage (wrongly reporting it to be $2.80 for much of the 1990s when $2.80 was the minimum wage for tipped positions only) and asked what the legal basis would be for contesting termination of employment in reprisal for workplace organizing. The tentative grasp of employment law by these workers presented problems for organizing against the numerous workplace abuses they endured.

Second, the workers' undocumented status made them loath to mount challenges that engaged government agencies or which would bring their status to light. The images of deportation were vivid enough and the scope of potential loss was large enough to silently check actions that might have led to legal residency status coming into question. A recent immigrant from Mexico's Gulf Coast narrates the chilling effect of these threats:

> You know your boss can't call *la migra*. You know that there are too many of us Mexicans here for them to deport us. . . .

> But in the Spanish media it's on the news all the time. You can't stop yourself from thinking about it. . . . When I'm working, I'm always worried. It's always in my mind that they might deport me.

The third way in which undocumented status curtailed workers' bargaining power was the most pervasive. Because the overwhelming majority of Illinois Foods' workers had border crossing debts, family support burdens, and monthly remittances abroad to fund, they feared losing their jobs or having their hours cut. Their employer often made these fears real by scaling back hours and terminating workers. Several workers had their hours cut for weeks at a time simply for requesting time off to care for a sick child or relative. Others were penalized for getting sick themselves, and still others were stuck at an hourly wage of $4.50 (when the federal minimum was $5.15) after years on the job because their department manager had deemed their effort insufficient. The recent immigrant from Mexico's Gulf Coast sums up the atmosphere as follows: "If somebody complains, or does something, they're gone" (Si alguien se queja o alguien se hace algo, se va).

Wage cuts, reductions in hours, and the *threat* of those cuts helped to create an atmosphere in which employees labored at a high rate and asked few questions. Some workers suffered on-the-job injuries as a result. In one case an employee was instructed to use an industrial cleaner on hot surfaces day after day—without gloves, a mask, or other safety equipment.[9] After weeks of using the cleaner, the worker developed severe bumps and lesions on his arms and hands. The employer, who had instructed the worker to continue working regardless of his physical well-being, now reversed course by dramatically cutting his paid hours and reassigning him to jobs in which the physical ailment would not be visible to customers. In other cases workers were prohibited from leaving the premises in order to get medical care and, instead, ordered to patch themselves up with items from the store's small pharmacy section.

A final workplace practice institutionalizing a rapid pace of work was consistent verbal abuse from department managers. Much of the abuse took on a distinct racial tone. When workers made errors on the job, one common refrain was to stop thinking "like a Mexican." A disfigured worker was always referred to as "ugly guy." In some of their more literary renditions, the managers suggested that the workers had cacti for brains.

### *A Neighborhood-Based Organizing Campaign Fails*

Workers at Illinois Foods simultaneously pursued a narrow union-organizing and a broader community-organizing campaign for better wages and working conditions. Both failed, but the two organizing failures were independent of one another. Workplace dynamics and straightforward employer violations of multiple labor laws ultimately undermined the union campaign. The broader community-organizing campaign was undermined, however, by Illinois Foods' ability to identify itself with the neighborhood and against outside political pressure.

Illinois Foods' managers and owners used three straightforward tactics to win the union election, each one supported by the asymmetrical workplace power outlined in the previous section. First, they began to dismiss and cut the wages of many prounion workers.[10] Employee dismissals during union campaigns are most typically accompanied by formal, albeit spurious, justifications, such as claims that the employee violated obscure and unevenly enforced work rules (Mehta and Theodore 2005). No such justifications were given at Illinois Foods. Employees simply were told that there was no longer work for them or that their paychecks would be smaller in the future. The informality with which workers were hired and dismissed makes it difficult to provide a definitive count, but the combination of dismissal, intimidation, and the scaling back of hours to the point that employees were forced (for financial reasons) to quit resulted in more than half of the prounion workers leaving Illinois Foods between the filing of the NLRB petition and the union election itself.[11]

A second, related tactic involved the punitive assignment of new work tasks to prounion workers. Two representative examples make the point. When the first prounion workers were dismissed, their work was reassigned to the existing smaller workforce—which was ordered to perform the jobs without receiving extra hourly pay or paid hours for their efforts. After the union publicized health code violations in the store as part of its campaign of broader union pressure, workers were ordered to clean the troubled areas of the store in deliberately minute and excessive detail and were then verbally abused when they had less time with which to perform their ordinarily scheduled work.

A third tactic involved the employer appealing more directly to workers nervous about their job security. As more and more workers were dismissed for their support of the union, the owner began asking the remaining workers to support a rival union under his own control. Several did, and the resulting confusion about which union to support helped to seal the election result.

Aggressive though these violations of labor law were, the union organizers at Illinois Foods were prepared. Drawing on long-standing partnerships with neighborhood religious organizations and CBOs, they organized a broad public display of support for the workers, particularly in the Spanish-language media daily consumed by the majority of Illinois Foods' customers. Prospects for a neighborhood-organizing strategy—built around efforts to associate Illinois Foods with labor exploitation among current and prospective customers—seemed particularly high given that Illinois Foods' owners were not Mexican coethnics but white businessmen.

Despite the involvement of these high-profile organizations, however, business at Illinois Foods remained stable, and the owners did not soften their antiunion stance. Two fundamental elements of Illinois Foods' competitive strategy kept it in the neighborhood's good graces despite the persistent public pressure.

First, the store's decades-long presence in a neighborhood underserved by the large chains endeared it to the community in spite of the owners' status as outsiders. For better or worse, Illinois Foods was identified with the neighborhood. By contrast, members of the CBOs that mobilized against Illinois Foods viewed the union and its allies in citywide workers' rights groups as outsiders. As other midsize supermarket entrepreneurs have stressed, the store's careful construction of Mexican ethnicity—replete in its name, product selection, aggressive customer relations, extensive butcher's counter, and on-site *taquería*—earned it deeply rooted customer loyalties.

Second, the low incomes of the neighborhood's households left them strongly devoted to Illinois Foods' low prices. As the director of one community-based organization explains:

> We might have had success if there were other options for our members. But they don't make a lot of money, and the next-closest supermarkets are more than a mile away. And they're a little more expensive. The community believed the workers and knew about Illinois Foods' labor practices. It didn't matter.

This is the second main prong of the midsize competitive strategy: targeting low-income consumers likely to have great fealty to low prices. The very aspects of ethnic identity and material compulsion that built Illinois Foods' customer base and competitive strategy ultimately helped it convince customers to identify as consumers rather than as laborers.

### *Wage-and-Hour Violations and Heavy Workloads at Neighborhood Food Basket*

Around the same time that labor conflicts at Illinois Foods came to a head, workers at a recently opened branch of Neighborhood Food Basket also reached out to organized labor and community-based organizations to seek recourse for workplace abuses. The first of several planned Chicago branches in a national chain of midsize supermarkets, Neighborhood Food Basket was a different type of retailer and employer than Illinois Foods. Its price reductions, though substantial when compared with those of the large chains, were smaller, and its status as a nationwide retailer was clear to both its customers and the neighborhood's community-based organizations.

Neighborhood Food Basket's outsider status, combined with its higher overall meat and produce costs, put its profit-making model on shaky footing and ultimately laid the ground for a potent community-organizing campaign. The firm's competitive strategy, its expropriation of the gains from low-cost labor, and its inability to convey ethnic authenticity opened community-organizing possibilities that had been unavailable to labor advocates in the case of Illinois Foods. Neighborhood Food Basket's workers, the vast majority of whom were undocumented immigrants, faced a relatively common set of workplace violations. As is the case in many midsize supermarkets, the hourly wages ($7 to $8 an hour) were higher than the then-legal minimum ($5.15). But labor law violations and selective application of the store's reported rules were rampant. Most basic, the hours employees worked each week fluctuated, and the biweekly paychecks did not always match. Additionally, Neighborhood Food Basket employees worked especially long weeks before and during the store's highly publicized grand opening but received overtime pay only episodically.[12]

On their own these wage-and-hour problems were relatively commonplace within the industry. At Neighborhood Food Basket they were magnified by severe scheduling fluctuations and cutbacks in hours after the store's opening—which received heavy publicity as a result of elected officials' promises that the market would generate many jobs.[13] As the grand opening faded and customer levels receded, Neighborhood Food Basket quickly reversed its promises of full-time employment. Many workers' wages were cut from the initial $7-to-$8-per-hour level. More than forty workers were dismissed outright. And the hours for remaining workers were cut substantially. A few months after the opening, total employment had fallen below sixty, with the majority of those workers employed fewer hours than they had been at the beginning. Part-time workers had extremely limited schedules, typically totalling around only ten hours per week.

For the workers who remained at Neighborhood Food Basket, virtually every aspect of employment changed for the worse. Jobs that once promised (relatively) stable employment, full-time work, and (comparatively) high wages of eight dollars per hour had become insecure, predominantly part time, and low wage. As sales fell, the employer used job termination, hours cutting, and wage cuts to intensify the pace of work in an effort to make up for low initial sales.

As part of a large national corporation, Neighborhood Food Basket offered health benefits, vacation benefits, and sick time—employment perks rarely seen in midsize supermarkets. Workers could not easily make good on these benefits, however. Requests to take sick days and vacation time were met with veiled threats about employment termination and further reductions in work hours. Workers who had fallen out of favor with managers had their paid weekly hours arranged as inconveniently as possible—twelve paid hours spread out over three different shifts over three different days or four-hour shifts separated by eight hours off—and were asked to perform extra work. A few months after the grand opening, the remaining Neighborhood Food Basket workforce was laboring more intensely and at lower pay than it had at the inception.

### *Community Pressure Leads to Business Decline*

Workers contacted union organizers and several of the neighborhood's vocal CBOs as soon as the post–grand opening job and wage cuts began. Neighborhood Food Basket's employees never filed for union recognition with the NLRB. Instead, they encouraged a broad community–labor campaign on their behalf and stood by as Neighborhood Food Basket's falling reputation—in terms of not just labor practices but also prices and quality—took its toll on the employer.

Although the tales of employer abuses at Neighborhood Food Basket were decidedly milder than those at Illinois Foods, the public campaign against it was easier to construct. Neighborhood Food Basket's status as a national chain and outsider—and its lower-quality, higher-cost meat and produce—helped to turn community sentiment against it. The head of the community-based organization that struggled to persuade its members to boycott a neighborhood supermarket explains the genesis of the campaign:

> It went well because of the outsider/corporate angle. There was a sense that they [Neighborhood Food Basket] were not of the community, and that they were trying to make profits just by holding down labor costs. . . . The support the workers felt was something you could really see. Towards the end, we had some big public rallies at which current workers were speaking [openly]. They'd finish the rally and go back to work. It seemed like they were immune [to reprisal] because the support for them was so obvious.

Whereas community organizations struggled to paint the Anglo-owned Illinois Foods as an outsider, establishing Neighborhood Food Basket as a corporate predator was relatively easy. As the organizer for a workers' rights organization explains,

> [Illinois Foods] looks Mexican. You'd think it's one of ours. You have to really look around to figure otherwise because they have the right stuff and at the right prices. . . . . [Neighborhood Food Basket] just didn't look authentic. They had all the right colors and the right music; they had chilies and everything they were supposed to stock. I can't explain it, but they just didn't pull it off.

Neighborhood Food Basket's failure was not an isolated incident. To the contrary, it is not alone in terms of the Chicago market. Both of the city's major chains have attempted—and failed—to develop Hispanic-format stores. Additionally, other national chains have failed in their attempts to cater to immigrant populations in northeast Illinois. A recent incursion into the market by an international grocer is likewise noteworthy for its failure to incorporate ethnic specialties into the raft of goods it purchases cheaply in its country of origin.

Like those other firms, Neighborhood Food Basket's use of many of its parent chain's formats and displays easily marked it as an outsider. Problematic though it was, that outsider status alone was not sufficient to curtail Neighborhood Food Basket's fortunes and swing community sentiment. Despite the successful mobilization of community organizations against the employer, the organizers involved agree that the bottom-line reason behind the success of the campaign was more material. An organizer from a regional workers' organization explains:

> Their prices were high from the get-go. You have to remember that they're owned by a large corporation and have high overhead costs. Even in the first few weeks, people thought the prices were high. . . . This reinforced the idea that they were outsiders. . . . Their meat and produce weren't as fresh, either. And after we started the campaign, they sold less. So the stuff they did sell was older. That sent their reputation further downhill.

Even a high-ranking union official—someone sympathetic to higher costs if they support higher wages—expresses surprise at the low quality and high price of the fresh foods:

> The butchers said that a lot of the meat they were throwing out was ten days old. And that was the stuff they were throwing out! When the sales fell, things just sat on their shelves forever. . . . And they were charging almost $4 for skirt meat [the industry standard for skirt steak at the time was $2.50 to $3 per pound in midsize supermarkets and $5 at the large chains]. I mean [laughs in disgust], come on!

These quality and price problems in turn provide additional insights into the lack of public rancor against Illinois Foods. The director of the community-based organization involved in the campaign reflects:

> It's a funny thing. Illinois Foods aired all their dirty laundry in public. You could see the foremen standing, glaring at the workers.

> They didn't even pretend to treat them well. . . . . The owner's sons would drop hints of deportation and lord the undocumented stuff over the workers. . . . But I couldn't stop our members from going there on the way home. I couldn't even tell them not to. Everything has gone back to normal there. They're centrally located; their prices are good; and their food is good.

The ends to which community sentiment against Neighborhood Food Basket was swayed, it must be noted, were not those originally envisioned by the workers and organizers. After the employer began to cut hours and wages and intensify work, the campaign stopped seeking wage and benefits improvements and, instead, took on the goal of forcing Neighborhood Food Basket out of the neighborhood.

The different outcomes of these community-organizing campaigns reflect the different underlying competitive models used by Illinois Foods and Neighborhood Food Basket. By any estimate Illinois Foods capitalized its low labor costs and high work rates into price cuts. As an exploratory store for a large national corporation, Neighborhood Food Basket converted its cheap labor costs into higher corporate profits rather than cut-rate prices. Where very low profit margins of 0.5 to 1 percent are standard throughout midsize supermarkets, Neighborhood Food Basket's parent corporation targets a rate of 2 percent (reflected in its comparatively high prices and lower-quality fresh goods). As the employer interviews presented at the beginning of this chapter suggest, the midsize supermarket industry is cost competitive first and foremost in terms of its differentials with the large chains and only secondarily in terms of head-to-head competition between similar supermarkets. As the community and union organizers discovered at Neighborhood Food Basket and Illinois Foods, employers maintain considerable discretion in their use of the cost savings of low-wage, highly productive labor.

## Coming to Terms with Multifaceted Competition

Cost competitive but prone to quality-based product differentiation, Chicago's food retail industry has restructured along multiple paths. Low wages and high work rates provide midsize independent retailers with the means to expand sales by selectively cutting costs. Yet this cost-based competition comes embedded in an indispensable skein of product quality, product differentiation, and ethnic affiliation. Convincingly portraying a store's ethnic identity—through product selection, attentive customer interaction, and the presence of coethnics on the workforce—may not be sufficient to make a living in this industry segment, but it certainly is necessary.

This hybrid competitive approach cannot readily be extracted from the classical restructuring theories that guide the analysis of manufacturing firms. The conceptual tools with which scholars and policy makers categorize firms and labor market strategies were inherited from a historically specific and long since lapsed model of manufacturing competition based on distant markets, large firm sizes, and extensive capital equipment costs. Retailers serve local markets. They can be large or small. And in food retail, as in other retail segments, start-up costs are covered by a check for the rent, a few days' of inventory, and a few vans. Recognizing that food retailers simultaneously pursue cost- and quality-competitive paths raises the question of whether their competitive strategies and employment practices can be shifted. Here, the theoretical components of restructuring theories carry direct policy implications. As the example of the parallel organizing campaigns at Illinois Foods and Neighborhood Food Basket in particular demonstrates, high-quality goods and persuasive appeals to ethnic identity can trump comparatively high prices and public outcry against the abusive labor conditions on which low prices are based. One of the most intriguing aspects of the midsize food retail sector is the plurality of ways in which employers shift back and forth between appeals based on the cost-competitive and quality-competitive sides of their business models. When the competitor in question was the major chains, Illinois Foods represented itself as a low-cost alternative, but when competition came from a second low-cost competitor or from a community–labor coalition seeking workplace changes, Illinois Foods instead was able to portray itself—convincingly—as a community-based retailer.

The fluidity between the two sides of the business model signals both challenge and opportunity for policy and organizing efforts. On the one hand, policy actions against degraded work practices in the industry can proceed with the certainty that cost-based competition is not absolute. Unlike cost-competitive manufacturing subcontractors, midsize supermarkets have at their disposal a number of ways to expand business and protect profits if their labor costs rise or work rates fall. On the other hand, policies and community strategies that seek improved wages and working conditions have to contend with both the economic and the cultural sides of the competitive model. In contemporary urban politics, concern for wages and working conditions in urban businesses is often overwhelmed by the broader imperative of remedying disinvestment and reversing the underservice of lower-income neighborhoods by food retailers (Short, Guthman, and Raskin 2007). In terms of community-organizing strategies, the case of Chicago suggests that formal opposition to low wages and poor working conditions will need to be tempered with the recognition of the role these retailers play in underserved neighborhoods. New York's Greengrocer Code of Conduct, which offers employers the ability to improve their public standing by voluntarily agreeing to a set block of wages and work practices, provides one possible template for these organizing campaigns. It is discussed in chapter 8.

Beyond economic restructuring and these practical questions of community organizing, the experiences of workers in Chicago's food retailers help to clarify some of the basic building blocks of degraded work practices. Across the midsize industry segment, the pervasiveness of workplace insecurity stands out as a defining feature. The effectiveness of this insecurity—insecurity of employment, of paid hours, and of wages—in securing rapid work rates and parrying workers' attempts to improve wages and working conditions in turn speaks to the impact of the deep segmentation of Chicago's low-wage labor market on employer strategy. In a labor market in which workers' primary options are poorly paid and often physically dangerous forms of contingent work—day labor construction, industrial temping, landscaping, part-time restaurant work—the lure of stable full-time employment holds extra power. Midsize food retailers describe their ability to give workers large numbers of paid hours per week as their primary tool for attracting a capable labor force. But the uneven enforcement of labor laws and the unwillingness of most undocumented workers to directly confront legal violations make it possible for employers to constantly threaten or effect the removal of this most basic incentive to employment. Thus, the persistence of degraded work strategies relies, as much as any other factor, on the chronic instability of employment options for undocumented workers.

Workers in food retail stand with millions of other workers facing similar problems in local-serving industries. Encountering these pre–New Deal working conditions within modern industry may come as something of a surprise. But degraded working conditions are less surprising in industries known for poor working conditions, including residential construction.

Seen from afar, the solitary day laborer who faces daily uncertainty in whether, under what conditions, and for how much compensation he will work confronts an even more dire set of employment circumstances. Nevertheless, organizing and policy remedies for the degradation of construction employment are more straightforward and more attainable. In an industry in which rapid access to workers equates to cost savings for contractors, laborers and their advocates have a stronger ability to pressure employers to improve wages and working conditions, despite the aggressively contingent organization of employment in the industry.

6

# Building Degradation

## *Dangerous Work and Falling Pay during a Construction Boom*

The grueling work of day laborers offers few certainties. When *jornaleros* rise well in advance of dawn to queue for work, they have no assurance it will materialize. When a contractor pulls his truck to the curb and asks, "¿Quién quiere trabajar?," no worker can be certain that he will be at the front of the line or that the pay on offer will be fair or that the contractor warrants trust. The day begins with the singular goal of finding work, and jumping into a contractor's truck is always a relief. But arriving at the work site brings on a set of less easily resolved challenges.

The uncertainties quickly reveal themselves. The first question is, how fast should the worker work? Each job stands as an implicit audition for future work with the same contractor, with that contractor's friends, and with subcontractors encountered on the work site. Few things make a favorable impression like a blistering work pace, especially on demolition and the other brute-force jobs with which day laborers are often tasked. After that comes the bind of hourly pay. *Jornaleros* must weigh the instinct to win future jobs by working quickly against the need to make the most of today's job. Fast work could mean more hours in the future, but it definitely means less pay today.

Whether that pay actually materializes is yet another uncertainty. Residential construction is and always has been a risky business. A contractor's optimistically low estimate for a job often falls apart as soon as work begins. When the drywall won't hold the heavy cabinets the homeowner purchased or the wall torn aside to install a new vanity reveals rust, faulty electrical work, and water damage that wasn't in the floor plan, the owner responds to the revised estimate by refusing to pay. When costs run over or checks fail to clear, day laborers are the first to have their pay delayed, cut, or simply revoked. If they are lucky, they end the day with sixty dollars in their pockets, sore backs, stiff fingers, and the inextinguishable worry that they won't be able to do the same thing again tomorrow.

Thanks to the day-to-day fluctuations in the labor and skills contractors need to complete even the simplest construction job, day labor is an old form of work organization, one long presumed to be an artifact from the pre-Fordist age. Intuitively, the highly visible return of day labor to the United States during the 2000s' construction boom signals a substantial change to long taken-for-granted labor market rules. More immediately, it helps to explain the rarest of events: a low-wage business boom.

The residential construction industry should have stood out as a favored employer during the distinctively inequitable 2001–7 business cycle. Houses, the new widgets of a financialized U.S. economy (Newman 2009), required skilled labor of the kind that had disappeared with manufacturing plant closings over the previous three decades. And the pace of the housing boom—the value of residential construction put in place in the United States rose from $5.85 trillion in 2000 to $8.8 trillion in 2005—triggered a remarkable expansion of demand for that skilled labor.[1] In other words, the boom should have been good news for workers. Orthodox and heterodox economic theories alike suggest that rapid industry growth enhances worker bargaining power and yields improvements in wages and working conditions. Yet wage gains never materialized for workers in residential construction occupations. Between 2000 and the apex of the boom in 2005, the median hourly wage of construction laborers actually fell, from $14.64 to $14.32.[2]

In many industry segments, particularly the residential remodeling subsector, these mild wage declines—remarkable in their own right in the face of industry-record growth—were just the most obvious component of a far broader transformation of workplaces and working conditions. During the expansion street corner shape-ups, in which workers offer their services to construction contractors, became a growing presence in local labor markets across the United States (Day Labor Research Institute 2001). Striking for the stark employment insecurity and spot wage bargaining it entails, day labor is only the most visible manifestation of degraded work in the historically low-wage residential construction industry (Philips 2003). Whatever the hiring mechanism—street corner shape-ups, worker centers, temporary agencies, or networks of workers and previous employers—workers at the bottom of the construction labor market frequently perform dangerous tasks without instructions or safety equipment, get misclassified as subcontractors or temporary workers, are underpaid or not paid for the agreed-upon work, and find themselves subjected to verbal and sometimes physical abuse by contractors (Valenzuela Jr. et al. 2006; Kelsay, Sturgeon, and Pinkham 2006). Because it plays an active role in lowering wages and working conditions, the growth of day labor and related degraded work explains much of the disconnect between the fortunes of the residential construction industry and its workers.

As a flash point for controversy over undocumented immigration and as a target for community organizing, day labor has become an important issue in community and economic development. As wages and working conditions have fallen in low-skill construction jobs immigrants' rights groups, workers' organizations, labor unions, and others have entered the industry as unofficial regulators of the employer–employee relationship. Operating at the local level, these organizations have established regulated hiring halls, through which they attempt to enforce floors on wages and working conditions and police individual instances of employer malfeasance (Theodore, Valenzuela Jr., and Meléndez 2009). The ability of these organizations to impact local labor markets rests in substantial part on their ability to prod and persuade individual contractors to change their employment and pay practices. In doing so, these organizations must engage the driving question of this book: which contractors degrade work because they can, and which do so because they must?

Where contractors degrade labor out of competitive necessity, public sector and community leverage remains limited. Forcing an individual employer to comply with employment standards higher than those of its cost-cutting competitors brings the risk of making that employer uncompetitive without changing the working standards in the industry as a whole. When contractors degrade labor out of convenience and opportunity rather than necessity, however, community efforts to raise wages and change working conditions run less risk of damaging the fortunes of compliant employers. Recognizing the difference between these two situations is crucial to the dozens of day labor worker centers and hundreds of CBOs nationwide that find themselves struggling to put a floor under wages and working conditions in construction.

## The Atomized Residential Construction Industry: Barriers to Regulation and Research

Conventional employer and establishment surveys do a remarkably poor job of describing residential construction. Small firm sizes (most residential contractors are assumed to be sole proprietors or employ no more than one or two workers), low barriers to entry into the industry, the millions of firms involved operating nationwide, and the general inadequacy of public licensing programs make efforts to measure the size and composition of the industry prohibitively difficult (Finkel 1997, 57–59). At the same time, the legal-reporting mechanisms and membership organizations through which this large and highly diffuse body of business establishments could be surveyed simply do not exist.

As a result, research on construction overwhelmingly focuses on the commercial construction industry segment, whose large firms and heavy regulation (by the Davis–Bacon Act and local prevailing-wage laws) enable traditional survey and data collection methods and guarantee a base level of reliable data. Research on residential construction remains comparatively rare and typically begins with caveats about the incompleteness of the data sources, the bias toward larger and more financially successful employers, the unknown size of the industry, and the overwhelming difficulty in distinguishing different types of contractors from one another (Finkel 1997, 56).

A close look at the available data sources for metropolitan Chicago illustrates these problems. According to the Economic Census and the Census Bureau's Nonemployer Tax Statistics (which capture sole proprietorships), the Chicago Consolidated Metropolitan Statistical Area alone had more than 100,000 residential construction contractors in operation in 2002 (U.S. Census Bureau 2003a). Although Census Bureau data sources provide rough snapshots of overall industry size, they offer no firm-level data and provide no means of assessing the key question of industry structure; they instead give estimated averages and cumulative sums that provide no information on the variance in operations and employment practices on different types of contractors. They say nothing about the structure of the industry.

As an alternative way to answer such questions, researchers would ideally turn to household surveys such as the Current Population Survey

(CPS), but again, problems emerge. The CPS substantially undersamples the immigrant and undocumented worker populations employed as day laborers; it also falters at broader levels of industry and occupational analysis by failing to split the construction industry into commercial and residential segments and recording data for only three different construction occupations. By these and other available statistical measures, research on residential construction fails to distinguish between general contractors, trade specialists, residential remodelers, and other types of contractors. Each such group of contractors occupies a distinct industry niche and has different labor market needs. Longitudinal data on firms and industry segments likewise come up short, as do data on the composition of different regional construction industries.[3] In short, even the most basic measures of industry structure lie beyond the reach of currently available data.

The poor fit between these point-in-time data sources and the fluid day-to-day operations of the industry further complicates matters. Many of the contractors operating in residential construction are unlicensed and do not report the earnings from their work. Indeed, my own fieldwork highlights the fundamental inability of day laborers and other construction laborers to maintain contact with contractors who lack business licenses and fixed addresses and who move back and forth between employment as general contractors, subcontractors, and laborers.[4] Even if these contractors were covered in the available data, classifying them would pose a problem of its own. At any particular moment a contractor might simultaneously be working as a general contractor on one home remodeling project, a skilled subcontractor on another, and a laborer on yet another. Classifying a contractor as simply one type or another misrepresents the data and imposes a false fixity on employment and contracting relationships that must be understood more relationally.[5]

No approach to studying residential construction can fully address all of these barriers. But given the open-endedness of the industry and the fluidity of contractors' roles, the case study approach used here fits the task better than others. Through primary and secondary data sources, interviews with contractors, regulators, and workers, and direct observation of construction work, the research presented in this chapter and the next works relationally. It begins by placing front and center the impact of labor-intensive work and small firm sizes on the bidding process and labor market relationships.

## Precarious Profits in an Industry Built from Unpredictable Work

The intricacies of the construction process and unpredictable spikes in industry demand make flexible employment a necessity of day-to-day residential construction work. Above and beyond other industries, construction faces built-in fluctuations in final demand. These play out over multiple and overlapping time periods. At the level of the business cycle, construction is hit much harder by fluctuations than is the economy as a whole. Accordingly, industry members mark the double-dip recession of the 1980s, which threw the industry into crisis, as a pivotal point in the basic institutional transformations shaping industry practice today.

Construction work also remains seasonally cyclical. Because much construction work involves digging into bedrock and completing complicated technical processes outdoors, job counts spike in warm months and plummet during cold ones. And beyond these built-in cyclicalities, the basic challenge of stringing together a steady roster of jobs dominates a contractor's work. Because of their limited size, most construction contractors have little capacity for redundancy. One cancelled contract or one cost overrun can result in a prolonged dry spell.

This instability attaches to the work process, as well. Unlike mass-produced manufactured goods, the product of residential construction is characterized by its uniqueness. Even when they are built from the same blueprint, no two homes are alike. Differences in location and terrain, quality of work in the initial construction, upkeep, and modification produce structures that differ in large ways and small. With the notable exception of Fordist new home construction in residential subdivisions, the residential construction process resists mechanization because every job differs (Finkel 1997).

John Dunlop best captures the importance of the fundamental indeterminacy and variability of construction work in his classic overview of the industry. "The work place of construction is highly variable," he writes. "The sites of work frequently change and no two projects are identical." In Dunlop's view the uniqueness of individual properties and structures produces unique labor markets. Contractors respond to the variability of their day-to-day work by maintaining flexible workforces:

> The technical conditions place great stress on organization building in management, since contractors must be continuously expanding or contracting a work force . . . and adapting an organization for

> new conditions. . . . These conditions place a great premium on a flexible and skilled work force, on continuously matching jobs and available men, on shifting the work force around among different contractors, and on uninterrupted operations. (Dunlop 1961)

The instinctive contrast is to manufacturing industries, which are built around the repeated production of the same item. With repetition comes returns to scale, realized through capital investment in expensive equipment (Sayer and Walker 1992, ch. 4). This production method favors large firms with a superior ability to maximize investment and versatility (Gordon, Edwards, and Reich 1982). By contrast, the sheer variability of residential construction work militates against the predictability that enables large firm size; at a basic level, "heterogeneity, worker recalcitrance, and project size and duration all work against mechanization" (Finkel 1997, 24). Even if the long-term payoff warranted investment in capital equipment, most firms would lack the resources to buy it and could not up-skill or substitute capital for labor.

The fundamental variability of construction work made employment flexibility a staple in the industry long before flexibilization arrived as a competitive strategy in production industries. From pipe fitting to framing to electrical work, the dozens of trade skills essential to the construction process cannot be retained in the form of full-time workers. These skills take a long time—often years—to learn and pose a talent-poaching problem for the training firm, which cannot promise the steady work needed to lock up as future employees the workers it trains. Thus, contractors subcontract for skilled specialists rather than employ them directly (Bosch and Philips 2003, 4).

Because the day-to-day work of construction proceeds through the project-specific combination of varied trade skills, labor, as opposed to technology, plays the role of fulcrum in the production process. Labor costs, measured by payroll and subcontracting, by a wide margin represent the top cost for residential contractors and remodelers (U.S. Census Bureau 2005a). They also are the most easily varied. Contractors stand at the whim of market pressures on material costs but can exercise real control over workers and the division of labor on their projects. Thus, construction contractors continually push to deskill the construction process (Erlich and Grabelsky 2005). This allows them to reallocate project costs away from expensive skilled subcontractors and toward interchangeable low-wage laborers who in addition to the cost savings they provide, are easier to find, hire, and manage.

The roots of day labor in construction have more to do with the unevenness of labor demand than with labor and cost control. Historically, day labor responded to the variability of construction demand across seasons and business cycles.[6] Long before the current period of day labor growth in U.S. cities, day labor shape-ups—populated by queues of job seekers like those seen in *On the Waterfront*—were common in places as varied as nineteenth-century Tokyo, early twentieth-century Sicily, and the Fordist United States (Valenzuela Jr., Kawachi, and Marr 2002; Lewis 1964; Theodore 2003). From the contractor's point of view, these day labor arrangements solved two of the problems endemic in running a business with small profit margins and little room for error. They allowed for *numerical* flexibility, or the ability to cut payroll in times of slack demand, at the same time that they enabled *functional* flexibility, or the ability to pull different specialty skills into the work process without maintaining a high payroll (Harrison 1994). These are important functions in a cost-competitive industry dominated by small firms with limited capacity for carrying overhead costs.

The historical prevalence of day labor in residential construction conveys something essential and inescapable about the industry itself. Absent heavy regulation, industry labor markets are characterized by (a) contingent employment, (b) deskilled work, and (c) skill-formation problems (Philips 2003). The industry today continues to be driven by small employers and word-of-mouth business recommendations. Work sites change frequently; the duration of most jobs remains short; and the ability of small contractors to keep on staff the dozens of specialty skills needed to complete most jobs tends toward nil (Finkel 2005). Apart from questions of labor control and workplace abuses, day labor employment delivers value to contractors who negotiate uncertainty and flexibility every day.

## Small Contracts and Low Payroll: The Lean Competitive Environment of Residential Remodeling

As outlined, small establishment sizes and labor-intensive work make labor flexibility essential and labor cost cutting pervasive in residential construction. These pressures take an especially intense form in the residential remodeling industry segment—the primary employer of day laborers. Remodeling almost exclusively consists of the most labor-intensive forms of construction work, such as demolition, drywall installation, and painting (Sassen 2001, 285). It is on these jobs that contractors stand to gain the most from employment informalization.

In residential remodeling, the especially small size of most of the available jobs magnifies the basic problems facing residential contractors. Because additions and alterations to homes typically cost much less than outright new construction, remodelers chase contracts much smaller than the industry average. In 2002 the typical remodeler in the United States had just 3.9 payroll employees, including the business owner.[7] Because employment figures skew right, the median, unavailable from the Economic Census, certainly is lower (U.S. Census Bureau 2005a).

In aggregate terms remodeling constitutes a small segment of the residential construction industry. In 2002 remodelers accounted for 15 percent of residential construction work nationally (U.S. Census Bureau 2005a). Remodeling permits accounted for 30 percent of the total value of residential work performed in Chicago between 2000 and 2003, a figure that suggests the industry segment which is the primary home to day labor and degraded work is about twice as large in Chicago as it is nationally.[8]

Whatever its size and relationship to residential construction at large, remodeling operates as a particularly deconcentrated and low-margin business. Nationally, 82,000 remodeling contractors employed just 320,000 construction workers in 2002.[9] By virtually every measure, remodelers occupy a less favorable financial position than other types of residential contractors. The typical establishment with payroll collects just over one-half million dollars per year in receipts (Table 10). It employs fewer than four workers and has a per-worker payroll of just $23,700. Remodeling work is the most labor intensive within residential construction (with value added totaling 40 percent of total receipts), and given the comparatively low volume of on-the-books subcontracting, it is the least likely to be subcontracted to trade specialists.

These data establish that licensed residential remodelers with payroll occupy a particularly labor-intensive segment of the residential construction industry. Yet remarkably, these data only cover the comparatively well-positioned subset of contractors with payroll. The hundreds of thousands of owner-operator contractors in the industry—sole proprietors who report their business earnings as income and have no formal employees—occupy an even more marginal market position. Invisible

TABLE 10

**National Employment, Receipts, and Expenditures by Residential Construction Industry Segment**

| | NEW BUILDING CONSTRUCTION | | | |
|---|---|---|---|---|
| | GENERAL CONTRACTORS | BUILDERS | REMODELERS | INDUSTRY TOTAL |
| Establishments and Employment | | | | |
| Establishments | 62,858 | 26,046 | 82,750 | 171,655 |
| Employees | 316,928 | 241,069 | 320,208 | 878,205 |
| Construction Employees | 206,871 | 120,071 | 207,637 | 534,578 |
| Accounts (Millions) | | | | |
| Receipts | $79,290 | $140,227 | $45,235 | $264,752 |
| Value of Construction Work | $78,600 | $139,221 | $45,034 | $262,855 |
| Total Worker Payroll | $5,416 | $4,116 | $4,929 | $14,461 |
| Value Added | $23,871 | $51,444 | $18,286 | $93,602 |
| Cost of Materials | $22,952 | $36,833 | $12,542 | $72,328 |
| Cap Expenditures, Excluding Land | $814 | $907 | $528 | $2,249 |
| Share of Receipts | | | | |
| Capital Expenditures | 1% | 1% | 1% | 1% |
| Subcontracting | 41% | 37% | 32% | 37% |
| Value Added | 30% | 37% | 40% | 35% |
| Per Establishment | | | | |
| Receipts (Millions) | 1.261 | 5.384 | 0.547 | 1.542 |
| Employees | 5 | 9.3 | 3.9 | 5.1 |
| Construction Employees | 3.3 | 4.6 | 2.5 | 3.1 |
| Payroll per Worker | $26,179 | $34,282 | $23,739 | $27,051 |

All figures in 2002 dollars. *Source:* adapted by the author from U.S. Census Bureau 2005a.

in statistical assessments such as the Economic Census, sole proprietors, who total more than 500,000 remodelers nationwide, collected an average of just $90,250 in receipts in 2002 (U.S. Census Bureau 2003a, 2004a, 2005b, 2006a).

In Cook County the amount of business that the standard owner-operator residential contractor does is considerably less than the national average—a finding consistent with the observation that these contractors work primarily on small remodeling jobs in older city dwellings (Table 11).

In Chicago, as in the United States, nonemployer contractors account for considerably more than half of all residential construction establishments. This population resists classification as any particular type of contractor or construction specialist. Some are general contractors; some, subcontractors; and some, essentially laborers. Whatever their place within the subcontracting chain, these contractors operate in a financially lean market niche. In terms of receipts, they bring less than one-fifth the revenues of establishments with payroll.

Because such industry-wide income statements are the only available source of data on these contractors, there exists no statistical means of assessing their internal cost structure in terms of payroll, value added, and subcontracting. The data on licensed contractors in Table 10 suggest, however, that labor subcontracting (likely to be an especially high cost in the case of employers without payroll of their own) and materials costs total 60 percent or more of the total receipts for residential contractors. Nationally, this conservative estimate (which does not account for overhead costs and capital investments) would leave a sole proprietor earning $100,000 in revenues in the booming housing market of 2003 and 2005 with just $40,000 after basic expenses. For Chicago's sole-proprietor contractors (who tallied annual receipts of just over $70,000), this would leave less than $30,000 in profit if no other costs were incurred.

The lean finances and limited leverage of these contractors rendered most unable to increase receipts during the 2002–6 housing boom. Nationwide, total receipts for sole-proprietor residential contractors did grow in tandem with the housing market, increasing by more than $10 billion

TABLE 11

**Financial Characteristics of Sole-Proprietor Residential Contractors**

| | YEAR | ESTABLISHMENTS | RECEIPTS | RECEIPTS PER ESTABLISHMENT |
|---|---|---|---|---|
| United States | 2003 | 451,130 | $40,259,185,000 | $101,333 |
| | 2005 | 526,995 | $50,265,309,000 | $102,039 |
| Cook County | 2003 | 12,859 | $815,999,000 | $72,056 |
| | 2005 | 15,770 | $1,061,557,000 | $72,014 |

All figures in 2007 dollars. *Sources:* U.S. Census Bureau 2004a; 2006b.

between 2003 and 2005 alone. More than 70,000 new contractors entered the industry, however, to take advantage of the favorable market. As a result, per-contractor receipts held more or less steady, growing by just $1,000 during that same period. The gains to contractors were even smaller in Chicago. Between 2003 and 2005, total receipts for sole-proprietor contractors in Cook County grew by 20 percent. But per-contractor receipts held flat as the result of nearly 3,000 additional contractors entering the market.

It is these industry dynamics that have led previous research on construction to label this industry segment a form of scarcely organized chaos and a near-textbook case of cost-based competition (Philips 2003; Finkel 1997). When residential construction is viewed as a low-margin and cost-competitive industry, the use of day labor and degraded work to gain competitive advantage appears inevitable. But a closer look at the industry, its institutions, and its restructuring over the past twenty-five years reveals that day labor and degraded work confer different benefits to different types of contractors and that newly elaborate subcontracting chains have intensified cost-based competition for some subcontractors at the same time that they have mitigated it for others. In short, the position of individual contractors within the industry goes far in determining their propensity for using and benefiting from degraded work.

## Restructuring Construction: Subcontracting Deepens as the Industry Booms

The deep roots of day labor in construction could suggest that the current surge in informalization amounts to a continuation of long-term trends in the organization of the industry. After all, employment flexibility in residential construction was a functional need long before the current era of cost-oriented workforce flexibility in the U.S. economy. But the residential construction industry in which day labor thrived in the early 2000s differed substantially from the nearly informal industry of the past. The cumulative impact of changes to the industry becomes visible in changes to contractors and the options available to them. Today, small residential contractors have available fewer and fewer of the tactics they long used to overcome the numerous obstacles to making a profit in their industry niche. Labor costs remain the most easily varied cost and a site of prime competition between subcontractors. Understanding this transformation is crucial to understanding why the 2000s' construction boom—which by any measure should have improved fortunes for residential contractors—has been marked by day labor employment and widespread degradation of wages and working conditions.

### *Where Immigrant Workers Fit*

The influx of immigrant and undocumented workers into residential construction—as day laborers, as subcontractors, and as unofficial employees—increases the number of vulnerable workers available to contractors. Studies of day labor have provided valuable information about these workers' demographic profiles, working conditions, and place within the residential construction labor market. Yet attempts to measure the scope of the phenomenon at an industry level are hampered by the difficulty of surveying the small subcontractors who employ day laborers. Treating day labor as synonymous with the growth of immigrant and undocumented worker populations in the industry provides an alternate way to gauge the scope of day labor in residential construction. In the United States more than 90 percent of day laborers are immigrants, and 75 percent lack legal immigration status (Valenzuela Jr. et al. 2006). The overlap between these populations makes it possible to use estimates of the total number of Hispanic and immigrant workers in construction as a basis for calculating the total size of the potential day-labor labor supply within the industry.

Nationally, foreign-born Hispanic workers constituted a large and growing segment of the construction workforce in the mid-2000s. They accounted for 13 percent of construction employment in 2000, growing to 15 percent in 2004, 17 percent in 2005, and 19 percent in 2006 (Passel 2006). A Pew Hispanic Center (2007) estimate of the population of undocumented Hispanic workers paints a similar picture of growth, from 9 percent of the construction workforce in 2000 to 12 percent in 2005 (Table 12).[10] The raw numbers identify the significant role immigrant and Hispanic laborers play in the industry. They mislead, however, because they treat immigrant and undocumented workers as evenly employed throughout the various segments of the construction industry. Most day laborers, immigrants, and undocumented workers work in the residential construction portion of the industry. A national survey of day laborers found that as of 2004 day laborers worked primarily for homeowners and residential contractors and most frequently in occupations—such as demolition and roofing—associated with residential construction (Valenzuela Jr. et al. 2006). Broader measures of the occupational homes of immigrant construction workers yield similar findings.

TABLE 12

**Foreign-Born and Undocumented Hispanic Employment in the U.S. Construction Industry**

| YEAR | 2004 | 2005 | 2006 |
|---|---|---|---|
| Foreign-Born Hispanics (000s) | 1,651 | 1,913 | 2,249 |
| Recently Arrived, Foreign-Born Hispanics (000s) | 386 | 592 | 847 |
| % Foreign Born | 15.3 | 17.1 | 19.1 |
| % Recently Arrived Foreign-Born Hispanics | 3.6 | 5.3 | 7.2 |
| % Undocumented | 10.0 | 12.0 | n/a |

*Sources:* rows 1–4, Passel 2005; 2006; row 5, Pew Hispanic Center 2007.

The occupations in which Hispanic construction workers are most strongly represented are mainstays of residential construction and, more particularly, of residential remodeling (Table 13). The laborer/helper occupation in particular grew (both in the aggregate and as a share of Hispanic employment) during the housing boom of the early 2000s (Center to Protect Workers' Rights 2002). Laborers perform menial and often grueling tasks, such as hand demolition and materials carrying, vital to the remodeling of homes. Taken together, the largest residential construction occupations—laborer, carpenter, painter, and roofer—alone account for more than half of all Hispanic construction employment. These same occupational data also indicate that few Hispanic workers have penetrated the highly skilled and management occupations associated with commercial construction. Foreman and managerial occupations, as well as skilled occupations such as welder, ironworker, and insulation, account for more than 30 percent of all construction employment but just 10 percent of Hispanic construction employment.

Whatever the specific numbers—and they remain elusive under existing data collection methods—it is clear that the residential segment of construction employs a large share of undocumented and Hispanic construction workers. Other available data sources are finely grained enough to make possible estimates of the representation of these workers in residential construction. Table 14 provides a range of estimates of foreign-born Hispanic and undocumented workers as a share of all residential construction workers. The bottom-end estimate calculates the share based on the

TABLE 13

**Hispanic Employment in Major Construction Occupations, United States**

| OCCUPATION | PRIMARY INDUSTRY SEGMENT | % OF ALL WORKERS EMPLOYED IN OCCUPATION | % OF HISPANIC WORKERS EMPLOYED IN OCCUPATION |
|---|---|---|---|
| Laborer/Helper | Residential | 11.5 | 21 |
| Carpenter | Both | 13.8 | 14 |
| Painter | Residential | 6.6 | 13 |
| Other | Both | 1.2 | 8 |
| Manager | Commercial | 16.0 | 6 |
| Drywall | Residential | 2.2 | 5 |
| Foreman | Commercial | 8.0 | 4 |
| Electrical | Both | 6.9 | 4 |
| Plumber | Both | 4.6 | 4 |
| Roofer | Residential | 2.1 | 4 |
| Administrative Support | Commercial | 6.3 | 3 |
| Operating Engineer | Commercial | 4.0 | 3 |
| Bricklayer | Both | 2.5 | 3 |
| Heat, A/C Mechanic | Both | 2.5 | 2 |
| Construction Trades, NEC | Both | 1.8 | 2 |
| Concrete | Commercial | 1.0 | 2 |
| Tile | Commercial | 0.9 | 2 |

Numbers do not sum to 100 owing to omitted occupations. *Source:* Center to Protect Workers' Rights 2002.

modest assumption that just one out of four of these workers employed in the construction industry works in the residential construction industry segment. The high-end estimate assumes that one out of two is employed in residential construction.

Because residential construction accounts for less than one out of seven construction industry jobs with payroll, the relatively small total immigrant and undocumented worker population in construction comprises a large portion of the residential industry segment. By the most modest estimate, at least one in five workers in residential construction in the United States is undocumented. A midrange estimate puts the number closer to 30 percent.

It is tempting to focus on day labor as the prime element of labor market

TABLE 14

**Estimated Employment of Foreign-Born Hispanics and Undocumented Workers in Residential Construction, United States, 2004–6**

| YEAR | 2004 | 2005 | 2006 |
|---|---|---|---|
| Construction Employment | 6,976,000 | 7,336,000 | 7,689,000 |
| Residential Construction Employment | 925,800 | 992,700 | 1,013,000 |
| Total Foreign-Born Hispanic Construction Employment | 1,485,888 | 1,687,280 | 1,922,250 |
| Estimated Undocumented Employment | 767,360 | 806,960 | 845,790 |
| Foreign-Born Hispanic Share of Residential Construction | | | |
| If 1 in 2 Foreign-Born Hispanics in Construction Works in Residential Construction | 58% | 63% | 72% |
| If 1 in 3 Works in Residential Construction | 38% | 42% | 48% |
| If 1 in 4 Works in Residential Construction | 29% | 32% | 36% |
| Undocumented Share of Residential Construction Workforce | | | |
| If 1 in 2 Undocumented Workers in Construction Works in Residential Construction | 41% | 41% | 42% |
| If 1 in 3 Works in Residential Construction | 27% | 27% | 28% |
| If 1 in 4 Works in Residential Construction | 21% | 20% | 21% |

*Sources:* author's calculations from Pew Hispanic Center 2005; 2006 and the U.S. Bureau of Labor Statistics' Current Employment Statistics. Undocumented employment estimates are based on an estimate in Passel 2006 that 11 percent of construction industry employment consisted of undocumented workers in 2005. The estimate of this share does not vary by year.

change in construction. But nationally, only 117,000 workers queue for (or secure) day labor employment every morning (Valenzuela Jr. et al. 2006). While this accounts for more than one-fifth of Hispanic immigrant employment in all segments of the construction industry, the other four-fifths of this new workforce labor under different employment relationships—as subcontractors, as occasional payroll employees of general contractors, and as contingent workers—that are so well integrated into industry networks that job seekers need not visit the day labor shape-up to find day work (Valenzuela Jr. et al. 2006).

Although immigrant employment in construction remains connected in the popular imagination with brute-force deskilling, migrants from Latina America often bring significant construction skills with them. The ways in which workers bend and build upon these skills to expand their opportunities within local labor markets vary depending on the prior institutional organization of those labor markets. These efforts to push above the bottom of the subcontracting chain shape the construction labor market in ways that limit some of the more intensive vulnerabilities the immigrant workforce faces. In Philadelphia and North Carolina, Iskander, Lowe, and Riordan found that workers were able to insulate themselves from the risks inherent in contingent employment by using their portfolio of skills to job jump between employers, a finding that echoes Valenzuela Jr.'s conclusions that some day laborers function as entrepreneurs (Iskander, Lowe, and Riordan 2010). The sociologist Ruth Milkman's study of the Los Angeles residential construction industry (2006) found, however, that immigrant workers often escaped the uncertainty of construction employment by converting themselves into labor barons, contractors who insulated themselves from risk by supplying builders with crews of immigrant workers whose precarious employment functioned as an outlet valve for the multiple uncertainties of the construction process. These findings only appear to be contradictory. The flexibility with which workers position themselves in the subcontracting chain often means that ascent to a higher skill level converts recently immigrated workers into contractors exercising a position of power over their peers. Day laborers in Chicago move in and out of a series of fluid employment relationships in the industry. Identifying the position of individual workers and workforce segments within the industry thus rests not on an a priori assumption of the structure of labor demand but rather on a careful reading of the multiple factors shaping employers' hiring practices.

## The Labor-Intensive Housing Boom: Demand for Unskilled Laborers Soars

From 2002 through 2007, low interest rates catalyzed a residential construction boom and a remarkable run-up in home values. Following the 2001 recession, the Federal Reserve Board of Governors cut the Federal Funds Rate from 3.5 to 2 percent and made clear its hope that housing growth and refinancing would spur the national economy. Federal Reserve Chairman Alan Greenspan put the point somewhat obliquely, testifying to Congress that "besides sustaining the demand for new construction, mortgage markets have also been a powerful stabilizing force over the past two years of economic distress by facilitating the extraction of some of the equity that homeowners have built up over the years" (U.S. Congress 2002).

Given that homes are the largest asset of more than half of all U.S. families, many homeowners took advantage of the deep interest rate reductions to undertake home improvements (Baker and Rosnick 2005). The housing boom provided a powerful stimulus not just to residential construction but specifically to the labor-intensive work of remodeling. Home sales prices grew by a remarkable 50 percent between 2000 and 2006 (Figure 4). From mid-2004 to mid-2007 alone, remodeling expenditures expanded by nearly 50 percent. As Saskia Sassen stresses, remodeling is especially prevalent in large cities dominated by financial and professional services sectors (Sassen 2001, 285).

Chicago was an enthusiastic participant in the boom. Between 2000 and 2006, the total number of residential units that underwent construction in Chicago more than doubled (Table 15). While growth was strongest among large housing developments (of five or more units), which typically fall under union construction rules, it also was quite strong in the two-, three-, and four-unit buildings on which day laborers most frequently work.

These data, however, skew toward new housing starts. Data on the type of construction work done, derived from permits filed with the City of Chicago Department of Buildings, suggest that the rate of remodeling growth equaled or outstripped overall rates of residential housing growth for the 2000–3 period (data on later years are unavailable). Over this four-year span, the total value of residential remodeling permits grew by 63 percent.[11] Assuming that the rate of remodeling growth tracks with the overall rate of residential construction growth in the 2004–6 period, then the total amount of remodeling work in Chicago alone more than doubled over this period. By any measure such an expansion of remodeling activity generates substantial labor demand.

Rapid growth in remodeling activity and the unique (and poor) competitive position of remodeling contractors suggest the need to understand the remodeling industry not just as an offshoot of residential construction but as a growth industry in its own right (Belsky, Calabria, and Nucci 2005). One

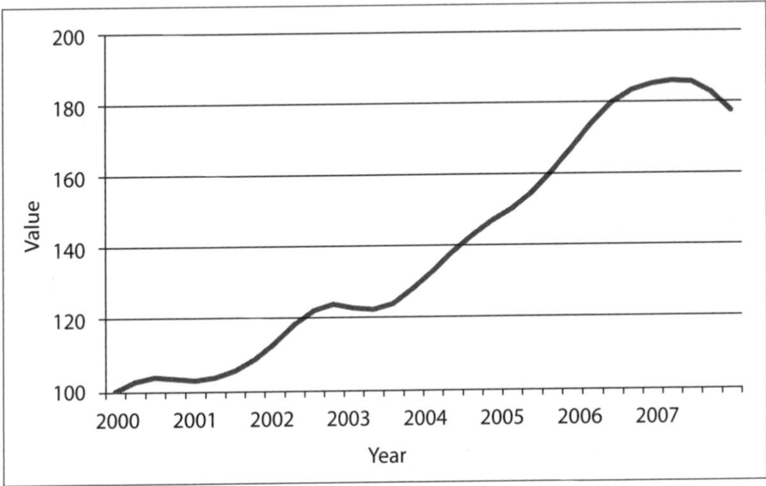


*Figure 4. Quarterly Residential Remodeling Expenditure Growth, United States. Indexed: 2000 = 100.* Source: *the three-quarter rolling average is calculated from Joint Center for Housing Studies 2007.*

of the defining aspects of residential remodeling is that compared with other residential construction industry segments, it is driven by the unique desires and abilities of homeowners, the end users of construction. The important contrast here is to large-scale suburban housing development and commercial construction, in which professionals with knowledge of the construction process negotiate with the contractors formally in their employ. Because homeowners' desire to build wealth despite stagnant incomes and job insecurity often drives remodeling activity, remodeling contracts historically went to the lowest-cost contractor (Bogdon 1996; Joint Center for Housing Studies 2005). But the extreme difficulties homeowners face in evaluating contractors' work proposals substantially modify this cost-cutting impulse.[12]

Many homeowners turn to do-it-yourself contracting texts to guide their interactions with contractors, and the leading texts in the field say much about those homeowners' dilemmas.[13] They emphasize licensing and references as the main elements of contractor selection and devote far more detail to helping homeowners decide what they want to request from a construction standpoint than they do to evaluating bids. Homeowners also receive guidance from state government publications explaining the intricacies of building codes and construction law, and these too paint

TABLE 15

**Growth in Residential Building Permits and Permit Values, Chicago, 2000–6**

| BUILDING SIZE (# UNITS) | | 2000 | 2006 | GROWTH |
|---|---|---|---|---|
| Single Family | Buildings | 1,334 | 1,415 | 6.1% |
| | Units | 1,334 | 1,415 | 6.1% |
| | Construction Cost ($000s) | $241,080 | $287,934 | 19.4% |
| 2 | Buildings | 65 | 121 | 86.2% |
| | Units | 130 | 242 | 86.2% |
| | Construction Cost ($000s) | $14,404 | $27,509 | 91.0% |
| 3–4 | Buildings | 326 | 521 | 59.8% |
| | Units | 1,056 | 1,657 | 56.9% |
| | Construction Cost ($000s) | $106,782 | $168,704 | 58.0% |
| 5+ | Buildings | 171 | 404 | 136.3% |
| | Units | 4,091 | 10,769 | 163.2% |
| | Construction Cost ($000s) | $302,937 | $991,811 | 227.4% |
| Totals | | | | |
| | Buildings | 1,896 | 2,461 | 29.8% |
| | Units | 6,611 | 14,083 | 113.0% |
| | Construction Cost ($000s) | $665,203 | $1,475,956 | 121.9% |

All figures in 2011 dollars. *Source:* author's calculations from U.S. Census Bureau 2000a; 2006a.

the contracting process narrowly. Written from the state's perspective and often with the state's needs in mind, these publications urge homeowners to evaluate contractor licenses and bonding and make only a cursory mention of bid specifications (see Washington State Department of Labor and Industries 2007; California Contractors State License Board 2004).

Overall, the demand generated by the housing boom was as distinctive as it was large. At the same time it created extensive demand for unskilled workers employed in remodeling, the boom placed the contracting process in the hands of cost-conscious end users who retained little familiarity with the details of construction work. These unique traits to the 2000s' housing boom intersected with longer-term changes in the industry to produce not just demand for less-skilled workers but also the means and (sometimes) necessity of hiring them. Because day laborers and other immigrant construction workers claim few formal skills and work for low wages, they are the laborers of choice for such jobs.

## Thinning Margins: How Technological Change Makes Contractors Reliant on Labor Cost Savings

Historically, residential contractors enjoyed a materials monopoly that helped to limit the risks of their work. The public had restricted access to most building materials, from drywall to pipes to prefabricated vanities. In addition to selling their labor and expertise, contractors sold these specialized materials, often at a considerable markup. The extra earnings from this minimonopoly improved margins and provided contractors with a source of profit generation beyond labor itself (Nicholson 2006; Federal Reserve Bank of Chicago 2000).

Changes in the building materials supply chain have greatly restricted contractors' ability to make these markups. The shorthand term *Home Depot effect* captures the transformation that has broken up the materials monopoly. The expansion of Home Depot and other do-it-yourself supply dealers makes building products directly available to the public, allowing the end users of construction to strip away contractors' markup on materials (Abernathy et al. 2004). As a result, contractors increasingly resell materials at low margins or at cost (Joint Center for Housing Studies 2005). The elimination of this source of income places pressure on labor cost reductions as a means of generating profit.

These same technological changes also provide contractors, however, with a new means of profit generation. The ready availability of premanufactured housing components has provided contractors new means of deskilling work—and thus, of cutting labor costs (Erlich and Grabelsky 2005). While on-site construction work remains mostly impervious to capital substitution, the manufacture of prefabricated housing inputs has improved to the point that many housing fixtures (such as doors and frames, cabinets and vanities) can be purchased as preassembled products. Whereas the installation of such fixtures in the past required at least some component of craft skill or contractor expertise, these projects can now be accomplished with minimally skilled laborers performing basic demolition, installation, and finishing tasks. In short, technological changes in the industry provide contractors with low margins to remedy and the means of doing so.

## Risk Rolls Downhill: Residential Contractors Subcontract to Vulnerable Workers

The contingent nature of construction work and the small size of most residential construction firms made subcontracting a staple of residential construction long before the modern era. Until recently, the construction process was coordinated and managed by a general contractor who bid the project, oversaw and coordinated the work of different specialty trade contractors, and directly employed at least a portion of the laborers involved (Weil 2005). This subcontracting arrangement centered risk on the general contractor and addressed the basic need for functional flexibility in the construction process.

Dating from the Reagan administration's withdrawal of support for collective bargaining and workplace inspections and enabled by the continued deskilling of the work process, this function-based subcontracting model (hereafter labeled the *general contractor model*) has given way to the labor contracting model of organizing construction jobs (Philips 2003; Finkel 2005). The signature innovation of the evolving model is the transformation of the general contractor into a project manager who oversees construction labor without necessarily participating in it (Weil 2005, 452).

Under the labor contracting model, general contractors possess greater ability to directly access low-wage subcontractors (Figure 5). The subdivision of work into small pieces limits the need for skilled subcontractors and creates extra opportunities for (indirectly) employing unskilled workers. This shift rests on the industry changes I have outlined: a growing supply of unskilled immigrant laborers, technological changes that allow for the deskilling of work, and consumer demand for labor-intensive and cut-price work. The rise of labor contracting subdivides the work process in a way that reduces general contractors' need for skilled subcontractors and increases the number of tasks for which unskilled labor can be used to bid down project costs. It is within this evolving model that the labor barons—bundlers of unskilled workers—growing in Chicago, Los Angeles, and other cities have carved out a distinctive industry niche (Milkman 2006).

As union density in residential construction has fallen and enforcement of labor laws has weakened, general contractors have added new levels of specialization to the subcontracting process in order to separate skilled from unskilled labor. This shift frequently succeeds in cutting skilled (and often union) subcontractors out of the work process. Historically, these subcontractors provided a bundled service of technical expertise, skilled

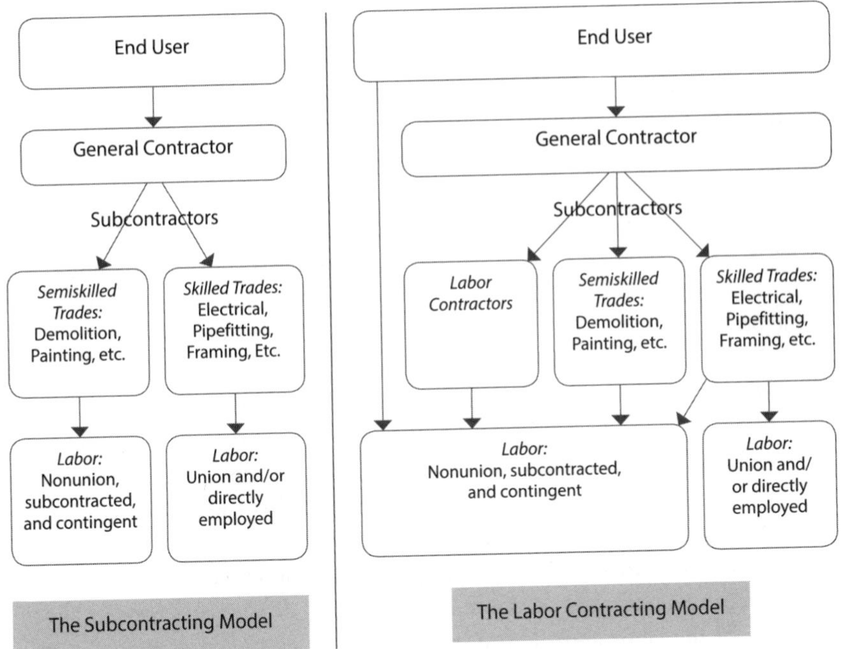


*Figure 5. Evolution of Residential Remodeling Production Processes.* Sources: *adapted by the author from interviews, Philips 2003, Weil 2005, and Ehrlich and Grabelsky 2005.*

labor, and unskilled labor—all at the same price. Electrical work, for example, entails the careful tailoring of circuits and wires to the construction work at hand, the skilled construction of electrical boxes, and the mostly deskilled work of pulling wires from box to box. Under the general contractor model, subcontractors enjoyed minimonopolies over their craft or trade area and charged the same rate for both the highly skilled and the fully deskilled components of their work. Under the labor contracting model, general contractors directly access unskilled workers and employ specialty subcontractors for increasingly limited portions of the construction process.

The labor contracting model has changed the operation of the residential construction industry in three basic ways. First, as Weil (2005, 452) explains, it mitigates the risk and improves the rewards of general contractors while unfavorably impacting risk-to-reward ratios for both homeowners and subcontracted laborers. Under the general contracting model, general contractors shared the end user's interest in cost control, but only to a point. General contractors' bids to end users were based on subbids from often unionized subcontractors. In order to turn a profit, the general contractors needed to mark up the total bid by including their own labor and materials (Weil 2005, 452). The labor contracting model aligns the interests of the general contractor and the end user. Because general contractors now turn a profit from managing the project rather than performing labor, they squeeze the labor and the materials costs they had previously worked to mark up in order to either push down the total bid estimate for the project or preserve their own profit margins as the work occurs.

The long-standing industry institution of subcontracting, which once served to coordinate the functional and technical complexities of construction work, makes an apt vehicle for squeezing costs. In fact, the (often Byzantine) elaboration of subcontracting chains is one of the contemporary construction industry's defining features. Rather than using subcontracting to align specialized skills that support overall construction goals, general contractors today use the subcontracting chain much as cost-competitive manufacturers use the supply chain—to isolate individual elements of the labor and the production process and play off prospective bidders against one another (Erlich and Grabelsky 2005).

In addition to these somewhat formal and structural changes to the subcontracting process, contractors have cut labor costs through another, often illegal, measure—the misclassification of directly employed workers as subcontractors. Because misclassifying workers as independent contractors makes them ineligible for nonwage benefits that drive up hourly labor costs, doing so straightforwardly reduces labor costs. In residential construction these nonwage labor costs include not just health care and payroll taxes but also expensive contributions to state workers' compensation and unemployment insurance funds. Studies of Massachusetts and Maine show that the rate of employee misclassification in construction significantly outstrips the rate for the economy as a whole (see Carré and Wilson 2004; see also Carré 2005).[14] In Illinois a minimum of 6,200 construction employers misclassified employees as subcontractors between 2001 and 2005 (Kelsay, Sturgeon, and Pinkham 2006). Given that firms that misclassify one worker typically misclassify several and that the strong union presence in commercial construction limits misclassification in that industry segment, it seems likely that a small segment of repeat-offender residential construction employers accounts for a large share of this misclassification (Weil 1991).

Cumulatively, these changes have transformed subcontracting practices, as well as labor markets themselves, in residential construction. Between 1967 and 1997, general contractors went from directly employing 34 percent of the residential construction workforce to just 24 percent (Bosch and Philips 2003). In the process they reorganized the distribution of risks and rewards in the industry. Today, "all risk and liability are shifted from the hands of the construction manager [i.e., the general contractor] to the subcontractors. The price for estimating mistakes, workplace injuries, materials delays or any of the other *standard* hurdles is borne entirely by the subcontractor, who is also responsible for the management of labor relations" (Erlich and Grabelsky 2005, 428).

Beyond the technical aspects of this type of industry reorganization, then, the labor contracting model functions as a means of shifting risk from general contractors to subcontractors. The growth of degraded work practices can best be understood with reference to these changes and the increasingly precarious position of most subcontractors.

### *Unions and Regulators Look Elsewhere*

Because of the industry's radically deconcentrated structure and small establishment sizes, the grip of employment laws have always exerted a weaker grip on residential construction than on other industries. Scholars of the industry emphasize the polarization between large builders and small general contractors and its built-in tendencies toward cost-based competition (Finkel 1997, 32; Philips 2003). Whereas large contracts, the Davis–Bacon Act, and unionization historically pulled commercial construction onto a high-productivity, high-wage path, residential construction remains difficult for most regulatory agencies to police.

In the era of strong labor unions and strongly enforced federal laws governing workers' compensation and subcontracting, the industry was better regulated than it is today. In the immediate postwar era, the strength of unions and regulatory institutions, combined with strong demand for new suburban housing, ensured both a steady stream of work and a reliable labor supply. Ample funding for OSHA, the Wage and Hour Division of the Department of Labor, and state-level agencies improved enforcement of basic wage laws and working conditions and guarded against misclassification of employees and off-the-books payment (Philips 2003). At the same time, inroads in unionization among residential builders strengthened the labor movement's presence in the industry, effectively providing an extra regulator capable of monitoring violations in employment law and alerting state agencies (Palladino 2005). From the mid-1940s through the early 1980s, residential construction suffered few labor shortages and saw wages rise somewhat steadily (Federal Reserve Bank of Chicago 2000). But even during this period of stability and fairly vigorous regulation, unions never made residential construction a priority.

A series of small regulatory and enforcement changes initiated in the 1970s gradually undercut this already weak regulatory settlement. Procedural changes to National Labor Relations Board rules in the late 1970s and early 1980s made union formation—which depends on picketing the work sites of mobile employers in residential construction—more difficult (Erlich and Grabelsky 2005, 432–24). Funding cuts to wage-and-hour enforcement and OSHA inspections initiated under the Reagan administration reduced the risk employers faced for misclassifying or mistreating workers (see Bernhardt and McGrath 2005).[15] These political-economic changes were amplified by the double-dip recession of 1981–82. This deep economic downturn, the most severe since World War II, chilled housing demand nationwide. Even in union-dominated labor markets such as Los Angeles, where the carpenters' union had recently boasted that "there isn't a nail driven in this area that isn't driven by a union man with a union card in his pocket," contractors began to double-breast (to supplement union work with nonunion work), and the union share of the construction market fell precipitously (Milkman 2006, 93). Chicago began with weaker union representation and saw area-wide unemployment rates top 12 percent in 1982, the local peak year for deindustrialization. To this day area labor officials view the ensuing falloff in housing demand as the force that broke momentum for unionization and set the industry down its current path. In their struggle to make ends meet, union contractors began to perform nonunion work at greatly discounted rates. Trade union officials identify this as a turning point in Chicago's construction industry. Employment data bear them out. During the next building boom, in the 1990s, union density diminished, and wage growth was virtually nil (Federal Reserve Bank of Chicago 2000).

By the time the 2000s' construction boom arrived, the regulation of residential construction was minimal at best. In the mid-2000s Laborers' International Union of North America president Terry O'Sullivan lamented that "we have virtually no presence" in the residential construction market (Erlich and Grabelsky 2005, 424).

## New Winners and Losers in a Thriving Industry

In cost-competitive manufacturing industries, firms began to pursue contingent employment practices and aggressive subcontracting arrangements as a desperate response to competition from low-wage competitors in the U.S. South and abroad. It was a defense measure. What, then, can explain residential construction contractors' aggressive embrace of day labor amid the biggest industry expansion in decades? It is tempting to characterize the growth of day labor as an offensive maneuver designed to build control over labor. But the question of contractors' agency—of the ability of any employer or institution to effect significant change in so disorganized an industry—suggests otherwise. A handful of manufacturing conglomerates and corporations with significant market share can remake an industry with aggressive action. But residential construction contractors have weak industry associations and a microscopic market share at the firm level. Employer strategy appears more likely to be reactive than constructive.

Opportunism provides a more satisfactory explanation. At the peak of the boom, the foreign-born population of workers in construction grew by more than 10 percent per year. Under normal economic circumstances, the industry would have had few mechanisms for incorporating this influx. But the 2001–7 business cycle was an outlier of dramatic proportions. Immigrant workers provided the raw labor and hours needed to sustain record contracting growth without the wage growth that ensues from tight labor markets. In order for this to happen, the industry had to be organizationally ready to incorporate an influx of unskilled workers. The prior rollback of union strength and the deskilling of residential construction work through reliance on prebuilt fixtures provided hundreds of thousands of subcontracted nodes through which these workers could be incorporated into the industry. While day labor unmistakably solved cost problems for contractors, it also provided an all-purpose labor supply that could be plugged into dozens of new spaces created in the industry's complex chains of contractors, subcontractors, and subsubcontractors.

The overall financial dynamics of the industry in the 2000s made it clear that workers' losses were contractors' gains. The simultaneous explosion of construction demand and contraction of laborers' wages released an enormous amount of free-floating profit into the contested subcontracting chains that regulated organization and competition within the industry. The institution of competitive bidding of contracts would suggest that the end users of construction claimed these profits in the form of price discounts from competing bidders. But this rarely was the case. As homeowners, general contractors, subcontractors, and laborers fought over the allocation of profit from a rapidly restructuring industry, the beneficiaries of day laborers' flexibility and fast-paced work varied from day to day and job to job. The key question in the industry is not whether day laborers take away jobs from other workers but rather who benefits from day laborers' work.

# 7

# A Perfectly Flexible Workforce

## *Day Labor in a Precarious Industry*

Seen from a distance, the residential construction industry of today appears to be a place-bound cousin of the globe-hopping industries commonly described by the epithet *sweatshop.* The extreme contingency of day labor and the quick physical toll construction work takes on laborers suggest a Hobbesian industry: nasty working conditions, brutishly low pay, and a short career. For good measure, employers have harnessed technology to deskill work previously thought to be immune from deskilling, a fact to which the high coincidence of day labor shape-ups with Home Depot parking lots testifies.

But the core reasons why scholars view residential construction as a premodern industry are much older. Recent advances in deskilling construction work come wrapped in a set of older institutional practices that seem ready-made for extracting highly productive labor for minimal pay. Long before economists insisted on grafting spot markets onto social and institutional relationships that had never previously needed them, construction contractors had developed the day labor shape-up as a way of quickly assembling the ever-changing labor teams a job required. Just as significant, contractors have long been accustomed to bidding against one another to win even small jobs. These basic mechanisms of market discipline, which other industries have incorporated through elaborate restructurings, were part of the essential organization of residential construction long before there was need for the terms *contingent work* and *labor flexibility.*

Fed by deskilling and day labor, contemporary residential construction jobs contain a substantial amount of free-floating profit extracted from workers who perform a broad range of essential construction tasks for low hourly wages. But the extraction of this profit does not complete an accurate analysis of the industry—it *begins* that analysis. Who realizes the profit from day laborers—how it is passed up and, sometimes, back down the subcontracting chain—is an open question that intensifies the ongoing negotiation and struggle among laborers, contractors, and homeowners.

Wages constitute only the most obvious dimension through which contractors realize a profit from day laborers. The complexity of the construction process makes day laborers desirable for ease and flexibility as much if not more than for simple cost cutting. The construction industry's exaggerated cycles of boom and bust make speed of work an especially important asset for contractors. When business booms, contractors overextend themselves to make up for the fallow periods that preceded the surge in demand. The typical sole-proprietor contractor who flourished during the 2000s' housing boom had scant capital resources, small networks of subcontractors, and minimal time to manage multiple concurrent projects.

The day labor corner—*la parada* (the stop) to the job seekers who spend their mornings waiting for work—solves multiple problems for this harried and overextended entrepreneur. The opportunity to pick up able and willing workers at virtually any time and with no advance notice allows contractors to minimize idle time on the work site and keep projects moving with minimal planning. *La parada* provides a ready solution to the surprises, mishaps, and delays that accompany remodeling jobs. When unexpected rot shows up behind a wall or delays in tearing out old fixtures from a soon-to-be-modernized building threaten the quick turnaround of the work, a trip to the day labor corner secures the extra hands needed to make the problem disappear and put the project back on track. The ongoing demise of the traditional general contractor model magnifies these benefits: virtually any contractor at any position on the subcontracting chain can slot day laborers into a project, and most can plug day laborers into multiple jobs at once.

This flexibility extends into other facets of the job. Licensed pipe fitters or carpenters work within narrow occupational boundaries and on their own terms. Day laborers work for the contractor, who can shift them between jobs at whim. With a bit of prodding—or often none, since day workers enthusiastically embrace their employer's demands in order to be invited back—the contractor can goad workers into working without rest or safety equipment and skipping lunch. And when cost overruns and a client's withholding of payment eat through the profit built into a contractor's initial bid, he can cut, withhold, delay, or outright decline payment for the work the day laborers performed.

On its own the managerial flexibility day labor provides would be sufficient to endear this reconfigured institution to contractors. But in addition to being flexible, day laborers are cheap. Depending on the job in question, hiring workers from the corner during the 2000s' boom netted contractors a wage savings of at least 40 percent and often more. Factoring in workers' compensation and other nonwage employer costs associated with construction suggests an even bigger cost differential. It is tempting to guess that these cost savings are illusory from the contractor's point of view. After all, the process of bidding for construction jobs should force contractors to capitalize these labor-cost savings into their bids, severely reducing or potentially even eliminating the direct profit gains associated with cheap labor.

But actual markets remain considerably more complicated than the stylized picture that appears in textbooks. Although construction subcontractors can ably price project bids to reflect the actual costs of materials and labor, those costs become inputs into a negotiation between a general contractor who knows a lot about construction work and a homeowner who knows little. As a result, the cost savings produced by low wages and efficient production rarely reach the end user of construction. During the 2000s' building boom, the day-to-day work of residential construction doubled as a process for negotiating which contractor and which segment of the subcontracting chain realized the substantial profits produced by day laborers' cheap and flexible work.

## The Cost Gap between Day Laborers and Payroll Employees

Popular debates about immigration and the U. S. labor market revolve around the notion that undocumented workers primarily function as a source of cheap labor for employers. The wage gap between unskilled immigrant laborers and others in construction is if anything larger than this debate would suggest. By most estimates day laborers earn less than $0.60 for every $1.00 other construction workers make (Figure 6).

These compensation data do not include common construction employment costs such as payroll taxes, employment benefits, and workers' compensation expenses. If these costs—which are borne by the employers of payroll construction workers but not by the contractors who hire day laborers—were brought into the equation, the cost differential would increase substantially. Regardless of the specific estimate, this gap in hourly labor costs reflects the dual labor markets of residential construction work

| Population | Occupation | Hourly Wage |
|---|---|---|
| Day Laborers | All | $10.00 |
| Payroll Construction Workers | Roofer | $17.25 |
| | Painters, Construction, and Maintenance | $17.26 |
| | Miscellaneous Construction Trades | $18.69 |
| | Drywall Installer | $19.09 |
| | Plumbers, Pipe Fitters, and Steam Fitters | $25.97 |

*Figure 6. Estimates of Hourly Construction Earnings by Worker Type, United States, 2004.* Sources: row 1, *Valenzuela Jr. et al. 2006 and author interviews;* row 2–6, *U.S. Bureau of Labor Statistics 2007.*

(Philips 2003). Union tradespeople and skilled specialists undergo a years-long formal apprenticeship that renders them highly skilled and increases the wages they command. Although the foundations of this apprenticeship system continue to crumble, these workers benefit from a labor market that helps to guarantee both the supply and the demand of highly skilled work.

Nonunion and low-cost contractors, by contrast, increasingly turn to day-labor labor markets, where hundreds of workers line up daily for work at street corner hiring sites. In northeast Illinois hundreds if not thousands more workers seek work through personal networks, temporary agencies, and the not-for-profit Albany Park (Day Labor) Worker Center on Chicago's Northwest Side. In a typical week day laborers in Chicago work three full days but seek work six or seven. Because moments in which labor demand outstrips labor supply are rare, contractors maintain a firm advantage in the labor market. When a contractor pulls up to a hiring site, workers instantly surround the car. If only one of these job seekers undercuts his peers, the wage floor they have attempted to set drops. Thus although day laborers can make hundreds of dollars in a good week, wages and employment vary in spot-market fashion (often hovering around eight to ten dollars per hour), and the impulse to undercut when negotiating with contractors cannot be avoided. Edgardo, a pseudonymously named and relatively skilled day laborer from South America, explains the permanent contingency of wage negotiations as follows: “What's the typical pay? There is no typical pay. It depends. It depends on the time of day, the season, how many workers are out there [on the corner], how much I have worked that week. At different times I receive ten dollars per hour and fourteen dollars per hour for doing the same work. It depends."

Workers routinely try to organize minimum hourly wage rates for individual types of work, but as Luís, a skilled day laborer from Mexico, explains, a single desperate worker can scuttle the agreement.

> You learn after awhile not to go below ten dollars per hour. But the new guys don't know that. They come to the corner, and you explain that there's a minimum wage [*salario*]. But then a day goes by, and they don't get work, and they'll run up to the [contractor's] truck and say, "Eight dollars," and get in.

As a result of the low wages paid to day laborers, many long-established specialty contractors—not general building contractors but firms dedicated to specific portions of the construction process—in the Chicago area experienced severe cost cutting from new competitors during the 2000s' housing boom. The waning fortunes of Jenkins Remodelers, a longtime union contractor on the North Shore, illustrate the realities of competition today. Benefiting from a popular reputation for high-quality plumbing and related work, Jenkins thrived through the postwar era and into the 1990s. But as housing prices grew at annual rates of 10 percent or more during the 2000s—a time in which remodelers should be expected to thrive, particularly in high-cost North Shore real estate markets—Jenkins actually lost market share, particularly on smaller and more labor-intensive jobs. The inability of unions to sign up new contractors, along with weakened enforcement of licensing laws, allowed nonunion low-wage firms to establish themselves with ease. In the mid-1990s Jenkins counted eighteen direct competitors in its unofficial service area. By 2007 it counted eighty-one, the vast majority of which it could not compete with on cost terms. One of the firm's long-tenured contractors explains:

> These guys charge maybe fifty cents on the dollar of what we do. Do you know how high our union rates are? Just to come out to your house, there's a minimum fee. Its forty-one dollars. We charge more than eighty dollars per hour for every hour after that. . . . Our work is made to last, and we're proud of it. But our up-front costs are so high it's hard to get a foot in the door. People keep quoting us competitors' rates, and it's like, "We can't compete with that."

Among the many problems Jenkins faces is the diminished allure of high-priced but long-lasting construction work. The firm, like the unionized construction industry, grew up at a time in which the norm (or at least the expectation) of long-term homeownership made investments in long-lasting work practical. As of 2007, fully 40 percent of the homeowners in Jenkins's area had moved into their buildings after the year 2000, and only 30 percent had lived in their buildings since 1990 or before.[1] Jenkins's long-term competitive strategy of offering durable work at high prices effectively priced it out of a market in which short tenure and high monthly mortgage payments oriented homeowners toward lower-cost contractors.

The contractors taking market share from Jenkins promise substantially lower costs to homeowners. Raj, a small contractor offering simple remodeling work—including the pipe fitting work Jenkins does, as well as drywalling, framing, and other work over which carpenters and other specialty trades usually held a near monopoly—exemplifies the strategy used by these competitors. In business since 2003, Raj has remained busy with his reputation for low-cost work. Unlike Jenkins Remodelers, Raj employs no workers himself. Instead, he functions as the overseer of a construction process run almost completely by day laborers and other recently arrived immigrant workers. When meeting with homeowners, Raj brings along a handful of immigrant construction workers with whom he routinely works. These workers operate as the de facto subcontractors and develop a bid based on low-cost materials from Home Depot and hourly labor rates of eight to ten dollars. Raj himself is not present for the work, which is almost solely conducted by the subcontractor (often a sometimes or former day laborer himself) and the day laborers that subcontractor hires for the job.

For small projects such as the installation of new bathroom fixtures (for example, a vanity, tile, and a tub), the subcontractors charge in the range of $3,500 to $4,000. Raj takes a generous markup, charging the homeowner around $6,000. For a similar job Jenkins Remodelers estimates its cost at $12,000 or more. Although the faster worker rates, high-quality materials, and general reliability of the work performed by Jenkins significantly offset this price differential over the long run, the sheer size of the gap between the two quotes places Jenkins at a severe market disadvantage, especially in cases in which homeowners are preparing homes for resale, as opposed to planning for long-term ownership.

These two examples represent extremes on the spectrum of remodeling labor costs. At a time in which many contractors have moved toward nonunion subcontractors, Jenkins remains committed to working with Chicago's trade unions and has in other ways refused to update its business model to the unique particulars of the 2000s' housing boom.[2] Similarly, Raj provides an extreme case of a nonunion low-cost contractor. Although the hourly rates Raj and his subcontractors pay day laborers are more or less the industry standard, many nonunion contractors perform a great portion of the work themselves and, accordingly, charge higher prices. But one way or another, nonunion contractors who hire day laborers cut hourly labor costs by large margins. This is the essential cost differential driving the remaking of low-end residential construction.

## Access to Day Laborers Speeds the Deskilling of Construction Work

Although the labor cost gap between day laborers and formally trained construction workers opens substantial competitive opportunities for cost-cutting contractors, these opportunities are restricted to certain types of jobs and certain contracting arrangements. The nature of construction work itself and the institutional organization of residential contracting continue to insulate many types of jobs from this competition. In many cases, the cost-cutting contractors who hire day laborers reap little direct benefit from the immediate labor cost savings, as these savings themselves must be passed on to a general contractor as a means of winning the right to perform work.

Union and other high-cost contractors face the greatest threat from cost-cutting competitors on smaller and comparatively deskilled jobs. This happens in substantial part because smaller jobs are easier to deskill. Large construction projects, such as the gutting and rehabilitation of a row house or the addition of a new room to an existing house, inevitably require high-level construction knowledge and experience with managing complex projects. Small jobs, such as painting an apartment or installing new cabinets or other fixtures, can more easily be performed, however, by workers with minimal experience and low skill levels. In fact, hiring day laborers at low wages is one of the few ways contractors can guarantee good returns from such small-scale work. "Most of the guys you see hiring day laborers, they're doing real small jobs—I'm talking $20,000 or less," explains a general contractor with decades of experience. "Those jobs just aren't worth it if you can't mark it up 100 percent [over anticipated costs]. If you hire day laborers, you save a lot on costs."

When contractors working larger jobs—such as gut/rehab and large-scale renovation projects costing hundreds of thousands of dollars—hire day laborers, the day laborers perform the most labor-intensive parts of the work process. On smaller jobs such as remodeling a kitchen, contractors periodically bring in day laborers to rip out old fixtures and walls, to cart out debris, and to paint, sand, and perform other basic mechanical work while the skilled contractor in charge of the job negotiates the intricacies of design, measurement, and customization.

Among day laborers work in entry-level labor and in less skilled occupations, such as painting, roofing, and landscaping, accounts for the majority of employed hours (Figure 7). Comparatively few day laborers (20 percent) do electrical work, and just one-fifth of all day laborers perform any other type of occupation.[3] With entry-level labor as the norm among day laborers, contractors must be able to deskill work in order to take advantage of this workforce.

Like their peers who perform small remodeling jobs, contractors responsible for much larger and more complicated projects have found ways to restructure the work process, the better to draw from this worker population. In general the larger the job, the more intricately the contractor rationalizes and subdivides the labor process. In order to cut labor costs on a multi-million-dollar residential rehabilitation in an upscale North Side neighborhood, a contractor I will refer to as Mike divided all skilled construction jobs into separate design components—assigned to licensed subcontractors at high hourly rates—and deskilled labor performed at the lowest possible cost (see Figure 5).[4] As he explains, in detail:

> I'm not going to go become a licensed electrician or plumber. But what I do is I have the electrician come in here and post his license and work as a consultant. He does the design work. But the actual putting in the boxes and running the conduit and running the fixtures before the drywall, the day laborers do that. So [the contractor] comes back in every once in a while, and at the end and says, "OK, fix that; the building inspector will be OK with that, but he's not going to like that." And so we change some things. . . . But the actual physical work of doing all that stuff? Why pay a contractor

| Construction Occupation | Percent Performing Occupation |
|---|---|
| Construction Laborer | 92 |
| Painter | 85 |
| Roofer | 81 |
| Gardener/Landscaper | 77 |
| Carpenter | 69 |
| Drywall Installer | 68 |
| Housecleaner | 67 |
| Other | 21 |
| Electrician | 20 |

*Figure 7. Occupational Employment of Day Laborers, United States, 2004.* Source: *Valenzuela Jr. et al. 2006.*

to do it? [The contractor] deserves to have some profit, but now I can strip down his profit percentage. Usually, a job like this house costs about $700,000 to do—just in pure, hard costs. If I do it with my own construction crew, I can strip out 45 percent of that in labor costs. I do that with someone like José and Juan [former day laborers now in his employ as off-the-books workers], who have enough experience and intelligence to do it.

In a project of this size and complexity, even the most aggressively cost-cutting contractors can incorporate day labor only partially and at the margins of work driven by higher levels of skill. Still, this ability to break down the work so minutely effectively intensifies the impact of the Home Depot effect on skilled contractors. Whereas these contractors historically were able to charge for design, materials, and labor, they can increasingly charge for only the most skilled, least labor-intensive parts of their work. In Chicago and its nearby suburbs, the practice of electricians loaning out their licenses and consenting to trade paid labor hours for a higher rate on smaller design jobs has grown both in frequency and in price, and contractors casually spoke about this extralegal activity during interviews. Waning union influence and enforcement power likewise make it progressively easier for contractors to replace portions of carpenters' and plumbers' jobs with day labor work.

Because the profitable employment of day laborers usually remains limited to the most deskilled jobs, competition between low-cost contractors and high-wage union contractors is more partial and indirect than it first appears. Although Jenkins Remodelers lost market share during the boom, it remains strong on large-scale remodeling and multifamily residential jobs, where competitors' ability to undercut Jenkins on costs is limited owing to the obvious complexity of the work and the need for skilled labor. Cost-cutting competition has more severely restricted Jenkins's ability to profit from small- and midsize jobs for single homeowners—many of whom now call to request that the contractor perform hours-long jobs installing fixtures already purchased rather than the lengthy design-and-bid jobs it formerly conducted. Similarly, the trade unions whose contractors and laborers work in Chicago's residential housing markets maintain a good hold on large condominium developments and expensive properties. But the ability of cost-cutting contractors to severely undercut union rates on single-family and smaller residential jobs has quickly reduced union market share in residential remodeling. Competition between day laborers and high-wage union workers remains confined primarily to residential remodeling and (comparatively) small construction jobs in single-family homes.

Because residential contractors can tap day labor only for certain types of activities, the incorporation of day laborers into the construction labor market has different impacts for varying kinds of contractors. Small contractors and contractors who specialize in labor-intensive work have the most immediate incentive and ability to hire day laborers. Although these contractors employ day labor workers the most aggressively, they rarely possess the capacity to keep those cost savings for themselves, instead passing them up the chain to the general contractors who commission them. The demise of the general contractor model and the growth of cost-competitive subcontracting in the residential sector place many subcontractors in the position of pushing down labor costs out of necessity.

## Homeowners Circumvent the Contracting Process

Chicago's day laborers work for three main types of contractors. The first is homeowners themselves. According to the National Day Labor Survey, private homeowners account for approximately 38 percent of all day labor employers (Valenzuela Jr. et al. 2006). Interviews with day laborers and with not-for-profit officials working with Chicago's day laborers suggest a lower figure in the Chicago area of perhaps 25 percent. Given the Home Depot effect and the growth of do-it-yourself renovation work, their role as employers resembles that of contractors themselves.

A sporadic demand for labor distinguishes homeowners as employers. Whereas contractors who hire day laborers typically prefer to form long-term working relationships with individual workers, homeowners lack the volume of work necessary to hire workers more than occasionally. From the point of view of day laborers and other entry-level construction workers, this makes homeowners useful but problematic as employers. On the one hand, they typically offer better working conditions (e.g., less monitoring, more frequent breaks, meals, a slower pace of work) than do contractors and are less likely to withhold or refuse payment for services. On the other hand, homeowners do not offer the promise of regular work and potential skills acquisition—a significant difference from the numerous contractors and subcontractors with whom many day laborers develop longer-term working partnerships. Although community-based organizations and workers themselves make dedicated efforts to tap homeowners as employers, they express continual frustration at the trade-offs this move entails.

The decision of homeowners to circumvent the contracting process by hiring day laborers directly reveals much about the struggle to capture the cost savings of low-wage labor. When viewed as contractors, homeowners stand on top of a simple contracting chain in which they access labor, normally with the intermediation of subcontractors. Owing to the asymmetric knowledge that shapes the bidding process, homeowners have no guarantee of benefiting from low labor costs when they hire a contractor. But directly hiring day laborers ensures a one-to-one link between homeowners' costs and labor costs. Accordingly, the homeowners who hire day laborers uniformly cite low hourly pay rates—and the prohibitively high cost of hiring a contractor—as their reason for turning to this workforce. Hiring day laborers cuts costs for these individuals not because it gets them access to day laborers' labor—they would almost certainly access that labor through the contractors who would otherwise be hired to do the job—but because it cuts the contractor and the contractor's margin out of the construction process.

The efforts of homeowners to circumvent the contracting process point to the intense conflict over the profits created during construction. As scholars of construction suggest, the conversion of a subcontracting process formerly based on skill into a cost-pressure system akin to the manufacturing supply chain has transformed the fortunes of contractors (Weil

2005; Finkel 2005). The strategies, labor practices, and predisposition to degraded work practices of the contractors who hire day laborers depend on those contractors' own position in the subcontracting chain.

## Opportunistically Degrading Work: General Contractors

The complexity of subcontracting places general contractors in a favorable position for profiting from degraded work practices. Perched atop the subcontracting chain, they benefit from information asymmetry within the different portions of the bidding process. When bidding out their own work to subcontractors, general contractors benefit from both an intricate knowledge of construction techniques and of the particular job being bid. Operating as professionals, they squeeze subcontractors for low costs (based almost exclusively on low-wage labor) and a fast pace of work.

But when they make their own bids to a homeowner or developer, this transparency disappears. Unlike contractors, homeowners know little about the construction process, evaluating bids, or pricing labor and supplies. The Home Depot effect does partially mitigate homeowners' positional disadvantage by allowing them to remove materials from the bidding process. At the very least, it allows aggressive end users to insist that materials be provided at cost. But the particulars of the work of construction itself—the difference between sound and shoddy jobs, the hidden labor in seemingly simple tasks, the potential to run into decaying foundations and materials shortages—eludes most homeowners. As a result, general contractors by and large do not incorporate into their final bids the cost savings earned by squeezing subcontractors. For these contractors, hiring day laborers and degrading work is not a matter of competitive necessity but rather a means of padding always-contested profit margins.

When asked whether general contractors use day labor to lower bid costs, contractors and industry members dismiss the idea. "Nobody knows what they're asking for from a contractor," explains the general contractor with decades of experience, "especially homeowners. . . . You're not going to cut your bid price because you've got Juan working for you. Nobody cuts prices because the homeowner's either going to accept your bid or not. The bid's not negotiable."

In theory contractors and, especially, experienced contractors understand the multiple contingencies of the building process and make carefully calculated bids with a knife-edge precision. They are high enough to cover the contractor for the unexpected problems that increase time and costs (such as alterations not visible in blueprints, rust and rot, material and labor shortages, miscommunication with subcontractors) but low enough to beat out other contractors in the marketplace. In reality bidding works much more heuristically. Rather than work these multiple contingencies into the bid and negotiate with potential clients, most general contractors follow a simple rule of thumb: bid high and work out the details later. "Especially on small jobs, if I'm a contractor, I ask for a sky-high amount," explains a workers' advocate and longtime contractor. "If I get it, great. If not, I'd just as soon not be bothered anyway. There are too many things that could go wrong, and the payoff just isn't worth it."

This approach often leads to bids that fail to cover the amount of work ideally involved. As a longtime union carpenter details, "Everyone's going to tell you they spend hours looking at the home and figuring out their bid. That's not how the contractors I know do it. It's the other way around. You make your bid and then work backward, trying to find the cheapest way to do it."

Another contractor, who abandoned a professional career to work full time on renovations during the 2000s' boom, echoes this logic: "Sometimes we run into a job where the homeowner quotes another guy's bid that's half as much as ours. . . . But it doesn't matter. The homeowner isn't comparing apples to apples, and we weren't going to win that bid anyway."

The large quantity of work available during the 2000s' housing boom helped contractors to keep bids high relative to project costs. With many jobs to choose from, bidding functions as a means of sorting through the multiple available opportunities and selecting the one with the highest margins. Even when construction demand lags, this approach is supported by homeowners and their trepidation about hiring a class of businessperson regarded as untrustworthy by the population at large. Just as contractors approach remodeling jobs with an eye toward the numerous technical risks involved, homeowners find themselves awash in nightmare-scenario stories about cost overruns and the unreliability of contractors.[5] The popular literature counseling homeowners on how to deal with contractors, a representative piece of which treats finding a reliable contractor as "the great mystery of home-owning in America," gives an apt characterization of the fears involved (Levinson 1992, 2). How-to guides remind homeowners that because contractors know everything about the construction process and "you know next to nothing, it's hard to ignore the suspicion that they might try to put something over on you, sell you something you don't really need, or over-charge you. . . . Your suspicions are well-founded" (Stephens 1998, xxviii).

Given the general climate of suspicion around contractors, it is not surprising that homeowners prioritize basic due diligence—checking the contractor's licensing and bonding, calling referrals, looking for evidence of unreliability—over the far more complicated mechanics of the construction work itself. The counsel that homeowners receive treats the details of construction work with a light touch, underlining the impossibility of homeowners understanding every type of job and gently pushing them to focus on a contractor's demeanor over his itemization of time and materials (Levenson 1992, 15–19; Stephens 1998; 27–28). In preparing themselves to evaluate contractors, homeowners thus have few tools for understanding a contractor's own cost structure and negotiating downward on price.

Given these risks, homeowners often rely on the information theory of pricing, but not in the expected way. Time and again, advice to homeowners urges them to avoid rather than seek out the lowest-cost bids for a project, counseling that "the extra money you spend [on a higher bid] may actually save you in the long run. . . . If an offer seems too good to be true—it is" (Levenson 1992, 29). Another manual, set up in the didactic fashion of a textbook, gives away the lesson before walking readers through the examples, lest they miss the point: "[In our examples] it will be obvious that the higher bid is the more accurate one" (Stephens 1998, 340). In response to these horror stories and reminders to be wary of low-cost bids, homeowners often treat lower bids as signaling low-quality work. In this environment contractors who convert the planned hiring of day laborers into a cut-rate bid will be more likely to knock themselves out of consideration than win the job.

## Degrading Work as Competitive Necessity: Subcontractors

For the specialty subcontractors—drywallers, painters, labor contractors, and others—hired to provide labor for general contractors, maintaining low labor costs is a matter of competitive necessity. On larger projects in particular, general contractors frequently subdivide work into finite and relatively deskilled tasks subject to easy cost comparison. "Remodeling has the most competitive bidding," explains a contractor turned subcontractor who has seen the bidding process from both sides. "You have to keep your costs down. The general contractors know the price they want when they look for a sub, and you either have it or don't. The problem is that you often bid too low compared to your labor costs."

For subcontractors this pressure to bid low has been increased by the growing availability of materials to nonspecialists and end users. Just as specialized general contractors, such as Jenkins, have lost much of their ability to charge homeowners a markup on materials, general contractors themselves now buy materials—particularly drywall and plumbing fixtures—that were once supplied by subcontractors at a considerable markup. The longtime union carpenter mentioned before details the resulting change to the industry:

> What you see now is a lot of these owner-operators [general contractors operating as sole proprietorships] cutting out the middleman. They buy materials themselves and no longer get charged for materials. Subs now make their profit only on labor. That's a lot of why the labor costs get squeezed.

The difference in estimated labor costs on the two sides of the subcontracting bid can be enormous. Drywall installation, a labor-intensive and frequently subcontracted task, provides a good example. The four-part task of installing drywall—cutting, hanging, taping, and finishing drywall sheets—happens in many residential remodeling jobs, particularly when contractors update old apartments to contemporary tastes by knocking out and moving walls or installing new fixtures.

As a general contractor, the aforementioned contractor turned subcontractor charges more than sixty dollars for each eight-feet-by-four-feet drywall sheet he installs. With drywall sheets typically costing around thirty-five dollars, this represents a twenty-five-dollar per-sheet markup for labor and overhead costs. But when bidding as a subcontractor, competition forces him to cut this margin to a bare minimum. Contractors typically demand prices of forty dollars or less per sheet, leaving a margin of just five dollars. With even the fastest workers able to install no more than three sheets of drywall per hour, this leaves little money for labor costs and virtually no margin for error. Other subcontractors confirm these cost-cutting dynamics for drywall work. In bidding to be a subcontractor for a small-scale remodeler of homes on Chicago's Northwest Side, a former day laborer turned contractor adds eight dollars per sheet for labor and overhead. Another day laborer and sometimes contractor marks up sheets seven dollars, and when he is not employed on his own construction jobs, he works for a large subcontractor who has expanded business by charging just $1.20 per square foot—or $38.40 per eight-by-four sheet—for drywall. In all of these cases, the workers performing drywall installation are either day laborers or undocumented immigrants who bundle together various jobs for low-wage contractors.

The thin margins on subcontracted work place firm downward pressure on labor costs. Across specializations subcontractors pay workers substantially less per hour than do general contractors, a necessity if they are to bring total costs in line with the per-hour rates demanded of them. Painting pays, for example, eight to ten dollars per hour when workers are hired as subcontracted labor for painting contractors but twenty dollars per hour when they are directly hired by homeowners or general contractors. Under direct employment, demolition pays ten to twelve dollars per hour, but as a subcontractor it typically pays eight dollars. As the contractor turned subcontractor explains in recounting a large rehabbing job on Chicago's Southeast Side, "I wanted to pay my workers at least a little more than the [accepted] minimum, but there was just no way. . . . I lost money on a lot of subcontracted jobs as it is."[6] Not surprisingly, day laborers prioritize work with homeowners and general contractors over subcontractors. The CBOs that work with day laborers likewise attempt to build workers' connections to homeowners and general contractors, hoping to avoid the lower pay and workplace problems workers encounter with subcontractors.

From workers' points of view, working conditions as much as wages constitute the main reason not to work for subcontractors. Because their thin margins leave little room for error and little opportunity to recover profits in the event of a construction problem or an unexpected interruption, subcontractors push workers in a number of ways that general contractors themselves do not. The aforementioned workers' advocate and longtime contractor has seen the damage this inflicts.

> At a lot of the jobs, I've seen, you'll see the *jornaleros* doing things they shouldn't be doing, like lifting drywall sheets from the back [as opposed to the knees]. You're going to wear your body out in a few years doing that. . . . But what are you going to do? The guys want to work, and they get what seems like a good hourly rate, and these contractors are happy to take it.

Because of these grueling conditions, day laborers such as Arturo, a recent immigrant from central Mexico, place construction low among their preferences for the types of work available from *la parada,* despite its comparatively generous pay and ready availability. "To me, moving is the best work. Nobody yells at you. Nothing really goes wrong. The problem is, you can only get it at the beginning and end of the month. But it's a lot better than construction."

One observer of the contested bargaining relationship between contractors and day laborers notes that above other factors, workers most commonly refuse jobs with contractors known for mistreating workers.

> I don't see too many problems with wage theft [nonpayment of wages]. It's really more things at work. A lot of the contractors . . . workers don't want to work for them because they have a bad reputation. They yell at them a lot, or they claim [the workers] stole their tools. Word gets out pretty fast, but that's a lot of the jobs out there.

Unfavorable and illegal workplace conditions are so widespread among residential subcontractors that workers single out only the most egregious problems for action; a generally high level of degraded work practices is broadly tolerated. When workers negotiate with contractors, the negotiation almost solely revolves around hourly rates of pay. Workplace features such as safety equipment and breaks rarely enter into the discussion. In assessing the merits of a particular subcontractor, workers focus on the core questions of whether a contractor is likely to pay what he owes and whether he screams, scolds, or otherwise mistreats workers. Still, these concerns often fail to prevent workers from accepting employment with a contractor, particularly when little work is available elsewhere.

The workplace issue most notable in its absence from negotiation is occupational safety. Contractors provide safety equipment and safety training so infrequently that workers rarely bother to note their absence (Buchanan 2004; Mehta and Theodore 2006). Similarly, workers experience injuries—and lose time to injury—so frequently that the problem escapes adequate measure. Nationally, one in five day laborers reports being injured on the job during the previous year (Valenzuela Jr. et al. 2006). But the high incidence of workplace mishaps leads workers to considerably narrow their definition of *injury.* The day laborers with whom I worked on Chicago's Northwest Side did not treat chronic back pain, aching joints, or abrasions, at least of the type that cleared up within a few days, as workplace injuries. Although few workers claim problems with injury, nearly all visibly suffer from maladies such as stooped gaits, restricted movement in the hands or fingers, stiff backs, and scarring.

## Working Conditions at the Bottom of the Subcontracting Chain

Workers often decline to contest these workplace problems, because they have larger problems to dispatch. In particular they struggle to collect pay owed for work they have performed. Few other problems so clearly mark the divergence of day labor work from payroll employment. Whereas professionals view the collection of paychecks as a routine formality, securing the compensation they were promised requires consistent vigilance on the part of day laborers.

Because they operate at the bottom of the subcontracting chain, residential subcontractors find themselves vulnerable to the threat of withheld payment—a common tactic used by homeowners and general contractors to protest work deemed of insufficient quality. The constant surprises provided by the construction process provide a never-ending stream of such disputes. Because even the most straightforward job is often complicated by unexpected changes to work plans, homeowners, contractors, and subcontractors frequently dispute the quality, quantity, and fair cost of work done. If a homeowner withholds payment from a general contractor or if a general contractor disputes the quality of the subcontractor's work, then the subcontractor often fails to collect the pay owed. The contractor turned subcontractor narrates a characteristic example from his experience as a subcontractor:

> A couple years ago, I took a framing job on a fourteen-unit building in South Chicago. I was new and didn't really know what I was doing, so I gave a very good price. . . . But I messed up and didn't look carefully enough at the building before I bid it. At one point a few weeks in, I realized I had to level the floor. It wasn't in the bid, but it had to be done. I told the GC [general contractor], and he said, "It's OK [to do it], I'll pay you later." Then later, the GC asked me to reinforce part of the framing in this one place. It had to be done, and again, he said, "Don't worry about it. I'll pay you later."

> I thought everything was OK. But in the end the GC's money ran out, and I didn't even collect on all of the original bid.

In agreeing to these extra, structurally necessary construction costs, the contractor turned subcontractor ran up dozens of extra hours for his own workers (who were hired as day laborers). In the end he paid them for their work and accepted a loss on the project. But the choice was his to make, and within the accepted practices of subcontracting, he could have withheld pay to his workers without facing viable retribution. For most subcontractors their own inability to collect from a general contractor or a construction end user fashions a legitimate reason for not paying the workers they have hired. Vincent, a suburbs-based contractor who owed the worker Lozano and his crew more than seven thousand dollars for work on a bungalow on Chicago's South Side, nonchalantly explains his decision not to pay Lozano, as if it were not a legitimate worry: "I know I owe Lozano and his brother-in-law or whoever he is that money. But I haven't been paid myself. They'll get it as soon as the owner's check clears. . . . Don't worry. I'm not one of those guys who doesn't pay his workers."

Five months after the work was completed, Lozano and his crew of four workers were finally paid. In the short term the contractor suffered no repercussions for his refusal to pay. Two workers from Lozano's crew, including his brother-in-law, continued to work for the contractor throughout the period, even as they sought outside help in pursuing him for nonpayment. Because it is so common, nonpayment of wages is rarely viewed as a reason for terminating a working relationship. Ezekiel, who fared better than many of his peers as a drywaller during the 2000s' boom, relates a characteristic incident:

> The last problem I had with wage theft [*robo de salarios*] was at the corner a few months ago. I worked doing plaster for a Pole for one day.[7] The Romanian who hired [the Pole] disputed the quality of the work and refused to pay him. . . . So we didn't get paid. . . . . But the Romanian felt really bad about it and hired me himself a few times to make up for it.

Contractors typically embed their refusal to pay workers within post hoc complaints about the quality of work performed or about the worker's behavior at the job site. From the point of view of Octavio, an undocumented Mexican immigrant who frequently found himself at odds with his employers, these disputes are just a pretext for denying payment. Rational persuasion and attempts to clarify the disputed events in the workplace do not work. The case of his dispute with Darnell, a contractor involved in a large multifamily rehabilitation project on the South Side, typifies the problem.

> We worked for [Darnell] on that building for months. All along, he kept paying us regularly. But now he's claiming that we didn't sand the floors right and that there is water damage in the bathroom, and he hasn't paid us for the last month. Whatever happened in there, we didn't do it. But he won't answer my calls anymore.

Octávio responded by seeking assistance from the Albany Park Worker Center, a CBO that functions as a hiring hall for day laborers and provides resources to help workers with pay and work disputes. Octávio pursued Darnell for months but never was able to maneuver around the contractor's claim that the work had been botched. His response demonstrates the reach of the subcontracting chain and its ability to push risk onto workers. After determining that Darnell would refuse to pay, Octávio kept the final check for himself and passed on the $2,500 in unpaid work to his own workers, colleagues from the day labor corner and the worker center.

The workplace and pay problems day laborers face arise from their subordinate position at the bottom of increasingly elaborate subcontracting chains in the residential construction industry. The zero-sum game of subcontracting dictates that whenever day laborers lose pay or work harder for the same compensation, a contractor further up the chain benefits by padding his profit margins, by shedding the risk inherent in his own subordinate position on the chain, or by staunching the decline of his own earnings.[8]

The glaring problems in the day-labor labor market—nonpayment, workplace injuries, and chronically unstable work—have drawn a number of CBOs into the residential construction industry's conflicts. Many of these organizations operate worker centers through which they attempt to regulate the bottom of the chaotic construction labor market. In Chicago these services are provided by the Albany Park Worker Center (APWC), opened in the early 2000s by the not-for-profit Latino Union of Chicago. Seeking primarily to draw workers from the Pulaski Avenue day labor shape-up on the city's Northwest Side, the APWC concentrates on the core functions of running a day labor hiring hall and collecting on unpaid wages or wages tied up in dispute. Like other worker centers, the APWC has incredibly modest resources in comparison with the industry it attempts to regulate. In its day-to-day operations, the APWC's limitations manifest in the difficulties it faces in luring contractors to its hiring hall and in the long odds that face efforts to collect unpaid wages for workers.

## When Low Pay Is the Smallest Problem: How Activists Regulate Degraded Work

Compared with pay rates in supermarkets, restaurants, and other service businesses, day laborers earn generous wages, often ten dollars per hour or more. But the extreme contingency of day labor work means these wages come at a cost. Because the availability of construction work is uneven, most day laborers manage to secure work fewer than three days per week (Valenzuela Jr. et al. 2006). Sustained success in the day-labor labor market requires securing long-term employment with a single contractor or developing a set of contractor contacts large enough to provide semisteady work. The workers' advocate and longtime contractor, who has worked with day laborers in Chicago for nearly a decade, explains their fundamental dilemma:

> *Jornaleros* are in a different position than contractors. Contractors want relationships with homeowners; *jornaleros* want relationships with *patrones* [patrons]—building owners, contractors. They're trying to get a rolodex of contractors—they need five to six *patrones* to stay busy full time, but that's really hard to do. If a contractor gets two to four months on a general remodeling job, the *jornalero* gets maybe six days out of that.

Unless problems with a contractor—such as unwillingness to disclose his name or his use of a visibly shoddy vehicle—are evident up front, workers set out to impress the contractor by asking few questions and working quickly and without complaint. This disposition makes them vulnerable to the subsequent withholding of wages. When they try to track down nonpaying employers, worker centers face the same problems that confound the Census Bureau and Bureau of Labor Statistics in their efforts to compile accurate information on construction. Contractors provide minimal information with which to track them down, and worker centers often begin their search for offending employers with no address, no permanent phone number, no last name, and no building permit number (although they frequently do copy license plate numbers). Without these basic data workers struggle to use the modest legal tools they have available.

At the work site itself, workers seek to make a favorable impression with contractors by working quickly—even when they are paid by the hour and stand to lose financially from finishing their work ahead of schedule. Individual workers' stories reveal the constant tension between maximizing the pay from a job in the short term and trying to secure a permanent job that altogether removes the problem of looking for work. This tension is epitomized in the incident related in the introduction. Jaime, a skilled painter who accepts demolition jobs when the supply of painting work dwindles, narrates the contradictions day laborers inhabit as they try to maximize their hours worked and daily payouts while facing pressure to minimize those same hours:

> We had an all-day demolition job in a kitchen for twelve dollars an hour. And [the other worker] starts working like a mule. He was tearing down the walls as fast as he could, really sweating. I said, "Hey, what are you doing? We're only going to get paid for five or six hours this way!" And he says, "Yeah, but if we finish the work fast, the contractor will hire us again."

In this case the contractor did not hire the workers again, and each lost an estimated two hours of paid work for their efforts to impress. Even apart from these calculated efforts to secure additional work, many day laborers internalize the impulse to work as fast as possible. Despite their enthusiasm for fast and cheap work, some contractors, including Tim, a residential remodeler working on the Far North Side, are frequently upset by the pace of work to which day laborers subject themselves.

> I had a real problem the other day with Ivan. I hired him to strip some radiators, and he just went nuts. He was working so fast, it was upsetting to watch. It was like he was in a race. He worked through his gloves after an hour or two, and when I went to check up on him, he was using the [chemical] stripper bare-handed. I finally made him stop and said, "Look, you have to take a break."

Although less tangible than low pay rates or wage theft, the eagerness of day laborers to work rapidly constitutes one of the workforce's prime assets in the eyes of contractors. Day laborers, they emphasize, are not just cheaper than other workers but also more productive. Like his peers, Mike, the contractor working on the multi-million-dollar redevelopment on the North Side, wonders how far he would have to push day laborers to find the limits of his authority as a boss.

> The results you get with these guys are amazing. If I took José and Juan up to the roof and told them to jump, I'd have to stop them and say, "No, no, just kidding." . . . There are only three times they've had to tell me no to something like that, and you can tell it just breaks their hearts to do it. They think they're going to get fired if they say no, which in a way is good. You want to keep them a little scared.

These benefits to contractors extend to the broader set of low-wage construction workers of whom day laborers are only the most visible part. As the contractor who gave up his white-collar career for remodeling explains, "We don't hire day laborers, but we do have the Polish connection, where you find a kid who works twelve hours for forty dollars, won't take breaks, and doesn't want to quit."

A rapid pace of work and near-total employer control over the work site and conditions of employment form unstated components of the contract between subcontractors and day laborers. In addition to instances where they deny payment after themselves failing to be paid by general contractors and subcontractors, contractors often withhold wages or pay in response to the perception that workers have given less than full effort. A 2006 wage theft case involving Marco and Adrián, two workers paid hourly for a weeks-long painting and cleanup job in a condominium development in the West Loop, typifies the problem. For the first two weeks, the subcontractor was pleased and paid the workers regularly. But at the end of the third week, the subcontractor withheld pay, claiming that Marco and Adrián had dropped their pace of work at the end of individual jobs when it became clear that they were on track to finish the day's work early. The subcontractor responded by refusing to pay the entirety of that week's wages, saying (inaccurately) that the law supported him.

Although the subcontractor could claim no legal basis for withholding the pay (about five hundred dollars for each worker), Marco and Adrián nonetheless were unable to collect. The struggles they faced in their attempts to be paid are commonplace in worker centers' efforts to guarantee pay and working conditions. Fundamentally, they lacked a legal mechanism to induce the subcontractor to pay. As was routine for wage theft cases taken up at the APWC, the workers filed a complaint with the Illinois Department of Labor, which had failed to respond after one year. Staff and volunteers at the APWC sent the subcontractor threatening letters and called to request meetings, but in the absence of a viable threat of sanction, the subcontractor simply ignored these requests.

Other efforts to recoup the wages were aborted owing not to the lack of viable legal mechanisms but instead to Marco's and Adrián's status as contingent workers who needed to seek work daily in order to earn a few hundred dollars per week. Because day laborers are obligated to queue early and long for available contractors, Marco and Adrián had to weigh a trade-off in their efforts to collect the money owed. Perhaps, their best option for getting paid was Cook County's pro se small claims court, where their case could be heard at no cost. Filing in small claims court would require them, however, to miss at least two days looking for work, one to file the petition and one to appear in court.

The payoff to that opportunity cost was uncertain. Even if the best-case scenario occurred and the judge ruled in their favor and the subcontractor had claimable assets, there was no guarantee that Marco and Adrián would recover their wages. If they lost the case or if the court could not compel the subcontractor to pay, then they would essentially trade two days of potential work for nothing. Like other day laborers who weigh the need to look for work against the sustained effort and long odds of recovering unpaid wages, Marco and Adrián chose to look for work. The experience of Alberto, a long-time drywaller, in confronting a similar problem highlights the wisdom of weighing the long odds of winning compensation against the need to secure and maintain work. Alberto opted to take time off from a recently secured full-time drywall job in order to file a small claims court case against a contractor who owed him $1,500. Upon requesting a second day off to amend the filing with proof of employment, he was dismissed by his new employer. This work-versus-activism trade-off also foreclosed the approach of organizing workers against the employer withholding Alberto's pay. Organizing actions such as protests had a guaranteed low turnout, since attendance would simply cost too many workers the opportunity to find work.

Armed with incomplete information on contractors and the jobs on which workers are employed and restrained by both the modesty of viable legal remedies and the need of day laborers to constantly search for new work, the APWC and other community-based organizations working with Chicago's day laborers can cite only a handful of successful wage recoveries among dozens of attempts over several years. The losses from unpaid wages add up for workers, but individual cases of nonpayment are simply too small and marginal for the legal system's modest safety net to catch them.

## The Appeal of the Street Corner: Worker Centers Struggle to Draw Contractors and Workers

Wage theft cases and political advocacy are important components of worker centers, but the day-to-day effectiveness of these organizations rests on their ability to broker connections between supply and demand in the construction labor market (Theodore, Melendez, and Valenzuela Jr. 2008). By requiring contractors to sign for services and providing documentation of the agents, the work assignments, and the pay rates of each construction job initiated on their premises, worker centers attempt to bring transparency to the day-labor labor market. In doing so, they set minimum wages, provide employees with a record of their employers, and prospectively head off wage disputes.

At their core worker centers depend on the draw of regulated employment to build foot traffic and draw workers into their broader political-organizing activities (Fine 2006). This in turn depends on the ability to promise regular work opportunities to workers. On this count the APWC struggled. In theory worker centers draw employers by screening workers and certifying the skills those workers will bring to the job. Faced with the prospect of picking up unknown workers on the corner or hiring vetted workers with guaranteed skills, employers should prefer the certainty of the worker center.

In practice, however, contractors learn to negotiate the screening process at the corner with relative ease. Bill, a contractor, who spoke no Spanish when he began hiring day laborers, negotiated the hiring process this way:

> You go there, and there's all these bodies, the place is overflowing with bodies. . . . As soon as people got the scent of you, you're just kind of surrounded. . . . And I said, "Guys, you've got to speak

> English," and everyone says, "Yeah," and you say, "No, really, I need you to speak English." . . . So I make them talk. Pretty soon, you've found the one or two guys who can keep up with your questions. You ask them how they'd do this or that job, and it's clear really quick who you want.

Although the day labor corner hosts a large number of daily transactions, individual contractors visit only infrequently. Through repeated contact with one another, contractors and workers develop networks that allow them to circumvent the need to hire daily, either at the day labor corner or through the worker center. Mike, the contractor working on the multi-million-dollar North Side property, relies primarily on references from other contractors and workers for hiring.

> When you do a lot of work like this and you know a lot of builders, you get together and ask, you know, "Who's a good drywaller?" I'll talk to the guy working on that house over there and ask, you know, "Who've you got that's a good concrete guy?" . . . I haven't been there [to the day labor corner] in a long time, because I was able to find four or five guys [who stuck].

The complexities of contracting and subcontracting repeatedly bring together in the workplace new combinations of employers and workers. Operating as industry outsiders, worker centers have limited capacity to become part of these networks, much less supplant valued worker references between contractors. For many of these same reasons, worker centers also operate at a disadvantage in terms of locking up labor supply. Because networks are an effective way to find construction employment and because worker centers cannot by themselves promise steady work, the day laborers who frequent the APWC treat it as one of a number of job search strategies (Figure 8). Individual workers may base their job search efforts out of a street corner hiring site or out of the worker center. But after an initial period of labor market adjustment and contact making, references—from friends, coworkers, and contractors—function as the primary means of job seeking.

The continuing importance of contractor networks may be one reason why the APWC has struggled to maintain a numerically significant presence with both day laborers and contractors. Three years after opening, the

| Number of Methods Used in Past Year | % of Workers |
|---|---|
| 1 | 0 |
| 2 | 72 |
| 3 | 16 |
| 4 | 27 |
| **Types of Methods Used** | |
| Worker Center | 63 |
| Street Corner | 50 |
| Temporary Employment Agency | 47 |
| References/Direct Solicitation | 100 |

*Figure 8. Means of Securing Employment for Chicago Residential Construction Laborers. N = 32.* Sources: *author interviews with Chicago day laborers. Only a subset of workers was asked about 4 method. Totals do not sum to 100.*

number of regular workers looking for work at the center had dwindled to just ten (although far more workers used the other services it provided). On any given day these workers were more likely to find employment through their own networks of contractors and workers than through contractor visits to the center. Revealingly, the APWC maintains its strongest connections with homeowners, who cannot easily tap contractor networks for hiring references.[9]

Among the workers who patronize the APWC, the center's connections to homeowners provide a strong draw. Yet the limited returns on the center's homeowner focus raise the question of how it (and other worker centers) can better insert itself as an intermediary in the construction labor market. In targeting homeowners, the experiences of the APWC and many of its workers point to the risk-laden position of the subcontractors at the bottom of the subcontracting chain and the limited potential of worker centers to impact the overriding pressures of cost-competitive bidding. Interestingly, this focus accepts the viewpoint that contractors seek day laborers almost exclusively because of their low hourly cost.

A closer inspection of the relationships between contractors and workers suggests, however, other reasons why contractors seek out day labor. Long before the contingency of day labor came to be used to hold down labor costs, contractors turned to contingent and temporary workers for the more basic reason that the construction process itself depends on labor flexibility. In addition to cutting labor costs, the availability of day laborers aids contractors in reengineering the production process in other important ways. First, it helps them to maneuver around the production bottlenecks that occur when routine but unforeseeable problems arise. Consider the case of the contractor Mike, who used a day labor work crew to reengineer the entire process of rehabilitating a planned two-million-dollar single-family home in a high-income Chicago neighborhood. In one revealing example, he explains his strategy for employing day laborers to wring high-cost contractors and idle time from the construction process:

> Let's say the plumbing contractor comes in and cuts through stuff, and instead of running [the pipe] up here [points to the ceiling], he has to put it down here [points to the junction of the ceiling and the wall]. And now we have to build this little soffit here. I'm not going to call the framing contractor, who's off building houses, to come build a little soffit. Do they have time? No. So you get one of your [day labor] guys who's a good, capable, general utility guy who can do some carpentry, can do some drywall, etc. . . . So, we've gone from being a 100-percent-subcontracted firm to a 10-percent-subcontracted firm with a core of four to five full-time guys who fill in the gaps and patch stuff up. I could come up with a list of about one hundred different things you could use day laborers for.

For Mike the availability of day laborers at low costs has thus made it possible to cut a number of high-cost subcontractors out of the building process and to forge ahead at tasks that would otherwise be delayed while waiting for skilled specialists to fix problems. The low hourly cost of day laborers enables these efforts, but the benefits extend much further. Contractors working in other market niches similarly describe the problem of coordination. As the former white-collar worker who found success as a contractor outlines:

> We don't have to go that route [hiring day laborers], because we know how to do everything ourselves. Contractors who can't do everything [e.g., carpentry, plumbing, drywall] are in a bad position. You have to wait for the drywall contractor. Then, you have to wait to put plumbing in. So many delays are built into the job. It costs money.

Hiring day laborers helps these contractors to pad their profit margins in ways that using the subcontracting chain to squeeze hourly costs does not. Day labor allows the contractor to dispatch problems that under normal circumstances would delay planned work, to avoid paying idle subcontractors while those contractors wait for other subcontractors to do work that must proceed theirs, to avoid paying high-cost subcontractors for less-skilled work, to smooth scheduling problems with other laborers and subcontractors, and in general to avoid the costly problem of idle time. This strategy itself is not new—contractors have long worked to coordinate their labor force and relationships with subcontractors—but it forms a novel tactical response to long-standing production problems.

## Targeting the Top of the Subcontracting Chain

For worker centers struggling to maximize the impact of their limited resources, targeting specific segments of the residential construction industry to the exclusion of others promises valuable outcomes. Although subcontractors at the bottom of the subcontracting chain can easily incorporate day laborers into their work, the subordinate position of these contractors increases the likelihood of degraded work practices in the workplace and limits the ability of any community organization to raise employment standards in addition to policing individual cases of workplace problems.

In Chicago residential construction contractors can be divided into four groups, each of which promises distinct benefits and drawbacks for workers. As Figure 9 suggests, each employment assignment for a worker offers a different trade-off between skills development, job security, and pay. Employment with general contractors and developers can provide months of steady work at a time and often offers workers the opportunity to learn new parts of the construction process. It also offers, though, few opportunities to develop a list of *patrones* capable of providing a steady stream of work opportunities. At the opposite end of the spectrum, working for a homeowner provides numerous opportunities for employment, few pay problems, and references to other homeowners. But the limited terms of these jobs leave workers to seek employment again the next day, and the work does not provide the opportunity to learn transferable skills. It should be noted that these divisions in Chicago are not necessarily representative of the broader structures of the residential construction labor market. Specifically, workers elsewhere are more likely to work for homeowners and general contractors and less likely to work in rehabilitation (Valenzuela Jr. et al. 2006).

Yet to limit the question of worker center intervention simply to targeting individual types of contractors means overlooking other potential abilities of worker centers, which have at their disposal more leverage than is readily apparent. This leverage derives from two basic sources: worker centers' ability to remove the spot-market pressures of the day labor corner and the desirability of their worker-screening functions for contractors that seek functional flexibility from day laborers in addition to labor cost reductions.

The spot markets created each morning on day labor hiring sites depress wages for workers who would be a bargain to many contractors at substantially higher prices. Employment instability often induces workers to toil at a breakneck pace—effectively shortening the tenure of their job assignments. And perhaps most important, day labor fills a valuable *functional* need for residential contractors seeking to improve the pace and precision of work by juggling their workforces and easily accessing high-productivity or suitably skilled workers.

## The Challenge of Precarious Work in a Precarious Industry

The complex reorganization of residential construction employment in and before the 2000s' boom provides definitive confirmation that local-serving, place-bound industries restructured with all of the vigor of manufacturing sectors. If anything, the remaking of construction has been more complicated than was the restructuring of steel, the automotive industry, or the other durable goods sectors whose variability and susceptibility to policy intervention lie at the center of the contemporary practice of economic development. Unbound by the limits of payroll, incorporation, and long-term investments in plant, property, and equipment, construction contractors find themselves free to experiment with new work models almost at will. As the result of these experiments—themselves structured by the persistent risk contractors face—the sector has forcibly incorporated several restructuring elements first seen in manufacturing sectors.

Most significant, the long-existing institution of contracting and subcontracting relationships has been reworked to function like the supply chain in production industries. Critics of the supply chain as an organizational form argue that it doubles as both a means of coordinating the work

| Contractor Type | Employment Term | Leads to Future Jobs | Skill Development | Payment Problems | Hourly Pay |
|---|---|---|---|---|---|
| Developer | Months | Rare | Moderate | Rare | $12 |
| General Contractor | Weeks or Months | Rare | Moderate | Rare | $12 |
| Subcontractor | Days or Weeks | Frequent | Minimal | More Frequent | $10–$12 |
| Remodeler | Days or Weeks | Frequent | Minimal | Frequent | $10–$12 |
| Homeowner | Days | Rare | None | Rare | $8–$10 |

*Figure 9. Characteristics of Day Labor Work by Contractor Type. N = 45. Sources: compiled from contractor, worker, and industry expert interviews.*

process and a bluntly effective system for devolving risk from powerful firms at the top of the value chain to dependent subcontractors locked into lean bids that provide minimal profits and place intense downward pressure on wages and working conditions (see Harrison 1994). Residential construction contractors have not grafted supply chains onto preexisting forms of industry organization but rather reworked subcontracting chains to carry out the same regulatory role.

As in manufacturing, deskilling and tailorization constitute critical conditions of possibility for this shift. They work in tandem with employment flexibilization, which converts modest changes in technology into bigger changes in the workplace. Residential construction work has deskilled only minimally. The Home Depot effect produced by preassembled fixtures amounts to a significant development not because it dramatically reduces labor hours but because residential construction work long resisted even this modest level of mechanization. Firms with fixed boundaries would likely struggle to recognize significant gains from this modest mechanization, as only large-volume jobs would offer a quantity of work sufficient to meaningfully subdivide to a large set of subcontractors and payroll laborers. But contractors' ability to hire day laborers at low cost and without further commitments makes it possible to divide even small jobs into component parts that can be readily assigned the lowest-cost labor, materials, and design. Even on small jobs with a limited payout, contractors can bring in day laborers for a few hours at a time or to handle a series of general labor tasks spread out across a range of previously self-confined specialty areas. On kitchen remodeling jobs, for example, day laborers can tear out the old fixtures and floorboards, install many of the preassembled replacement fixtures, hang drywall, and haul the ample debris such a job generates. The flexibility—in terms of both hours and work tasks—of the day labor workforce allows contractors to squeeze the trade specialists who previously commanded a high markup on portions of those tasks and further minimizes idle and down time on the job. For price takers in a risk-prone industry, this hypersubdivision of the work process represents a new and creative strategy for finding stability.

The picture of residential construction that emerges from this analysis stands at considerable odds with the sector's reputation for naked cost-based competition. Industry organization and structure matter not just as abstract questions but because they shape the strategies and tactics that interested parties use as they attempt to push back against the insistent degrading of work. In residential construction as in food retail, an industry perspective suggests frictions, interfirm rivalries, and weak points not readily identified by stylized depictions of a hypercompetitive industry. Mapping industry structure, risks, and competitive practices stands as an indispensable first step to reregulating industries in which basic labor laws go unenforced. But this only begins the process of taking action to reverse the growth of degraded work. In order to effectively intervene in these industries, workers, unions, community organizations, and public officials eager to address the problem need a framework to match potential organizing and policy actions to the distinct challenges and opportunities offered by each industry.

# 8

# New Answers to New Problems

## *The Creative Work of Reversing Degradation*

The solutions to the problem of degraded work are clear. Scholars and practitioners routinely point to the importance of raising the minimum wage, improving funding for workplace enforcement, stiffening penalties for violations of labor laws (and especially union-organizing laws), and passing immigration reform legislation that removes legal grey areas that make undocumented workers easy to exploit. But political barriers keep these measures beyond the realm of possibility. That fact should be no surprise. Inequalities of the scale visited upon the U.S. labor market in recent decades do not happen latently or because politicians and the body politic somehow remain ignorant of them. Degraded work stands as one of the outcomes of the decades-long political project of repealing the postwar Fordist political-economic settlement that produced favorable working conditions for a majority of the population. Plans to restore a fair labor market must take this new political and institutional landscape into account. Labor activists, community groups, and policy makers with limited organizational and economic resources not only must persuade individual employers to reform or hostile business interests to alter institutional arrangements from which they benefit but also must respond to the political and economic project that produces the conditions for degraded work.

My analysis of labor-sweating industries and the experimental responses to workplace degradation suggests that political feasibility is both a core tactical question proworker coalitions must address and a broader problematic through which reform efforts can be systemetized and expanded. The unifying concept of degraded work provides a means to meld place-, industry-, and organization-specific advocacy activities into a coherent, reproducible approach to workplace problems. It enables us to identify their shared strengths and logics.

The diverse set of political and organizing tactics on which worker advocates rely already incorporates such a critical analysis of industries and institutions. But their shared characteristics remain difficult to see because we lack a common language with which to synthesize them and because these approaches by necessity originate in the context of individual organizations, industries, and labor markets. A day labor worker center in Phoenix and legal reforms to home care work in New York share much more in common than the fundamental goal of improving wages and working conditions. We can better understand these organizations and their capacity for expansion by making explicit the implicit analyses of industries and institutions on which they rely.

Because of the sheer diversity of organizations engaged in labor advocacy, the basic tasks of enumerating and organizing their activities represent a challenge. Because labor advocates begin with the specific—a worker with a complaint, an employer with a bad reputation, an industry segment in which labor degradation accelerates—in order to build a more systematic set of reforms, understanding them from the bottom up is crucial. In the following examples, I focus on worker centers and, specifically, day labor worker centers in order to illustrate the key themes that shape and limit proworker reforms. These themes include the development of new institutions to match the changing organization of work and labor markets, the local focus of most organizing efforts, and the importance of sectoral, or industry-specific, strategies as a vehicle for refining advocacy practices and moving from local organizing campaigns to broader reform efforts.

Understanding worker centers provides a basis for analyzing a broad range of proworker organizing activities. This in turn allows a detailed examination of how these organizations work and whether, when, and why they succeed. Successful workplace reform efforts share the common trait of organizing groups of motivated workers with shared characteristics. Because worker populations often overlap with electoral boundaries, these organizations excel at developing relationships with elected officials. Seen this way, the bottom-up focus of worker organizing campaigns positions them to overcome the problem of political feasibility—to circumvent the hold of hostile business interests on national-level politics—in a unique way. Because the local focus of worker advocacy organizations gives them concentrated access to city- and state-level elected officials and because they target industries in which employers are deconcentrated and *less* organized than workers' organizations, asymmetric access to political institutions often works in their favor. When reforms are pitched at the national level and when they cover all industries and workers, business interests enjoy superior organization and funding to proworker interests. But this dynamic is often reversed when worker advocates target individual industries and when they do so at the state or local levels. Moving the question of political feasibility to the center of the analysis makes clear the extent of this surprising advantage.

## Inventing New Institutions and New Approaches

Understanding the growing nationwide response to degraded work begins with understanding the organizations working to reregulate local labor markets. The easiest of these organizations to understand is worker centers, whose dual focus on service delivery to marginalized workers and advocacy for broader reform uniquely positions them at the pivot between locally constituted workplace problems and political-economic challenges inscribed at the scale of national politics.

Worker centers' day-to-day activities represent a characteristically adaptive response to the unique challenges of degraded work. Because they deal with a population of contingent workers employed in a precarious industry, their basic operations and operating hours differ from other organizations'. Worker centers that engage the construction industry open their doors by 6:00 a.m., and few worker centers of any description approximate a nine-to-five schedule. Among their essential functions, they assist workers in confronting employers who at will rearrange the schedules and the employment status of the low-wage workforce. But this instability—the very instability worker centers seek to regulate—forms a barrier to scheduling, planning, and organizing public actions carried out by the same workers whose schedules have been made unpredictable. They confront these problems by mixing service provision (legal tutorials, English as a second language courses, and limited skills training) with organizing activities aimed at law-breaking employers and local, state, and national regulators with the capacity to reregulate low-wage industries.

That worker centers succeed at all seems remarkable. As labor scholar Janice Fine shows in *Worker Centers* (2006), her nationwide study of the phenomenon, they face the burden of policing industries in which small firm sizes, minimal unionization, and scant labor enforcement budgets have made degraded work arrangements a commonplace occurrence.

Despite these limitations, worker centers have managed to bring some order to chaotic low-wage labor markets, to steer regulators' resources toward law-breaking employers, to win back-wages for wronged workers, and, increasingly, to enact state-level legal reforms. Important in their own right, worker centers provide a conceptual point of entry to the task of identifying key approaches and techniques that workers and workers' advocates operating out of any institutional base can use to address the problem of degraded work.

Worker centers are not the only or necessarily the best response to the problem of degraded work. But the challenges they face—in finding local solutions to global problems and in attempting to achieve with scant resources what large regulatory agencies cannot—illustrate in particularly clear form the fundamental challenges confronting efforts to upgrade the low-wage labor market. Similarly, their successes employ tactics, strategies, and regulatory logics that can benefit organizing drives and political campaigns executed under the aegis of other organizations. Worker centers help to illuminate the path forward for both themselves and others.

## Thinking Locally: The Organization and Mechanisms of Campaigns against Degraded Work

In the absence of viable state- and federal-level responses to the expansion of degraded work, a varied set of urban-scale organizations combine community- and union-organizing techniques to persuade employers to abide by the law and, where possible, raise wages and working conditions above the minimum legal standard. The exact composition and division of labor among the coalitions pursuing these goals varies from campaign to campaign. Many organizing campaigns pursue the goal of a collective bargaining agreement. Unionization stands as a logical focus. After all, these problems were caused in substantial part by the systemic weakening of unions over several decades. At the level of the workplace, union representation provides workers the means to bargain for improved wages, benefits, and working conditions; it also insulates them against the employer reprisals that workers in degraded working arrangements have developed a strong reason to fear (see Freeman and Medoff 1984; Weil 1991). The collective voice unionization provides in the political process is equally important: the stronger the aggregate union representation in politics, the greater the chances that proworker legislation will pass.

While unionization represents an intuitive goal for most workers' advocates, the increasing brazenness with which employers violate union-organizing laws—by illegally firing, threatening to relocate, or otherwise intimidating employees—makes collective bargaining a singularly difficult outcome for an organizing campaign to achieve. The growth of the community–labor coalitions working to unionize low-wage workers marks a response to that very problem. Because employers can flout the National Labor Relations Act with minimal fear of incurring penalties, successful union-organizing campaigns devote significant amounts of time and resources to publicity designed to persuade businesses to obey the law. Industry analysis helps to identify where employers are vulnerable and plays a crucial role in this process. Community organizations ably provide this public pressure (the need for which says everything about the astonishingly long odds union-organizing campaigns face) and help deepen the ties between the prospective union workers and potential allies among neighborhood residents and elected officials. Even though the cold reality of resource availability remains a strong factor in the success of these coalitions, they have proven adept not just at achieving their own goals but at expanding workers' and community members' involvement in supporting one another's causes (Nissen 2004).

The community coalitions involved in unionization drives often embrace other, more open-ended organizing campaigns. Like unions, these community coalitions—which I discuss through the vehicle of the worker centers that best exemplify them, even though successful coalitions take other forms—begin their efforts by organizing workers around a shared trait. Unbound from individual workplaces, community coalitions organize more broadly than unions. This allows them to build a base that links individual worker populations that might otherwise remain isolated. Many groups organize geographically. In Chicago the Albany Park Worker Center targets workers in the eponymous North Side neighborhood, just as the Pomona Economic Opportunity Center serves and organizes workers in California's San Gabriel Valley and Casa de Maryland serves workers from the Washington, DC, suburbs. Just as frequently, these organizations make ethnic appeals, as did Chicago's Filipino Worker Center and Los Angeles' Korean Immigrant Worker Advocates. Others, such as the Washington Alliance of Technology Workers or New York's Restaurant Opportunities Centers United, target specific industries and occupations.

These targeted approaches form the basis for organizing workers and identifying advocacy goals. At first, defensive actions designed to mitigate the most obvious workplace abuses dominate the roster of activities. Many current worker centers began as community-based organizations that were drawn into proworker advocacy campaigns in response to complaints from their members. Others began their work at the request of workers, residents, or even the police, particularly in cases in which the high volume of traffic around a day labor shape-up raised safety concerns (Theodore, Valenzuela Jr., and Melendez 2009). Worker centers episodically and experimentally proceed from this starting point, focusing on sites, industries, and employers that feature frequent conflict and workers' complaints. This experimentation produces technical sophistication. Day labor worker centers began, for example, by setting up hiring halls—sometimes near or at an existing shape-up and sometimes in their own building—in which they experimented with ad hoc techniques for attracting workers and employers and assigning jobs. As those centers evolved they shared ideas, incrementally refining rules for matching employers to workers and then turning toward advocacy within local political systems (Theodore, Valenzuela Jr., and Melendez 2009).

As worker centers evolve they complement this focus on organizational practice with efforts to scale up or formally link on-the-ground service delivery and advocacy to systemic pressure for political reform. The process of scaling up often begins by forming relationships with regulators and elected officials. These relationships bring in formal political pressure capable of reforming the problematic workplace rules worker centers seek to enforce. For example, in Chicago the Albany Park Worker Center built a relationship with administrators in the state's department of labor in order to help ensure that complaints against law-breaking employers were prioritized by the agency. More promising, the National Day Laborer Organizing Network developed a formal partnership with the politically powerful American Federation of Labor–Congress of Industrial Organizations in 2005.

Though organizing a core of impacted workers who double as organizers and activists lies at the center of the worker center approach, it is these outside relationships with sympathetic elites and public officials that make it possible to enact legal reforms and systematically pressure law-breaking employers into improving working conditions (Fine 2006). Regardless of arguments for the preferability of worker-driven bottom-up strategies, building relationships with influential individuals and institutions makes sense as a corrective to the *structural* origins of individual workplace problems. Simple resource constraints limit the ability of these organizations to systematically address the degradation of low-wage work; worker centers approach the problem with neither the funding nor the police power of labor regulators, and the ineffectiveness of those regulators is one of the main reasons the problem thrives. Targeting organizing efforts toward influential elected officials and individual legislative bodies presents a substantially more favorable mix of rewards and risks.

Emphasis on this top-down approach has spurred the creation of several national networks that formalize the engagement of similar locally based worker centers and community coalitions with the problem of degraded work. They all embrace the logic of regulating industries rather than employers. Some of these, such as the Chicago-based Restaurant Opportunities Centers United, grew out of an individual worker center. Others, such as the National Day Laborer Organizing Network, developed as advocacy organizations attached to a particular workplace problem. Still others, such as the National Domestic Workers Alliance and Warehouse Workers Alliance, focus less on the institutional form that organizing takes and more on the workplace problems themselves. These networks join diverse sets of community advocates, worker centers, and unions to organize against specific local and national workplace problems. As the collective focus of these proworker organizations expands beyond the service delivery model in which worker centers were initially anchored, the institutional form advocacy takes matters less than do the guiding principles and strategies of that advocacy. And the strongest guiding principle is the very theme of this book: digging deeply into an industry's competitive practices in order to identify the friction points that provide workers' advocates an entry point for changing wages and working conditions.

## Sectoral Approaches Maximize Impacts by Targeting Industries

The most substantial victories won for workers take a sectoral approach focused on individual industries. By bringing an array of organizing and advocacy resources to bear on a single industry, sectoral campaigns amplify the reach of worker advocacy organizations and provide an institutional framework for transferring the knowledge those organizations develop. Two aspects of these sectoral campaigns mark them as especially promising approaches to the problem of degraded work.

First, sectoral campaigns allow worker advocates to develop specialized knowledge and industry-specific organizing and policy practices. This specialization results in technical and strategic innovation. For example, focusing on the day-to-day operations of residential construction has helped day labor worker centers to develop a surprisingly complex set of measures for governing labor market uncertainty. These include rules governing the job queue—when workers must arrive and how late they must stay to be eligible for hire on a given day—and the development of realistic minimum wage rates, hours requirements, and skill levels for a dozen-plus basic construction activities. The experimental nature of this process is evident today in the heterogeneity of worker center practices (Theodore, Valenzuela Jr., and Melendez 2009). A sectoral focus, facilitated by the advocacy of the National Day Laborer Organizing Network and the advocates whose advice and ideas it circulates, speeds the development of these detailed job-sorting technologies.

The impact of knowledge-sharing activities is clearer in assessments of worker centers' advocacy activities, particularly on the issue of wage theft, a staple activity for organizations engaged with degraded work problems. Here, the mechanisms worker centers across the country use to resolve wage disputes have converged over time. The difficulty of tracing contractors makes this task especially difficult in the construction industry. Worker centers respond with education programs that train workers to vet contractors in advance and obtain core information (including license plates, phone numbers, and business addresses) about prospective employers. Building on this basic information, they then move into direct advocacy, escalating from phone calls to the contractor to protests to claims and complaints filed with state departments of labor and small-claims court systems. These techniques do not always succeed, but the successes they register owe to the refinement of the wage theft remediation process through a tight industry focus. The example of day labor worker centers provides just one illustration of an industry-themed approach that benefits workers' organizations engaged in many other sectors of the economy.

Second, a sectoral approach helps workers' organizations develop and strengthen relationships with institutions, regulators, and elected officials, all of whom provide access to the policy-making process and extend the reach and effectiveness of organizing campaigns. The New York State Department of Labor's Wage and Hour Watch Program, for example, formalizes a decade's worth of collaboration between the state and six workers' organizations, each of which agrees to train a Wage and Hour Watch member who educates firms on labor laws and directly reports violations over a period of two years (Fine and Gordon 2010). In many other cases, the partnerships are less formal. For example, Chicago's Albany Park Worker Center developed a valuable working relationship with the Illinois Department of Labor administrators responsible for pursuing complaints against employers and with the state attorney general's office, which sought ways to publicize the problem of wage theft by construction contractors.

Relationships between workers' organizations and elected officials have in some cases led to successful legal reforms. Working from Chicago's Humboldt Park neighborhood, the San Lucas Worker Center used its strong relationship with some members of the Illinois General Assembly to secure the passage of Illinois Public Act 820 ILCS 125, the Illinois Day Labor and Temporary Services Act, which mandated the licensing of temporary employment agencies, explicitly forbade common wage-and-hour violations perpetrated by those agencies, and established a registration system for firms that contract with temporary agencies.

Other workers' organizations likewise use these relationships to influence the law and the outcome of organizing campaigns. Key examples include the Service Employees International Union's successful use of pressure from pension fund investors to persuade developers and janitorial firms to recognize a union and the successful push by a New York community–labor coalition to ensure the passage of a legally binding code of conduct for corner store greengrocers that frequently violated a slew of workplace laws (Bloom 2010; Ness 2005). Narrowing the focus of organizing activities to a single sector constitutes a crucial step in converting political relationships into reform.

Taken together, the knowledge-sharing and relationship development of a sectoral focus provides scalable techniques that can be systematically adopted by peer organizations. Networks such as the National Day Laborer Organizing Network and Restaurant Opportunities Centers United formalize this process by linking organizations and, in the case of the latter, developing organizing tools with the explicit goal of exporting them. But the most promising impact of scaling up is less formal. Narrowing the approach to a single industry enables workers and their advocates to systematically adapt, test, and evaluate the utility of a broad mix of industry-analysis tools and policies capable of persuading employers and industries to change their practices.

## How Workers' Advocates Use Industry Leverage

Because they engage the competitive models and regulatory pressures that shape industries, sectoral strategies support a surprisingly diverse set of organizing and advocacy techniques. The problem is not identifying them—individual success stories are easy to catalog. Instead, the main challenge lies in identifying their shared traits. Existing categorizations of worker advocacy campaigns, such as Amanda Tattersall's typology of community–labor coalitions, typically draw distinctions among the types of actors that comprise proworker movements (Tattersall 2005). But classifying the *activities* those actors pursue provides a clearer framework for evaluating practice and outcomes. Three general approaches are worth noting. *Union-authorization strategies* seek to level the playing field within workplaces and industries through collective bargaining. *Legal-realignment strategies* close regulatory loopholes, modify laws that indirectly support or degrade work, and target legal enforcement toward strategic points where its influence on firms will be greatest. *Institutional-formation strategies* create new third-sector institutions, public institutions and laws that penalize, restrict, or otherwise provide a basis for advocating against common degraded work practices. Each of these strategies addresses the fundamental challenge of mitigating labor market inequalities in its own way. All of them embody a distinct logic for narrowing the range of probusiness opposition to reform in order to achieve a measurable victory. And they all address problems anchored in specific workplaces and industries by realigning the legal and institutional frameworks through which interfirm competition is regulated. Although the social, political, and economic realities favoring individual strategies will vary across regions and industries, each approach has yielded positive results for low-wage workers.

Community–labor organizing campaigns constitute the most easily grasped of these responses. They are intuitive: because the waning power of unions enables the spread of many degraded work practices, reversing deunionization is an obvious step. But the goal of unionization also has the benefit of being concrete: it engages a specific legal process; union formation campaigns carry a discreet end date; and the end result applies to individual workplaces in a way that broader reforms do not. The Service Employees International Union's (SEIU) Justice for Janitors campaign represents the most prominent example of these partnerships and their potential. After launching the Justice for Janitors campaign in Denver in the mid-1980s, the SEIU and its allies succeeded in unionizing tens of thousands of janitorial workers across the country. Justice for Janitors campaigns combine the hallmark elements of community–labor organizing with great effectiveness: they mobilize community organizations to provide high-volume turnouts at protests and to spread their message effectively, and they use relationships with clergy and public officials to intensify pressure on high-profile employers. Significantly, the highly public nature of these campaigns tends to make employers bashful about illegal antiunion activities that they might pursue with great fervor if the public's attention were directed elsewhere. The campaign's origin in low-union-density Colorado was auspicious, as Justice for Janitors has since organized cleaning services in historically antilabor Los Angeles, Houston, Miami, and, newly, Indianapolis, the site where legislators later made Indiana a right-to-work state (Lerner, Hurst, and Adler 2008).

The noteworthy successes of Justice for Janitors and related campaigns stand, however, as exceptions to the more common outcome of a failed union election. As the food retail community–labor campaigns discussed in chapter 5 attest, threats of dismissal and wage cuts can quickly quell prounion sentiment, even in cases where the organizing drive is a matter of public record. Just as important, the community interests engaged in these campaigns are not unitary. In the abstract, community support for union recognition promises to provide the necessary pressure for a fair union election. But in practice the complex and conflicting interests from which that community is composed—community advocates are simultaneously workers and consumers; they often share ethnic identification with the employer being targeted; and their identification with specific neighborhoods or ethnic affiliations can lead other cooperating community organizations and, especially, unions to be viewed as outsiders—often cut short the campaign from the inside. Furthermore, in right-to-work states and in cases where union officials lack elite allies, union authorization simply may not be a realistic goal. This leads to a search for other approaches.

The expansion of legal-realignment strategies represents a response to this problem. These strategies provide a different mix of risks and rewards and may be more favorable to workers' organizations skeptical of their ability to secure union authorization. Worker centers and their peers can simultaneously pursue multiple realignment strategies, an approach that increases the likelihood of making at least some concrete progress against workplace problems. In contrast to symbolic, highly charged union-recognition campaigns, some of the most effective of these strategies, such as closing loopholes in the coverage of labor laws, are small and work incrementally.

This incremental approach can be effective in remedying the inevitable loopholes and enforcement gaps in national workplace laws. Under the United States' distinctive system of federal policy making, the large number of veto points for virtually every law provides employer advocacy organizations the leverage to weaken and carve out numerous exemptions from labor regulations. State-level minimum wage laws, for example, often exclude workers under the age of eighteen, allow lower wages for tipped employees, and provide for limited training periods during which employers can exempt themselves from wage floors (Zatz 2008). As demonstrated by the *Hoffman Plastics* Supreme Court decision, which makes undocumented immigrants ineligible for compensation from employers who illegally dismiss them during union-organizing campaigns, immigration status now constitutes an additional de facto class of legal exemptions. Virtually every workplace law carries exemptions of this type, and removing or limiting them strengthens the regulatory coverage whose shrinking scope has enabled the expansion of many degraded work practices.

Several recent campaigns have successfully shrunk these exceptions. New York's Domestic Worker Bill of Rights, passed in 2010, mandates vacation days, temporary disability benefits, time-and-a-half overtime wages, and other measures for domestic workers who had previously been exempted from labor laws whose coverage was limited to formal payroll relationships. Similarly, the aforementioned Illinois Day Labor and Temporary Services Act explicitly bans several common temporary agency practices not explicitly prohibited by labor laws that had been designed for other industries—specifically, charging workers for transportation to job sites and for safety equipment. When these formal and legally binding measures fail, workers' organizations have succeeded in working with the offices of state attorneys general and departments of labor to convene special task forces devoted to addressing the misclassification of workers as subcontractors and other related issues (Ruckelshouse and Leberstein 2011). Other recent cases of success in realigning legal coverage include a California law explicitly reversing the *Hoffman Plastics* decision's exemption of undocumented workers from compensation for illegal dismissal during union-organizing campaigns, the SEIU's creation of a public employer of record whose existence immediately converted 90,000 Los

Angeles–area workers from subcontractors with dubious employment rights into standard payroll employees, and the passage of California's Assembly Bill 633, which assigns a portion of the registration fees garment manufacturers pay to a fund from which industry workers can draw in the case of wage theft (Zatz 2008). As these examples suggest, this branch of legal-realignment strategy functions less as a formal set of measures ready to copy than as a range of approaches to engaging sympathetic elected officials and lawmakers.

Industry-level analysis underpins another primary focus of legal-realignment strategies, the targeting of regulatory and political resources to key strategic points in an industry's supply chain or prevailing competitive models. These pressure points are more numerous and easier to identify than typical accounts of the economy-wide shift from Fordist manufacturing to atomized service industries suggest. Cost-competitive businesses often find themselves attached to the supply chain for a single industry or firm. In mass-produced residential construction, for example, a handful of large, highly visible builders often accounts for a significant minority or a plurality of market share. Many low-wage employers are also tied to nationally branded chains, such as hotels or restaurants, and many others are linked together by common purchasers of services (Weil 2009).

The Los Angeles–based Justice for Janitors campaign effectively targeted these four traits of industry organization to organize workers in the 1990s. Researchers involved in the campaign used a supply chain analysis to link labor-sweating janitorial subcontractors to high-market-share contractors serving downtown businesses and skyscrapers. These businesses and skyscrapers maintained a high public profile that helped focus public attention on the advocacy drive. A related scan of regulatory pressure points revealed that the Los Angeles Community Redevelopment Authority, the regulatory body authorizing new office construction, had the Los Angeles County Federation of Labor on its board. This enabled the campaign to pressure all newly constructed office buildings to accept union janitorial crews (Milkman 2006, 157–58). Beyond the case of this Los Angeles–based campaign, permitting appears to offer a widely available point of entry for regulation. To take one example of many, the Chicago supermarkets whose law-breaking practices are chronicled in chapters 4 and 5 typically rely on assistance from city hall to assemble the sites for their operations, license additional parking, and assist with the navigation of the city's complex permitting procedures. This suggests that aldermen with control over permitting could intervene to frustrate the expansion plans of employers with a track record of labor law violations. Such an approach would build on a long community-organizing tradition of using permitting to extract concessions from employers. Examples range from so-called Type II economic development mandates, which require developers to make dedicated contributions to city funds in exchange for zoning variances, and Boston's Flynn-era linkage fee policy, which required developers of large commercial properties to contribute to an affordable-housing fund (Goetz 1990; Clavel 2010).

Previous efforts by federal regulators to regulate employers via the supply chain itself suggest additional new terrain for legal-alignment policies. In the mid-1990s the Wage and Hour Division of the Department of Labor began using a little-known "hot cargo" provision of the Fair Labor Standards Act to seize apparel goods during whose production wage-and-hour laws had been violated (Weil and Mallo 2007). Because the retailers selling these goods could not afford the supply chain disruptions resulting from seizure, they took on some of the enforcement burden themselves, pushing contractors to improve their labor practices. The strategy of targeting the supply chain represents another model on which to base future legal-alignment strategies.

Still, the main value in legal-realignment strategies lies more in the ease with which they can be executed than in the breadth of their benefits. For that reason, worker advocacy organizations have deepened their focus on institutional formation strategies designed to alter the rules in a more systematic way. Some of these institutions do not require public authorization. For example, the Maintenance Cooperation Trust Fund, established jointly by the SEIU local union representing Southern California's janitors and three of the region's largest unionized contractors, revived an old organizational form established by the Taft–Hartley Act to serve as an industry watchdog and advocate for reforms favoring unionized and higher-wage employers (Muñiz 2010). The trust fund monitors the industry to document labor law violations and uses connections to state regulatory agencies to increase the likelihood that legal violations will be prosecuted. It is credited with helping to expand union coverage in the industry and fight against efforts to chip away the region's valuable employer settlement on labor issues. Because it helps to minimize the impact of new competition on existing labor standards, this type of approach promises to be especially useful in cases where an industry's union employers face threats from nonunion competitors who obtain a market advantage by paying subminimum wages.

Other approaches are more direct. The firmest examples again originate in California, where state and federal inspectors in the 1990s joined to form the Targeted Industries Partnership Program, built to identify, fine, and extinguish sweatshops (Lee 2006). The program faltered by the end of the 1990s, as did a later effort to establish the dedicated California Office of Low-Wage Industries under the direction of the Department of Labor (Fine 2006, 163–69). Undermined by the absence of ongoing financial support but valuable in concept, these efforts represent basic steps to target one-size-fits-all enforcement budgets toward industries known for serial violations of labor laws.

The most promising institutional-formation strategies culminate in the passage of laws that explicitly address recurrent problems in low-wage industries. These efforts include the Illinois's Day Labor and Temporary Services Act and New York's Greengrocer Code of Conduct, a voluntary but legally binding document that compels signees to provide wages and working conditions well above the industry minimum. The main obstacle to such efforts is employers themselves—when they can organize and press their case to legislators. Thus, the fundamental challenge in forming new regulatory institutions is identifying instances where the political will to do so exists.

## Getting Organized in the Policy Process: When Workers' Organizations Have Strong Access

Because industry regulation generates broad benefits to workers by imposing targeted costs on employers, it poses a significant *political* challenge to workers' advocates. Employers in targeted industries can easily see their stake in potential workplace laws. The superior funding and organization of business interests are common knowledge to anyone who has ever confronted a state-level chamber of commerce in a political or organizing campaign, and this imbalance will only grow as union density and the political will to fund basic workplace inspections continue to decline.

Despite this unfavorable institutional imbalance, however, legislation benefiting workers at the expense of management does pass. As David Weil argues, workers' advocates tend to win legislative battles when capital is *disorganized* when compared with labor (Weil 2008). This disorganization frequently takes the form either of the impacted industries having ineffective institutional organization or of capital's interests being split between rival factions. At the national scale examples of disorganization are few. Capital very strongly and effectively organizes against union-related issues, and the interemployer rifts exploited by workers' advocates have secured laws with limited scope, such as the Worker Adjustment and Retraining Notification Act (Weil 2008).

At the level of cities, counties, and states, the disorganization of capital is both more common and easier to see. In fact, several workers' rights initiatives initiated by worker centers and their peers, including many of those outlined in this chapter, have skillfully exploited such disorganization. The most prominent cases originate from instances in which workers' advocates target industries with poor institutional representation in the political system. Illinois's Day Labor and Temporary Services Act, for example, embodies the problem of regulation in exaggerated form. Because the temporary-staffing industry it targeted had just 1,400 establishments statewide at the time of passage, the costs of the law fell on an extremely narrow employer population. But the bill passed with little fanfare or controversy largely for that same reason. The legislation was too narrowly defined for the Staffing Services Association of Illinois and other industry representatives to succeed in mobilizing broader business organizations against it. At the same time, the staffing agency workers represented by the San Lucas Worker Center *were* well organized: the San Lucas Worker Center and the Illinois General Assembly members with whom it had built relationships concertedly worked to secure the passage of the bill. Domestic worker bills of rights based on the model of New York's legislation follow a similar logic. Because domestic workers are employed by unnetworked, unorganized households, workers' advocates face less organized institutional opposition at the level of state assemblies.

In some cases proworker legislation succeeds because it targets practices that business organizations cannot in good faith protest. In recent years the states of Illinois, New York, New Mexico, Washington, and Texas have passed legislation addressing the problem of wage theft. At the urban scale Miami/Dade County, San Francisco, and other municipalities have also passed wage theft laws. The diverse geography of this regulation suggests its ability to circumvent employer opposition (Wage Theft 2012). Legislation redressing the frequent practice of employee misclassification (which results in unlawful exemption from workers' compensation laws and other measures) in construction has found even broader purchase, most likely because these problems are concentrated in unorganized residential construction contractors rather than politically connected commercial construction firms (Philips 2003).

Asymmetric access to the political process normally works against the interests of workers for the simple reason that employers are better funded and better able to articulate unified interests. But smaller asymmetries—between workers organized by worker centers and the fragmented industries employing them—provide opportunities for workers' advocates to push state- and local-level legislation without facing the vigorous opposition that meets broader-reaching laws governing unions and other hot-button issues. Because degraded work problems take their strongest form in atomized, deconcentrated industries, this suggests that proworker organizations may possess a systematic advantage in accessing the legal system.

Despite their promise, rallying support for legal reforms takes significant time and faces considerable risks, not just from oppositional employers but from the intricacies of state-level political bargaining processes that often dilute or stall legislation. Securing regulatory changes *outside* the auspices of the political process represents a potential alternative to these uncertainties. That approach was taken by the community–labor coalition responsible for New York's Greengrocer Code of Conduct. The passage of the code, along with its unique mechanics and the industry-specific regulatory logic it embodies, makes it stand out as an especially useful example of the ways that proworker organizations can push against degraded work arrangements.

## Regulating Disorganized Employers: The Greengrocer Code of Conduct

The Greengrocer Code of Conduct grew out of a spontaneous community–labor campaign against common labor-law violations, including subminimum wages, lack of overtime pay, employer abuse, unsafe working conditions, and illegal dismissal of workers in many of New York City's greengrocers. Greengrocers—large corner stores selling fresh produce, deli items, ready-to-eat meals, and basic groceries—operate within the same basic competitive constraints as supermarkets and with the further competitive accelerant of small firm sizes and a deconcentrated industry structure (Bodie 2003). They have few variable costs and, as stand-alone stores, little leverage with which to generate discounts from suppliers. These factors, as well as widespread cost-based competition between the hundreds of establishments operating in the city, provide the basic incentive and means to degrade work. Since the late 1990s, this pressure has been intensified by rapidly escalating property values and rents, which increase fixed costs in Manhattan's service industries without increasing consumers' willingness to bear higher prices on goods purchased (Bodie 2003).

The New York attorney general's office began to chart a sharp uptick in complaints from greengrocer workers in 1999. Soon after, a community–labor coalition, anchored by a Union of Needletrades and Industrial Textile Employees local and the Community Labor Coalition of the Lower East Side, elevated these problems to a matter of broader public concern. Following a familiar approach among organizations engaged with low-wage workers, the coalition built relationships with the state department of labor and attorney general's office and began to funnel complaints to those agencies. Staff members in the attorney general's office were quickly struck by the similarity in workers' complaints across establishments and concluded that the effective pay standard in the industry was two hundred to three hundred dollars for a seventy-two-hour week, or three to four dollars per hour (Bodie 2003). Following standard procedures, regulators stepped up inspections in greengrocers and vigorously prosecuted violations.

But the limits to this standard strategy soon became clear. Although effective at producing fines, the increased workplace inspections did not shift the greengrocer industry as a whole toward broad compliance (Bodie 2004, 2). In response the attorney general's office eventually began to build the Greengrocer Code of Conduct. Based on input from the community–labor organizations involved in the campaign against greengrocers, as well as input from other workers' advocate groups, the attorney general's office put into effect the voluntary code of conduct.

Although it may not be obvious at first, the individual components of the Greengrocer Code of Conduct directly respond to both the challenges regulators face in enforcing laws within a deconcentrated industry and the competitive threats and opportunities that regulation poses for employers. To begin with, the code is legally binding once signed by employers—but employers retain the option not to sign. This approach allowed the attorney general's office to enact the code swiftly and circumvented the political conflict likely to have come from proposing regulation with an obvious industry target. Two rewards induce businesses to sign the code. First, signing results in immunization against prosecution for previous violations of labor laws. Second, firms who sign the law use compliance as a competitive asset. As customer-facing businesses, greengrocers rely on positive interactions with customers, many of whom are aware of the industry's persistent labor violations. Reversing the common problem wherein firms gain market advantage by breaking labor laws, compliance with the code instead confers a competitive advantage on firms that operate within the law.

Once firms have signed, they are obligated to comply with existing labor laws and to provide additional workplace benefits, including paid vacation and sick days, not required under federal law. Given the small budget of wage-and-hour enforcement personnel relative to the number of firms in the industry, legal compliance remains a risk even after firms have signed the code. The most creative component of the Greengrocer Code of Conduct responds to this challenge. Fines incurred by New York's greengrocers now fund a separate, dedicated workplace monitor tasked with making unannounced visits to greengrocers in order to ensure compliance. In other words, the Greengrocer Code of Conduct channels dedicated resources to legal enforcement in a segment of the economy poorly covered by status quo regulation.

Two years after its inception, regulators and workers' advocates in New York deemed the code a success. Although noncompliance with labor laws did not completely disappear—the workplace monitor hired by the attorney general's office found employer records of hours worked to be subpar and reported frequent clashes between workers and employers over issues such as breaks—pay violations in particular subsided, and workers and workers' organizations voiced strong approval of the code (Bodie 2004, 25).

The Greengrocer Code of Conduct combines two of the main strategies—legal realignment and new institutional formation—used by organizations confronting degraded work, and it fits these strategies to the competitive pressures of a customer-facing industry in which firms have a tangible incentive to comply with the law. Well tailored to the industry it targets, the Greengrocer Code of Conduct illustrates the benefits of several pro-worker reform strategies. By pursuing relationships with regulators and targeting a disorganized industry incapable of deploying mass political opposition, workers' advocates secured a tangible reform of the type that would rarely succeed if pursued through normal legal channels. Just as important, that reform realigned existing regulatory institutions to better focus on a law-breaking industry. The Greengrocer Code of Conduct is not a straightforwardly transferrable regulatory fix—if pursued elsewhere, it would need to be adapted to different regulatory arrangements, different relationships between community organizations and regulators, and the distinctive operation of other industries degrading work. But it makes plain the mechanisms through which such reforms can be achieved.

## How Industry Analysis Identifies Leverage

This book argues that embracing the dynamism and instability of local-serving industries yields strategic insights workers' advocates can use to reregulate sectors of the economy characterized by sliding wages and deteriorating working conditions. To that end, the cases of the food retail and residential construction industries in Chicago suggest several productive ways in which the mix of regulatory strategies used by these organizations can be tailored to solve workplace problems elsewhere. Identifying those measures sheds significant light on the policy-relevant characteristics these industries share with others. These insights do not just inform the questions organizers face in Chicago—they identify linkages spanning many low-wage industries.

First and most noteworthy, consumer-facing industries in which low-wage workers daily interact with customers provide distinctive and valuable opportunities for intervention. Because local-serving industries mark out their submarkets through customer service and the development of specialized relationships with targeted demographic groups, they find themselves uniquely susceptible to campaigns that call their reputation into question. The advocacy focus on customer-facing industries is growing: the Justice for Janitors campaign, the campaigns undertaken by Restaurant Opportunities Centers United, and the organizing efforts orchestrated by the Retail Action Project all pressure businesses by complicating their relationships with consumers.

Understanding the intricacies of an industry provides opportunities to deepen and complicate these appeals. Most consumer-targeted campaigns proceed along the familiar terrain of appeals to fairness, justice, and good corporate citizenship. As the organizing efforts in Chicago's low-wage supermarkets demonstrate, these campaigns often fail to persuade, particularly when consumer attachment to low-cost retailers springs from material need. As income inequality intensifies and the share of low-income households continues to grow, the effectiveness of such campaigns seems likely to weaken. My work with food retail workers and the United Food and Commercial Workers in Chicago suggests an altogether different approach. Rather than engaging consumers on the basis of abstract ideals, workers may benefit from pointing out that low-wage supermarkets often fail to undersell their unionized competitors. Based on the industry competitive models charted in chapters 4 and 5, a 2011 price survey of Chicago Walmarts and unionized chain supermarkets found that the low-wage employer generally charged as much or *more* than unionized firms for fresh meat and produce (Nathalie P. Voorhees Center 2012). Why? Walmart employs a business model that generates deep price discounts from the low-cost sourcing of processed and packaged foods. But this same business model deemphasizes the fresh foods that make up a large portion of consumers' purchases in low-income areas. This suggests that organizers in the industry can appeal to consumers' pocketbooks instead of abstract formulations of justice that fail to resonate.

The importance of permitting for supermarkets and construction projects alike provides a second leverage point. Profits in supermarkets grow with larger facilities and expanded parking. Each of these requires assistance and/or approval from elected officials. Similarly, every residential construction project requires a permit, although permit enforcement in practice has proven highly uneven. Following the model of Boston's linkage fee ordinance or the garment industry supply chain model developed by the U.S. Department of Labor in the 1990s, day labor organizers and union organizers have the opportunity to tie permitting to compliance with basic labor laws. The potential for this approach extends far beyond Chicago and these industries.

Additionally, my research on these industries identifies the central importance of *time* to their business models. Workers in midsize supermarkets begin the day with trips to collect fresh meat and produce, just as construction contractors assemble and reassemble work crews from a combination of day labor shape-ups and existing networks of workers. The day labor shape-up and the open-air markets on which these firms depend thus represent strategic sites workers' organizations can pressure in order to induce systematic legal compliance among individual employers that workers' advocates would otherwise struggle to bring into compliance with the law. The effectiveness day labor worker centers have demonstrated in regulating shape-ups attests to their importance to the industry and potential as an intervention point.

These potential strategies remain untested and unevenly applied. Like any policy idea, they will encounter flesh-and-blood challenges that remain invisible during conceptualization. But the organizational apparatus with which to test them is growing; the need is strong; and they build on a developed body of work enacted by the community organizations confronting labor degradation daily. The structural mismatch between a polarizing national economy and minimally resourced workers' organizations with a local scope obligates workers and their advocates to investigate any potentially effective solution to the problem.

Conclusion

# Building a Fair Labor Market in Postmanufacturing Economies

Workplace inequalities in the United States widened during the Reagan years. They widened further during the celebrated 1990s economic boom. Workers fell behind during the anemic 2001–7 business cycle (which treated upper-echelon professionals and financiers kindly) and fell further behind during the disastrous 2007–9 recession. Three years into an anemic economic recovery, unemployment remains high, and labor force participation rates remain low. Union membership and health care coverage continue to fall, and workers' organizations across the country report the ongoing violation of basic labor laws by employers in a broad range of industries.

This litany of bad news makes it clear that inequality on the job is doing fine. But for the first time in recent memory, public discussion about inequality has grown in tandem with the real thing. As unionized manufacturing jobs vanished and low-wage service positions took their place during the 1980s and 1990s, critics of the United States' distinctive and mounting inequalities found themselves exiled to the margins of politically acceptable discussion. As the current, weak economic expansion slowly fills the hole carved by the employment dislocations of 2008 and 2009, income inequality has taken a central place in news and politics. Unfortunately, engaging the problem of income inequality, no matter how aggressive, provides no guarantee of addressing its root causes.

Academic critics of inequality know this problem well. Channeled into the concepts of social and economic polarization, inequality has for decades served as a central analytic in urban scholarship. It yields extremely valuable work: the economic polarization that scholars chart in research on deindustrialization and the growth of finance industries is historically specific and empirically nuanced. Furthermore, the conceptual frames articulating these inequalities—*labor market polarization, dual cities,* and *global cities* stand as particularly potent examples—establish the problem at hand with clear images and appropriately tidy concepts. But even as they steer attention toward a crucial problem, these structural formulations often lead to analytical and practical dead ends. What options does a student, activist, or scholar engaged at the urban scale have for addressing a global structural problem?

The theories of inequality used to analyze U.S. cities were developed through research and concepts rooted in *global* analysis. These global origins generate various conceptual, methodological, and policy mismatches for individuals using structural theories of inequality to organize action at the urban scale. A useful analysis of the diverging fortunes of high- and low-wage earners necessarily begins with the assessment of global trends: the decline of manufacturing employment in OECD nations, the rising power of financial industries, and the strategically crucial role played by central business districts that coordinate finances, design, and production for global firms. But the analysis becomes mechanistic when the urban scale is treated as a simple by-product of these global transformations.

Theories of global cities and service sector economic growth are useful but incomplete and misshapen as tools for analyzing specific industries, labor markets, and cities. As Michael Peter Smith, Angus Cameron, and Ronan Palan forcefully argue, the structuralism in these theories often has the unintended consequence of persuading elected officials and community activists that workplace polarization is so powerful and so fully determined by forces operating at higher spatial scales as to be completely beyond their control (Smith 2001; Cameron and Palan 2004). Identifying the global origins of these problems helps to establish their significance, but it does not suggest ways to address them.

The concept of degraded work provides a way to bridge these globally derived theories with research, theorization, and action at the urban scale. The growth of degraded working conditions originates in global and national transformations, including immigration, the fragmentation of the consumer bases targeted by local-serving industries, and the ascent of small workplaces that fall through the cracks of a workplace regulatory system built around large business establishments with hundreds of workers. But the actual form degraded work takes depends specifically on local factors—the competitive geographies of the industries targeting low-wage workers, pockets of excess labor supply, and local industrial and institutional histories. There can be no formula for identifying these arrangements, and the work of charting the competitive practices of local-serving industries will always be messier and more open-ended than the foundational concepts of national economic inequalities. But that messiness is an asset, not a liability. The fluid and contingent character of research on individual industries reflects the instability of the industries themselves. And that instability in turn provides workers and workers' advocates discreet opportunities for local action against structural economic transformations that provide few obvious organizing targets. The essential first step to this analytical leap is treating local-service industries as dynamic and worthy of the same scrutiny that manufacturers receive.

## Local-Serving Industries at the Center of Inequality

The problems embedded in globally derived theories of inequality become most evident in their treatment—or neglect—of the low-wage industries that account for a growing share of urban employment in the United States. Manufacturing industries and, increasingly, finance industries continue to be the targets of careful and finely grained analysis. Meanwhile, analysis of local-serving industries proceeds outside the analytical frameworks of economic development and critical industry analysis. For example, research on the food retail industry, which repeatedly features in many studies of degradation, focuses on the questions of food access and firm location. Job quality and the fit between competitive practices and working conditions do not figure in the discussion.[1]

Labeling service sector growth, rather than service sector restructuring, as the main cause of workplace degradation naturalizes wages and working conditions that are not intrinsic features of the industry. This creates many problems. The biggest is practical: treating degraded working conditions as inherent to the industry leads to a misallocation of community organizations' resources. Every manufacturer retains the ability to flee its existing location; victories won to ensure factory jobs today can always be undone through future capital flight or threats of capital flight. But local-serving industries cannot relocate without shedding the consumer bases and relationships on which they depend. On purely pragmatic grounds, workers and workers' organizations stand to benefit from focusing their efforts on employers who cannot flee regulations favorable to labor.

Scrutinizing these employers' competitive models and business practices illuminates industries that bear much in common with the manufacturing sectors on which critical scholars typically focus. Neoclassical economists and Marxians alike treat residential construction, security, food retail, and other local-serving industries as close to perfectly competitive: with so many firms bidding for so little market share, market dynamics are likely to keep profit margins to a minimum. For workers and unions, these competitive dynamics would make efforts to upgrade wages and working conditions at individual employers extremely risky. If the market really were perfectly competitive, then employers paying above-market wages or extracting below-average productivity from their workers would lose market share and potentially be pushed out of business. Although economy-wide reforms such as minimum-wage hikes and improved workplace enforcement would benefit employees in such industries, employer-specific organizing campaigns run the risk of inducing unintended and very negative consequences.

Digging into the actual operation of these industries suggests a different picture. In retail and customer-facing industries, market-fragmenting power protects firms from the whims of intense competition. The food retailers sweating labor on Chicago's Northwest and Southwest Sides serve miniature markets segmented by neighborhood, ethnicity, and income. Increasingly, they organize themselves as chains to develop economies-of-scale purchasing power and shared overhead cost structures that provide an advantage over the competition. As the fierce bidding over sites for new supermarket establishments and the evident nonrelationship between wage levels and price levels suggest, the industry is far from perfectly competitive.

The factors protecting residential construction contractors from intensive competition are different, but they perform the same function. Informational asymmetry between contractors and the end users of construction can build significant profit margins into the bid. At the same time, the growing organization of residential construction work around de facto supply chains assigns different ratios of risk and economic reward to various participants in the industry. Competition still matters, but that competition is deeply structured—and in ways that provide far more opportunities for organizers and regulators to change an industry's competitive organization than does the naked cost-based competition of the local-serving industries that appear in economic development textbooks.

Accepting the complexity of profit-making models in local-serving industries suggests a straightforward shift from documenting the *fact* of service sector growth to assessing *how* individual firms and industries adapt their business models to changing product markets, competitors, and labor markets. This in turn suggests the necessity of engaging the actual workplace practices through which degraded work practices are enacted.

## How Firms Sweat Labor: Working Conditions Matter as Much or More Than Wages

The experience of working in America has changed profoundly and predominantly for the worse since the early 1970s. These changes are too broad reaching to be readily cataloged with any moniker, but the realities of research and advocacy have forced critics of the problem to adopt a moniker regardless. As the buoyant but distinctly inequitable 1990s economic expansion gave way to an even more problematic boom in the early 2000s, critics in academia and in the public discourse adopted *income inequality* as the catch-all measure of the problem. In many ways it was a productive move. Foregrounding income inequality as a problem places the two-tier organization of the labor market front and center. The term also inserts a normative stance into public discussion. Terming inequality a problem neatly reverses the dominant economists' argument that unequal outcomes are a necessary market signals that facilitate needed economic change.

Although there are merits to focusing on income inequality, these are increasingly undercut by the fact that income-based measures on job quality substantially *underreport* other kinds of workplace inequalities. For example, rising labor force participation rates mask the extent to which a day's work fails to provide the benefits it once did. As U.S. households began to earn less for their labor in the 1970s and 1980s, they responded by working more aggregate hours. Spouses augmented unwaged domestic work with wage labor; family members working part time took full-time jobs; and survey data showed an unmistakable trend toward multiple job holding for primary earners. At the end of the last business cycle, in 2007, a twenty-fifth-percentile household earned five dollars less per hour than it did in 1973—a transformation that income inequality statistics ably capture. Less noted but equally important is the fact that the same lower-income household worked ten hours more per week for its diminished pay. Expanding our focus just a bit further to incorporate diminished pension eligibility, the replacement of defined-benefit with defined-contribution pension plans and the free fall in employer-provided health insurance coverage (accompanied by a mirror-opposite rise in prices) reveals the concept of income inequality to fall far short of measuring overall changes in job quality.

The data needed to measure these changes exist, but they are scattered, multidimensional, and often qualitative—they can never be effectively incorporated into a single unified measure of inequality. Yet the degradation of *nonwaged* aspects of work is in many ways the essence of the problem. A generation ago, food retail paid marginally better than it does today. But the typical worker also enjoyed job security, employer-paid health insurance, time-and-a-half pay for overtime, and working conditions free from verbal abuse and endless coercion to increase productivity. *In other words, working conditions are deteriorating much more quickly than are wages.* Throughout this book I have documented many negative changes to working conditions in construction and retail employment. I have shown how inequality takes dozens of forms, including the increasing instance of legal or de facto contingent employment status for workers; routine use of unpaid or underpaid overtime by employers; the routinization of just-in-time shift schedules that frustrate efforts to combine paid employment with child rearing and household needs; unpleasant and unsafe working conditions ranging from hundred-plus-degree temperatures to temperatures below freezing to employers mandating that workers use dangerous tools for which they receive no training; illegal fines and paycheck deductions for job training, safety equipment, and uniforms; fines, reduced hours, and retributive pay cuts for workplace errors; and the use of all those measures, plus others, to coax a breakneck pace of production from workers. Given that the United States has the lowest minimum wage among industrialized nations, employers stand to gain less from pushing on wage levels and more from remaking other, nonwaged aspects of the employment relationship. This argues for moving alternative measures of job quality—health and safety, the capacity for upward mobility, potential educational gains, job security, the absence of employer intimidation—to the center of the discussion.

Continuing to omit these issues from scholarship on income inequality does not just lead to the systematic underestimation of the extent of workplace inequality. It also blocks the identification of effective responses to the problem. Investigating questions of working conditions, law breaking, employee intimidation, and selective reward mechanisms within the workplace shifts the discussion away from abstract concepts and toward specific questions about how and why employers are changing workplace practices. Rather than focusing on the highly abstracted concept of an aggregate nationwide labor market, the empirical work on these issues suggests that the answers instead lie in workplaces themselves.

Scrutinizing employers improves our understanding of workplace problems in several straightforward ways. They are the entities that directly profit from sweating the labor of workers, undocumented and otherwise, and they represent a more logical place to begin the investigation than are global trends. Day laborers, industrial temps, bleary-eyed security guards, and the other familiar figures of America's low-wage boom work for employers who integrate access to vulnerable workers into a broad range of sophisticated business strategies that solve many organizational problems in addition to cutting labor costs. The *complexity* of employer strategy, as well as the way this complexity differs from textbook-simple ideas about employers paying low wages and speeding the pace of work simply because they prefer to, raises important questions that remain invisible when our attention drifts to the workers themselves. Treating these firms as low-wage employers suggests a textbook-simple analysis, in which labor-cost cutting stands as a central management goal, divorced from questions about skill level, flexibility, the work process, and productivity. Considering the full range of degraded work practices undertaken by local-serving industries obligates us to investigate multidimensional competitive strategies and the various historical, institutional, and social factors conditioning an employer's use of labor.

Examining a broader array of competitive strategies for employers in turn provides a clear way to incorporate the dimension of urban space—absent or read off from top-down models of polarization—into industry analysis. Firms in local-serving industries, like firms in all industries, operate spatially. But they do so within the confines of finely grained local markets and submarkets. Firm-level analysis of businesses in local-serving industries requires scholars to meld an analysis of urban space and the social and economic processes operating through it to basic questions of production and profit making. This approach productively foregrounds the very kinds of local specificity notably absent in top-down models of workplace polarization writ large.

## Segmented Labor Markets in the Twenty-First Century

Workers in low-wage labor markets toil in workplaces where regulators enforce basic labor laws selectively, erratically, or not at all. The very problem of degraded work is marked by circumstances in which taken-for-granted rules do not apply. Rhetorical frames built around employment polarization and income inequality deemphasize this rupture, instead suggesting that low-wage workers labor in marginal conditions within a labor market whose rules and norms cover all types of waged work. We would do better to think of these workers as challenged by a discreet labor market with its own distinctive rules for allocating jobs and setting compensation. Emphasizing the discontinuity between the conditions of degraded work and the more orderly labor market constructed by one-size-fits-all employment statistics and references to a nationwide labor market provides a more honest accounting of the problem and a clearer starting point from which to identify solutions.

Critical scholars have long used the productive analytical framework of labor market segmentation to understand the uneven rule regimes governing work. Like the concept of restructuring, theories of labor market segmentation today suffer from confusion about their historical origins and current applicability. The concept has its roots in a forty-year-old study of manufacturers in which the economists Peter Doeringer and Michael Piore distinguish a primary labor market characterized by job security, steady promotion, and guaranteed wage increases from a secondary labor market in which workers simply have no potential for advancement, regardless of their skill levels or tenure on the job (Doeringer and Piore 1971). Labor researchers have since expanded this single, historically specific concept of dualization to explain the intrinsic discontinuity and institutional regulation of all labor markets.[2] This refashioned analytic of multifaceted segmentation and market discontinuity clarifies basic measures that make degraded work distinctive from the standard employment relationships on which most labor market research is tacitly based.

Low-wage labor markets function by their own set of rules primarily because the existing workplace regulatory apparatus of the United States allows them to. The modernizing labor market regulations of the New Deal were designed to upgrade working conditions in a manufacturing-based economy dominated by large workplaces. Tellingly, the United Auto Workers' years-long effort to organize General Motors' Dearborn assembly plant was a key moment in this history. The Dearborn assembly complex covered more than one square mile and employed thousands of workers. A single labor inspector could ensure compliance at this plant. Often, inspectors needed not even visit, since a vigorous union documented employer violations by itself and kept management vigilant with the threat of a strike or negative public attention.

Seventy years later, organized labor has been decimated by decades of coordinated antiunion action by employers, and the construction contractors and corner stores thriving in urban areas employ just a handful of people apiece. But the old regulatory infrastructure lingers. It is increasingly underfunded and cannot effectively enforce laws even under the best of circumstances; the construction contractors interviewed for this book contend that OSHA, the Fair Labor Standards Act, and the rest of the basic bundle of labor laws operating in the United States have never exerted a meaningful impact on their industry.

With a low ratio of inspectors per establishment and minimal penalties for noncompliance, evading the law is not a covert competitive tactic in service industries—it's a basic, uncontested business practice on public display. The other factors segmenting these labor markets are very important in their own right, but the basic nonenforcement of core laws provides the binding framework for the day-to-day operation of workplaces.

Today, labor supply likewise plays a key role in structuring low-wage labor markets. Owing to their immigrant and often undocumented status, noncitizen workers in Chicago's food retail and residential construction industries, as in low-end jobs elsewhere, have a limited de facto ability to exit their jobs. They face two substantial barriers to doing so, and both relate to immigration status. First, hefty border crossing fees effectively increase the need to remain employed at all costs. Interest on debt to *coyotes* accrues rapidly, and for most workers the family poverty that drove them to cross into the United States remains a powerful incentive to send substantial monthly *remisas* to extended family abroad. A gap—any gap—in employment threatens to upend the precarious financial balance that makes this assistance feasible.

Documentation status and formal skill requirements also place higher-wage and more comfortable jobs off-limits to immigrant and undocumented workers. This amounts to labor market segmentation in the literal sense: a sharp cleavage between low-wage, dog-eat-dog jobs for which legal documentation is optional and better paid, highly skilled jobs available to native-born and naturalized workers only. Even for workers who can provide evidence of work authorization, jobs that require a bachelor's or a master's degree or certificate degrees recognized by a construction trade remain off-limits, especially when day-to-day subsistence needs crowd out the ability to augment a rigorous work schedule with other training.

This multiple segmentation of the labor market explains a riddle that confuses orthodox labor market analysts: why do substandard working arrangements persist? After all, workers should be able to vote with their feet, using the market to punish employers who provide low wages and substandard working conditions. Understanding these workers and their dilemmas makes the answer clear. Unable to depart for better jobs and frightened of interrupting their income, workers in low-end labor markets base their actions in the workplace on the goal of staying in the employer's good graces. In many ways the work degradation cataloged in chapters 5 through 8 was internalized within workers. Construction day laborers, for example, work at fast rates even when doing so threatened to shorten the number of hours for which they were paid—the underlying logic being that hard work today might translate into stable employment tomorrow. Food retail workers likewise curtailed their complaints about pay and the systematically unfair application of workplace rules in order to avoid the job loss routinely threatened by their employers.

Among the more notable traits of Chicago's midsize food retail industry segment is the awareness of both workers and employers that the jobs at issue are, within the narrow labor market negotiated by recently arrived immigrants, good jobs. Many employers keep an open-door policy on previously employed workers for this reason. Just as surely as they know workers will grow frustrated and depart for what they hope are better jobs, they know those workers will return after working elsewhere with fewer guaranteed hours and more uncertainty.

The undocumented status of most workers in this labor market both enables its segmentation from the primary higher-wage labor market and intensifies the impact of that segmentation. Workers in both industries have repeatedly sought to move to stable, salaried jobs in which they could convert hard work into steady pay without constantly negotiating the basic bundle of workplace uncertainties that currently characterize their employment. But every time they attempt to move up, they are held back by the absence of legal work authorization.

Segmentation is admittedly a technical term, but its application to low-wage labor markets is above all *pragmatic.* Recognizing the extent and impact of this deep segmentation of urban labor markets is crucial for the various planning actors—CBOs, unions, policy advocates, state officials, and others—seeking to put a floor under wages and working conditions in construction, retail, and other industries where the standards of employment are changing. These actors struggle day to day with the labor-intensive work of policing individual cases of the violation of workplace laws. On their own terms, such programs are remarkably effective. Yet they remain small compared with the scope of the problems involved. Using their political and policy powers to support changes not to individual employers but rather to the broader regulation of industries and workplaces is essential. To this end the theoretical concept of labor market segmentation is helpful because it identifies concrete factors (immigration status, nonenforcement of labor laws, and the general inability of workers to opt out of employment even over the short term) these organizations can begin to address in order to change the balance of power in low-wage workplaces.

## The Path to Fair Workplaces

Those who wait for the low-wage labor market to self-correct will wait in vain. Good jobs—the jobs wrongly conflated with manufacturing industries in the past—happen when policy, organizing, and labor market dynamics mitigate the bargaining imbalances that favor employers over workers. The fondly remembered high-wage manufacturing jobs that Chicago lost a quarter century ago and that the Sunbelt is busy shedding today were not inherited. They were made by collective bargaining agreements that took wages out of competition and allowed workers to negotiate for benefits, vacation days, and control in the workplace; by vigorous unemployment insurance and public welfare programs that allowed workers to pass on low-paying and undesirable jobs; and by consecutive decades of economic expansion and wage growth that saw employers bidding for scarce workers, as opposed to the other way around. It is no accident that popular discourse today refers to a job market instead of a labor market. Jobs, not labor, are the scarce resource the market allocates.

The prospects for improving the experience of work appear bleak against this backdrop. The work of building a fairer labor market proceeds anyway. One major factor bodes better for workers and workers' advocates today than it did a generation ago: the identity of the employers striving to roll back New Deal wages and working conditions. The firms sweating labor today are deeply tied to place. They cannot relocate without losing their customer bases. And their ties to suppliers, neighborhood populations, and local regulators provide multiple points for workers' advocates to pressure. It is impossible to say where the path forward ends, but it begins by taking seriously the competitive complexity of local-serving industries.

# Acknowledgments

I am indebted to many individuals and organizations who assisted in the preparation of this book. I owe a particular debt to Nik Theodore and Rachel Weber, who first pushed me to study urban economies and who later made sure that I conversed equally well with scholars and practitioners. The University of Illinois at Chicago (UIC) provided an amazing intellectual community as I worked on this book. As members of my dissertation committee, Phil Ashton, David Perry, and Joe Persky all poked and prodded at my work in distinctive and useful ways. The benefits to being at UIC were just as often informal. Dennis Judd asked a number of characteristically direct questions that forced me to clarify my ideas and arguments. I was also fortunate to clarify and refine my basic view of cities, labor markets, and organizing through ongoing day-to-day conversations with Janet Smith, Sharon Mastracci, and Brenda Parker. It might have been possible to produce this book in another academic environment, but I doubt it.

I benefitted from a terrific cohort of graduate students engaged in research similar to my own. Many of the questions I take up, as well as the engagement with economic restructuring that underpins them, emerged from an intense and wonderful graduate student experience shared with Greg Schrock, Nina Martin, and Heidi Sally. The ideas here might be mine, but there can be no mistaking the social process through which they were produced.

The research itself was aided by many individuals and organizations fighting for a fairer labor market. At times it seemed that Moisés Zavala had made me an honorary member of the United Food and Commercial Workers Local 881's organizing staff. In addition to introducing me to many workers and advocates, Moisés efficiently steered me toward the industry's most important challenges and helped me refine ideas and suppositions through endless, generous conversation. Also at 881, Ron and Steve Powell, Elizabeth Drea, and Kristen Ryan answered my questions, supported my work, and, flatteringly, attempted to put my conclusions to use.

From 2005 through 2007, I spent a lot of early mornings and slow afternoons with Latino Union and its members at the Albany Park Worker Center. The construction research would not have happened without Jessica Aranda, Eric Rodríguez, B. Lowe, and Antonia Dempsey, who introduced me to so many workers and contractors and who provided a suitably tough audience for my ideas and conclusions. To the *jornaleros*: I can't name you individually, but you were good company and good interviewees. I hope my efforts helped.

Chicago has an amazing social infrastructure of community and labor organizations dedicated to solving problems locally. At Mexico Solidarity Network, Tom Hansen made more introductions than I deserved and opened my eyes to many issues I would have otherwise missed. I am indebted to Ari Glazer and the San Lucas Worker Center, Tim Bell, Adam Kader, José Oliva, and many others whom I either cannot name or (shame on me) have forgotten.

As students of Chicago know, UIC and the Center for Urban Economic Development (CUED) are part of that infrastructure. CUED was an amazing environment. Among others in the CUED family, José Torres, Sandra Morales-Mirque, and Nina Martin accompanied me on interviews and tied trends in food retail to happenings in other low-wage industries. In a better world, Esteleta Cameron would be here to read the many results of our late and great community at CUED.

Many of the ideas and chapters in this book had a previous life touring conferences and universities. Along the way, Robin Boyle, Susan Christopherson, Charlie Hoch, Natasha Iskander, Bob Lake, John Landis, Faranak Miraftab, Rob Olshansky, Frank Popper, Ananya Roy, Betsy Sweet, Mildred Warner, and David Wilson asked smart questions that helped me to clarify the stakes, mechanics, and scope of my argument. You may not remember asking them, but your questions mattered.

This manuscript was reworked so thoroughly it is difficult to imagine that it began as a PhD dissertation. All who read it provided excellent comments. In particular, I wish to thank Chris Tilly, who provided a close reading that helped me to see its strengths and correct its weaknesses. David Wilson helped identify the strongest arguments and pushed me to fill in the gaps between them. Long before the manuscript reached their capable hands, Nik Theodore flagged its basic strengths and glaring weaknesses, and Rachel Weber helped me to find a foothold in academic conversations I did not expect to enter. Sara O'Neill-Kohl's enthusiasm for the manuscript did a lot to propel this work forward. Greg Schrock's comments sharpened chapter 4 considerably, and Jessica Greenberg kept me on track everywhere else.

I give special thanks to Jason Weidemann at the University of Minnesota Press. His detailed comments on the manuscript improved the writing significantly and helped make my rookie trip through the conventions of book writing painless. The entire University of Minnesota Press staff was a pleasure to work with.

Talking about the manuscript at home was one of the basic pleasures of this project. Jessica Greenberg has no need to read this book, since she's broken down every argument, empirical strategy, and writing challenge with me. I'm so damn lucky. To Gabriel, I'm counting on cognitive development to blunt your memories of my distraction as I worked on this. To Julian, please know that your dad once wrote a book. I'll be flattered if either of you ever reads it.

# Notes

## 1. New Inequalities

1. Calculated from U.S. Bureau of Economic Analysis 2011. Data coding may be slightly discontinuous owing to the shift from Standard Industrial Classification codes to North American Industrial Classification System codes in 1997.

2. See Castells 1997 and Van Kempen and Marcuse 1997 for examples. The essential formulation that manufacturing job loss and service sector growth entails structural inequality fails to hold if service sector jobs can be upgraded.

## 2. Beyond Low Wages

1. The author helped to orchestrate this campaign.

2. The number of undocumented immigrants dropped, with great publicity, to 11 million by 2009. But despite the commonplace stories of reverse immigration, the current estimate of the unauthorized immigrant population is still on par with 2005 levels.

3. For example, one of the supermarket employees interviewed for this book informed the author that he worked at a supermarket paying the minimum wage of $2.85 between 1998 and 2003. That was the tip-credit wage applied to a non-tipped position. The Illinois minimum wage during that period was $5.15.

4. A comparison with the auto industry is instructive. By the end of the twentieth century, a large number of U.S. manufacturers—including Nash, Studebaker, and Packard—had given way to the Big Three of GM, Ford, and Chrysler. But even if ownership of retail establishments is consolidated, the importance of geographical differentiation will insure the maintenance of a large number of establishments. Seven-Eleven might buy out other convenience store chains, but it will not consolidate them into a single store.

5. Economists, including those affiliated with Michael Porter's Initiative for a Competitive Inner City, put a more intellectual spin on the project, declaring fragmented urban demographics to signal the presence of undervalued areas that should logically attract ample business investment (Initiative for a Competitive Inner City 2002). In these cases and others, the heuristics of space and geography

lay bare the ample potential for market fragmentation in local industries, especially in the large cities of prime interest to urban scholars.

## 3. The City That Sweats Work

1. This estimate, based on the U.S. Census Bureau's 2009 American Community Survey, does not control for age, education, or occupational structure; it simply documents the aggregate difference in personal earnings between native and foreign-born workers.

2. The median household income of Hispanic-headed foreign-born households in 2009 was just $35,400.

3. A main exporting industry in these neighborhoods is the temp industry, which establishes storefronts in Hispanic neighborhoods with large numbers of unemployed and daily ships those workers to Chicago's factories and office complexes (see Peck and Theodore 2001).

4. As an example, access to the 2011 Occupy Wall Street marches was organized through this system. To participate in the march, individuals reported to a starting point set by the union or advocacy organization with which they were affiliated.

5. Target had already opened new food retail establishments on the Southwest and Northwest Sides and has since expanded further.

6. The author's calculations are from TradeDimensions 2005.

## 4. Oases in the Midst of Deserts

1. A number of Walmart supercenters are planned or are operating in Chicago and other large cities, but these stores can pursue an economies-of-scale/warehousing strategy due to the availability of substantial public sector planning efforts aiding in the assembly of full-size sites (see Boarnet et al. 2005).

2. The author's calculations are from TradeDimensions 2000; 2001; 2002; 2003; 2004; 2005. TradeDimensions provides the most reliable data on market share and composition in food retail, despite significant limitations that result in the overrepresentation of large, well-capitalized supermarkets in the market share estimates. These include selection bias in favor of firms that participate in a national barcode scanning program and limitation of the sampling frame to firms that self-identify as food retailers (as opposed to membership warehouses such as Costco or drug stores that sell food).

3. The author's calculations are from TradeDimensions 2001; 2006.

4. Product selection is based as much on the retailer's ability to get a good bulk purchase price on an item as it is on the retailer's reading of the local market's needs.

5. The author's calculations are from InfoUSA data.

6. Private mail sources, employer interviews, and visits to the neighborhoods themselves suggest that midsize independents are substantially underrepresented in most data measures. Note that Map 3 and Figure 2 are derived from different data sources (InfoUSA and TradeDimensions, respectively). Currently, no single data source offers both detailed establishment-level employment data on both employment and market share.

7. Although coethnicity is de rigueur for the workforce, it need not extend to store ownership. More than half of the owners of the supermarkets that target immigrant consumers, particularly Hispanic consumers, are assimilated white ethnics.

## 5. "They're Happy to Have a Job"

1. See Massey et al. 2003 for a particularly influential summation of this argument.

2. For years the large chains have attempted to push down prices on meat and produce, most prominently by replacing on-site butcher departments—and the attendant labor costs—with prepackaged case-ready meats prepared off site by nonunion butchers (American Meat Institute 2003). Nevertheless, meat and produce costs in Chicago's large chains are typically twice as high as they are for midsize competitors.

3. See Perkins 2004 and Faura 2004 for a more detailed breakdown of demographically inflected purchasing patterns.

4. Precise wage rates cannot be estimated, because wages vary with position, worker tenure, and the collective bargaining agreement under which workers were hired. All figures are in 2006 dollars.

5. These figures were determined on a store-by-store basis through publicly available collective bargaining agreements for union chains and through employer, worker, and community organizer interviews for nonunion stores.

6. Community organizations engaged with low-wage workers suggest that scheduling will soon become a major point of contention in workplaces. The value to employers of juggling hours and moving workers from fixed to variable schedules is especially strong in retail industries in which employers have few other types of day-to-day flexibility available. Carré and Tilly 2008 finds that stores shift, juggle, and rearrange hours so extensively that work schedules have become a "primary dimension of job quality in retail" (10).

7. Beyond the tangible cost-saving benefits it offers the employer, this practice allows Chiapas to maximize staffing during the food retail industry's heavy business periods (at the beginning and end of the month, week, and day).

8. More than two-thirds of workers supported the union at the time the election petition was filed with the NLRB.

9. Similarly, all butchers were trained on the job and without gloves or other safety equipment.

10. The (illegal) dismissal of workers is a staple in nearly half of all union elections in the United States (Bronfenbrenner 2009).

11. Here, the human subjects requirement of anonymity rules out the possibility of providing exact counts from documents with the NLRB.

12. Raises were frequently promised during this period but mostly failed to materialize.

13. Neighborhood Food Basket's managers followed an industry standard labor-stacking strategy at the store's opening. Because market share in food retail is highly contested, new entrants into a market orchestrate their grand openings to generate maximum attention and to pull in large numbers of customers.

## 6. Building Degradation

1. The author's calculations are from the U.S. Census Bureau's Value of Construction Put in Place surveys. All figures are in 2011 dollars.

2. Residential construction workers can most readily be classified as construction laborers, whereas their licensed trade specialist counterparts in commercial construction typically fall under other occupational classifications. The author's calculations are from the U.S. Bureau of Labor Statistics's Current Population Survey; Merged Outgoing Rotation Groups. All figures are in 2011 dollars.

3. This hampers researchers' ability to use national-level construction data from the Economic Census and Nonemployer Statistics, which in some cases provides more detailed measures than do state and regional accounts. Regional differences in union density, building materials (brick and wood in the northeast, stucco in the southwest), the age and design of housing stock, and residential reinvestment alter the composition of contractors, subcontractors, and trade specialists in regional and local construction industries. Attempting to read off the structure of a local industry from these national data begs the very questions researchers set out to answer.

4. These contractors also pay day laborers exclusively in cash, directly supporting the notion that wage payments will appear in neither contractors' official financials nor in the nonemployer tax data that serve as a proxy for owner-operator contractors (see Carré and Wilson 2005; Kelsay, Sturgeon, and Pinkham 2006).

5. The ability to move back and forth between laborer, subcontractor, and general contractor roles is particularly important for day laborers. One of the key strategies used by worker centers consists of building bidding and contracting experience for day laborers in order to allow them to bring in their own construction jobs in addition to being hired on as labor for other contractors.

6. This variability most acutely impacts small contractors, who lack the ability to pursue the large number of jobs necessary to guarantee a steady flow of work.

7. As defined by North American Industrial Classification System Code (NAICS) 23321, Residential Building Construction. These NAICS codes separate work on residential buildings from new building construction. Given that NAICS also provides a separate code for residential developers, this supplies a reliable estimate of the contractor population primarily engaged in remodeling.

8. Because a large portion of residential remodeling work is conducted without licenses and permits, any estimate of this type is likely to understate the actual size of residential remodeling. The author's calculations are from Chicago Area Housing 2005.

9. The author's calculations are from U.S. Census Bureau 2005a.

10. Passel and the Pew Hispanic Center use slightly different estimation methods.

11. The author's calculations are from Chicago Area Housing 2005.

12. The goal of reselling at a markup in the short term also means that homeowners are less inclined to pay higher prices for materials and labor that will hold up over the long run.

13. For a representative example, see Levenson 2002.

14. Given that misclassified workers are typically paid in cash, Valenzuela Jr. et al.'s 2006 finding that the overwhelming majority of day laborers is paid in cash supports the notion that misclassification is rampant in residential construction.

15. Reductions in enforcement have the greatest impact on smaller, hard-to-police establishments, like those in construction.

## 7. A Perfectly Flexible Workforce

1. The author's calculations are from the U.S. Census Bureau's 2007 American Community Survey.

2. For example, although rival contractors routinely push Jenkins out of bidding situations by offering no-cost estimates, Jenkins continues to charge more than one hundred dollars for a house visit and estimate.

3. And virtually none of the laborers doing electrical work is licensed, a fact that restricts their potential customer base and hourly rates.

4. In a related example, the firmly prounion Jenkins Remodelers scoffed at union rules requiring the use of forty-dollar-per-hour union labor for digging holes on public works projects, saying, "How much are you going to pay somebody to dig a hole?"

5. The title of one of the best-selling home improvement guides, *Hiring Contractors without Going through Hell,* depicts this position ably.

6. This institutionalized downward pressure on labor costs extends beyond

formal and licensed subcontractors to day laborers themselves. On the day labor corner and through their networks of contractors, day laborers are often asked to put together small crews of workers (typically two or three) for a few days' work. In their occasional role as sub- and subsubcontractors, day laborers pay the going rate (unofficial but broadly known) for work.

7. In the polyglot world of residential subcontracting, day laborers typically identify contractors by ethnicity over name. Contractors of eastern European origin are with few exceptions identified as "Polacos" regardless of nationality.

8. Note that the use of *his* here is apt, as every contractor discussed or encountered in my research was a man.

9. It is also worth noting that worker centers in Southern California appear to thrive in part because of the region's relatively deregulated residential construction industry and the attachment of many worker centers to day labor shape-ups at the site of Home Depot stores. Workers at these sites are directly hired by homeowners, who appear to derive more utility than do contractors from the labor-screening functions of worker centers.

## Conclusion

1. For such research, see Initiative for a Competitive City 2002, Pothukuchi 2005, Guthman, Short, and Raskin 2007, and Dunkley, Helling, and Sawicky 2004. These studies are solid on their own terms, and many deploy a sophisticated understanding of corporate decision making and industry geography. The problem is not that such analysis *cannot* incorporate questions of job quality but rather that it does not.

2. For the evolution of the concept, see Peck 1996, ch. 2.

# Bibliography


Abernathy, Frederick, John T. Dunlop, David Weil, William Apgar, Kermit Baker, and Rachel Roth. 2004. *Residential Supply Chain in Transition: Summary of Findings from Survey of Dealers.* Cambridge, Mass.: Harvard University Joint Center for Housing Studies.

Abu-Lughod, Janet. 2001. *New York, Chicago, Los Angeles: America's Global Cities.* Minneapolis: University of Minnesota Press.

American Meat Institute. 2003. *Fact Sheet: Case Ready Meats.* Arlington, Va.: American Meat Institute.

Appelbaum, Eileen. 2000. *What Explains Employment Developments in the U.S.?* Washington, D.C.: Economic Policy Institute.

Archer, Nicole A., Ana Luz Gonzales, Kimi Lee, Simmi Gandhi, and Delia Herrera. 2010. "The Garment Worker Center and the 'Forever 21' Campaign." In *Working for Justice: The L.A. Model of Organizing and Advocacy,* edited by Ruth Milkman, Joshua Bloom, and Victor Narro, 154–64. Ithaca, N.Y.: ILR Press.

Ashton, Philip. 2009. "An Appetite for Yield: The Anatomy of the Subprime Mortgage Crisis." *Environment and Planning A* 41, no. 6: 1420–41.

Baker, Dean, and David Rosnick. 2005. *Will a Bursting Bubble Trouble Bernanke? The Evidence for a Housing Bubble.* Washington, D.C.: Center for Economic and Policy Research.

Beauregard, Robert A. 1993. *Voices of Decline: The Postwar Fate of U.S. Cities.* Oxford: Blackwell.

Belsky, Eric S., Mark A. Calabria, and Alfred R. Nucci. 2005. *Survivorship and Growth in the Residential Remodeling Industry: Evidence from the Census of Construction.* Cambridge, Mass.: Joint Center for Housing Studies of Harvard University.

Benner, Chris. 1996. *Shock Absorbers in the Flexible Economy: the Rise of Contingent Employment in Silicon Valley.* San Jose, Calif.: Working Partnerships USA.

Bennett, Larry. 2006. "Chicago's New Politics of Growth." In *The New Chicago,* edited by Koval et al., 44–55. Philadelphia: Temple University Press.

Bernhardt, Annette, James DeFilippis, Nina Martin, and Siobhan McGrath. 2005. "Unregulated Work and New Business Strategies in American Cities." In *Proceedings of the 57th Annual Meeting,* edited by Labor and Employment Relations

Association, 188–96. Champaign, Ill.: Labor and Employment Relations Association.

Bernhardt, Annette, and Siobhan McGrath. 2005. "Trends in Wage and Hour Enforcement by the U.S. Department of Labor, 1975–2004." In *Economic Policy Brief #3.* New York: Brennan Center for Social Justice.

———. 2007. *Unregulated Work in the Global City.* New York: Brennan Center for Social Justice.

Bernhardt, Annette, Siobhan McGrath, and James DeFilippis. 2008. "The State of Worker Protections in the U.S.: Unregulated Work in New York City." *International Labor Review* 147, no. 2/3: 135–62.

Bernhardt, Annette, Ruth Milkman, Nik Theodore, Douglas Heckathorn, Mirabai Auer, James DeFilippis, Ana Luz Gonzales, Victor Narro, Jason Perelshteyn, Diana Polson, and Michael Spiller. 2009. *Broken Laws, Unprotected Workers: Violations of Employment and Labor Laws in America's Cities.* New York: National Employment Law Project.

Berry, Brian J. L., Irving Cutler, Edwin H. Draine, Ying-Cheng Kiang, Thomas R. Tocalis, and Pierre de Viese. 1976. *Chicago: Transformation of an Urban System.* Cambridge, Mass.: Ballinger.

Bloom, Joshua. 2010. "Ally to Win: Black Community Leaders and SEIU's L.A. Security Unionization Campaign." In *Working for Justice: The L.A. Model of Organizing and Advocacy,* edited by Ruth Milkman, Joshua Bloom and Victor Narro, 167–90. Ithaca, N.Y.: ILR Press

Blumenfeld, Hans. 1955. "The Economic Base of the Metropolis: Critical Remarks on the "Basic–Nonbasic" Concept." *Journal of the American Institute of Planners* 21, no. 4: 114–32.

Bluestone, Barry, and Bennett Harrison. 1982. *The Deindustrialization of America: Plant Closings, Community Abandonment, and the Dismantling of Basic Industry.* New York: Basic Books.

Boarnet, Marlon G., Randall Crane, Daniel G. Chatman, and Michael Manville. 2005. "Emerging Planning Challenges in Retail." *Journal of the American Planning Association* 71, no. 4: 433–49.

Bodie, Matthew T. 2003. "The Potential for State Labor Law: The New York Greengrocer Code of Conduct." *Hofstra Labor and Employment Law Journal* 21:181.

———. 2004. "The Story behind the New York City Greengrocer Code of Conduct: An Interview with Patricia Smith." *Regional Labor Review* 6, no. 2: 19–31.

Bogdon, Amy. 1996. "Homeownership Renovation and Repair: The Decision to Hire Someone Else to Do the Project." *Journal of Housing Economics* 5:323–50.

Bolen, Ed, and Kenneth Hecht. 2003. *Neighborhood Groceries: New Access to Healthy Food in Low-Income Communities.* Oakland: California Food Policy Advocates.

Bosch, Gerhard, and Peter Philips. 2003. Introduction to *Building Chaos: An Inter-*

*national Comparison of Deregulation in the Construction Industry,* edited by Gerhard Bosch and Peter Philips, 1–23. London: Routledge.

Boston Consulting Group. 1998. *The Business Case for Pursuing Retail Opportunities in the Inner City.* Boston: Initiative for a Competitive Inner City.

Braverman, Harry. 1974. *Labor and Monopoly Capital.* New York: Monthly Review Press.

Brenner, Neil. 2001. "World City Theory, Globalization, and the Comparative-Historical Method: Reflections on Janet Abu-Lughod's Interpretation of Contemporary Urban Restructuring." *Urban Affairs Review* 36, no. 6: 124–47.

Bronfenbrenner, Kate. 2009. *No Holds Barred: The Intensification of Employer Opposition to Organizing.* Washington, D.C.: Economic Policy Institute.

Buchanan, Susan. 2004. "Day Labor and Occupational Health: Time to Take a Closer Look." *New Solutions* 14, no. 3: 253–60.

Burns, William. 1982. "Changing Corporate Structure and Technology in the Retail Food Industry." In *Labor and Technology: Union Responses to Changing Environments,* edited by Donald Kennedy, Charles Craypo, and Mary Lehman. State College, Pa.: Pennsylvania State University Department of Labor Studies.

California Contractors State License Board. 2004. *What You Should Know before Hiring a Contractor.* Sacramento: California Contractors State License Board.

Cameron, Angus, and Ronen Palan. 2004. *The Imagined Economies of Globalization.* London: Sage.

Carré, Francoise, and Chris Tilly. 2008. *America's Biggest Low-Wage Industry: Continuity and Change in Retail Jobs.* Boston: University of Massachusetts at Boston Center for Social Policy Publications.

Carré, Francoise, and Randall Wilson. 2004. "The Social and Economic Costs of Employee Misclassification in Construction." A Report to the Construction Policy Research Center Labor and Worklife Program, Harvard Law School, and Harvard School of Public Health. Boston: McCormack Graduate School of Policy Studies, University of Massachusetts, Boston.

———. 2005. "The Social and Economic Costs of Employee Misclassification in the Maine Construction Industry." Boston: University of Massachusetts at Boston Center for Social Policy Publications.

Castells, Manuel. 1996. *The Rise of the Network Society.* Oxford: Blackwell.

Center to Protect Workers' Rights. 2002. "The Construction Chart Book: The U.S. Construction Industry and Its Workers." 3rd ed. Silver Spring, Md.: Center to Protect Workers' Rights.

Chicago Area Housing. 2005. "Residential Permits Database." Chicago Area Housing website, www.chicagoareahousing.org (site discontinued).

Clarke, Susan E., and Gary L. Gaile. 1998. *The Work of Cities.* Minneapolis: University of Minnesota Press.

Clavel, Pierre. 2010. *Activists in City Hall: The Progressive Response to the Reagan Era in Boston and Chicago.* Ithaca, N.Y.: Cornell University Press.

Cohen, Adam, and Elizabeth Taylor. 2000. *American Pharaoh: Mayor Richard J. Daley: His Battle for Chicago and the Nation.* Boston: Little, Brown.

Cornelius, Wayne A. 2005. "Controlling 'Unwanted' Immigration: Lessons from the United States, 1993–2004." *Journal of Ethnic and Migration Studies* 31, no. 4: 775–94.

Cotterill, Ronald W., and Andrew W. Franklin. 1995. "The Urban Grocery Store Gap." In *Food Marketing Policy Issue Paper No. 8.* Storrs: University of Connecticut Food Marketing Policy Center.

Davis, Elizabeth, Matthew Freedman, Julia Lane, Brian McCall, Nicole Nestoriak, and Timothy Park. 2005. "Product Market Competition and Human Resource Practices: An Analysis of the Food Retail Sector." Working Paper 05-03, Food Industry Center, Minneapolis.

Day Labor Research Institute. 2001. "Day Labor in San Rafael, California: The Feasibility of Uniting Contradictory Positions." Study Conducted for the City of San Rafael. Boise, Idaho: Day Labor Research Institute.

DeFilippis, James, Nina Martin, Annette Bernhardt, and Siobhan McGrath. 2007. *On the Characteristics and Organization of Unregulated Work in American Cities.* New York: Baruch College.

Dixon, Rebecca, and Mike Evangelist. 2011. *The President's FY 2012 Budget: Federal Priorities in Unemployment Insurance, Workforce Development, and Worker Rights.* New York: National Employment Law Project.

Doeringer, Peter, and Michael Piore. 1971. *Internal Labor Markets and Manpower Analysis.* Lexington, Mass.: D.C. Heath.

Doussard, Marc, Jamie Peck, and Nik Theodore. 2009. "After Deindustrialization: Uneven Growth and Economic Inequality in 'Postindustrial' Chicago." *Economic Geography* 85, no. 2: 183–207.

Doussard, Marc, and Greg Schrock. 2012. "Same Sad Song? Labor Market Restructuring and the Evolving Geography of U.S. Manufacturing, 1980–2007." Paper presented at the Annual Meeting of the Association of American Geographers, New York, February 24–28.

Dunkley, Bill, Amy Helling, and David S. Sawicki. 2004. "Accessibility Versus Scale: Examining the Tradeoffs in Grocery Stores." *Journal of Planning Education and Research* 23, no. 4: 387–401

Dunlop, John T. 1961. "The Industrial Relations System in Construction." In *The Structure of Collective Bargaining,* edited by Arnold Weber, 255–77. Chicago: University of Chicago Press.

Eaton, Adrienne, and Jill Kriesky. 2006. "NLRB Elections vs. Card Check: Results of a Worker Survey." East Brunswick, N.J.: Rutgers University.

Eisenhauer, Elizabeth. 2001. "In Poor Health: Supermarket Redlining and Urban Nutrition." *GeoJournal* 53:125–33.

Erdmans, Mary Patrice. 2006. "New Chicago Polonia: Urban and Suburban." In *The New Chicago*, edited by Koval et al., 97–104. Philadelphia: Temple University Press.

Erlich, Mark, and Jeff Grabelsky. 2005. "Standing at a Crossroads: The Building Trades in the Twenty-First Century." *Labor History* 46, no. 4: 421–45.

Faura, Juan. 2004. *The Whole Enchilada: Hispanic Marketing 101*. Ithaca, N.Y.: Paramount Market Publishing.

Federal Reserve Bank of Chicago. 2000. *Chicago Fed Letter, #155*. Chicago: Federal Reserve Bank of Chicago.

Ferguson, Bruce, and Barbara Abell. 1998. "The Urban Grocery Store Gap." *Economic Development Commentary* 1, no. 4: 6–14.

Fielding, Nigel G., and Jane L. Fielding. 1986. *Linking Data*. Beverly Hills, Calif.: Sage.

Fine, Janice. 2006. *Worker Centers: Organizing Communities at the Edge of the Dream*. Ithaca, N.Y.: Cornell University Press.

Fine, Janice, and Jenifer Gordon. 2010. "Strengthening Labor Standards Enforcement through Partnerships with Workers' Organizations." *Politics and Society* 38, no. 4: 552–85.

Finkel, Gerald. 1997. *The Economics of the Construction Industry*. Aramonk, N.Y.: M. E. Sharpe.

———. 2005. "The American Construction Industry: An Overview." In *The Economics of Prevailing Wage Laws*, edited by Hamid Azari-Rad, Peter Philips, and Mark J. Prus, 28–63. Farnham, U.K.: Ashgate Publishing.

Food Marketing Institute. 2007. "Key Facts: Food Retailers Net Profit—Percent of Sales." Food Marketing Institute website, accessed October 2007, www.fmi.org/facts_figs/keyfacts/chains.htm (no longer available on website).

Freeman, Richard B. 2001. "The Rising Tide Lifts?" Working Paper 8155, National Bureau of Economic Research, Cambridge, Mass.

Freeman, Richard B., and James L. Medoff. 1984. *What Do Unions Do?* New York: Basic Books.

Friedmann, John. 1986. "The World City Hypothesis." *Development and Change* 17:69–84.

Gautié, Jerôme, and John Schmitt, eds. 2009. *Low-Wage Work in the Wealthy World*. New York: Russell Sage Foundation.

Glasmeier, Amy. 2000. *Manufacturing Time: Global Competition in the Watch Industry, 1975–2000*. New York: Guilford Press.

Goetz, Edward G. 1990. "Type II Policy and Mandated Benefits in Economic Development." *Urban Affairs Review* 26, no. 2: 170–90.

Gordon, David, Richard Edwards, and Michael Reich. 1982. *Segmented Work, Divided Workers.* Cambridge: Cambridge University Press.

Graham, Stephen, and Simon Marvin. 2001. *Splintering Urbanism: Networked Infrastructure, Technological Mobilities, and the Urban Condition.* London: Routledge.

Grudin, Nicholas. 2004. "Grocery Union Negotiators Accept Two-Tier Pay Scale, Health Cost Payments." Knight Ridder, February 27.

Harrison, Bennett. 1984. "Regional Restructuring and 'Good Business Climates': The Economic Transformation of New England Since World War II." In *Sunbelt/Snowbelt: Urban Development and Regional Restructuring,* edited by Larry Sawers and William K. Tabb, 48–96. New York: Oxford University Press

———. 1994. *Lean and Mean: The Changing Landscape of Corporate Power in the Age of Flexibility*. New York: Basic Books.

Harrison, Bennett, and Barry Bluestone. 1988. *The Great U-Turn: Corporate Restructuring and the Polarizing of America.* New York: Basic Books.

Harvey, David. 1985. *The Urbanization of Capital: Studies in the History and Theory of Capitalist Urbanization.* Baltimore: Johns Hopkins University Press.

———. 1989. *The Condition of Postmodernity.* Oxford: Blackwell.

Hipple, Steven. 2001. "Contingent Work in the Late 1990s." *Monthly Labor Review,* March.

Hirschman, Charles, and Douglas S. Massey. 2008. "Places and Peoples: The New American Mosaic." In *New Places in New Faces: The Changing Geography of American Immigration,* edited by Douglas S. Massed, 1–22. New York: Russell Sage Foundation.

Hudson, Ray. 2001. *Producing Places.* London: Guilford Press.

Initiative for a Competitive Inner City. 2002. *The Changing Models of Inner City Grocery Retailing.* Boston: Initiative for a Competitive Inner City.

Iskander, Natasha, Nichola Lowe, and Christine Riordan. 2010. "The Rise and Fall of a Micro-Learning Region: Mexican Immigrants and Construction in Center-South Philadelphia." *Environment and Planning A* 42, no. 7: 1595–1612.

Joint Center for Housing Studies of Harvard University. 2005. "The Changing Structure of the Home Remodeling Industry." Cambridge, Mass.: Joint Center for Housing Studies of Harvard University.

Joint Center for Housing Studies of Harvard University. 2007. "Leading Indicator of Remodeling Activity (LIRA)." Joint Center for Housing Studies of Harvard Universitywebsite, http://www.jchs.harvard.edu/leading-indicator-remodeling-activity-lira.

Juravich, Tom, and Corinn Williams. 2011. "After the Immigration Raid: Evaluating the Campaign to Support Undocumented Workers in New Bedford, Massachusetts." *WorkingUSA* 14, no. 2: 201–24.

Kelsay, Michael P., James I. Sturgeon, and Kelly D. Pinkham. 2006. *The Economic*

*Costs of Employee Misclassification in the State of Illinois.* Kansas City: Department of Economics, University of Missouri–Kansas City.

King, Robert P., Ephraim S. Leibtag, and Ajay S. Behl. 2004. *Supermarket Characteristics and Operating Costs in Low-Income Areas.* Washington, D.C.: U.S. Department of Agriculture.

Knox, Paul L., and Peter J. Taylor, eds. 1995. *World Cities in a World-System.* Cambridge: Cambridge University Press.

Koval, John P. 2006. "An Overview and Point of View." In *The New Chicago,* edited by Koval et al., 3–15. Philadelphia: Temple University Press.

Koval, John P., Larry Bennett, Michael I. J. Bennet, Fassil Demissie, Roberta Garner, and Kiljoong Kim, eds. *The New Chicago: A Social and Cultural Analysis.* Philadelphia: Temple University Press.

Koval, John P., and Kenneth Fidel. 2006. "Chicago: The Immigrant Capital of the Heartland." In *The New Chicago,* edited by Koval et al., 97–104. Philadelphia: Temple University Press.

Lake, Robert W., and Kathe Newman. 2002. "Differential Citizenship in the Shadow State." *GeoJournal* 58, no. 2/3: 109–20.

Lee, Don. 2006. "Task Force in Tatters: State–Federal Tensions Hinder Garment Industry Crackdown." *Los Angeles Times,* August 4.

Lees, Loretta. 2003. "Super-gentrification: The Case of Brooklyn Heights, New York City." *Urban Studies* 40, no. 12: 2487–509.

Lerner, Stephen, Jill Hurst, and Glenn Adler. 2008. "Fighting and Winning in the Outsourced Economy: Justice for Janitors at the University of Miami." In *The Gloves-off Economy: Workplace Standards at the Bottom of America's Labor Market,* edited by Annette Bernhardt, Heather Boushey, Laura Dresser, and Chris Tilly, 217–42. Champaign, Ill.: Labor and Employment Relations Association.

Levenson, Ellis. 1992. *Hiring Contractors without Going through Hell.* New York: Walker.

Levine, Art. 2007. "Unionbusting Confidential." *In These Times,* September 24.

Lewis, Norman. 1964. *The Honored Society.* New York: G. P. Putnam's Sons.

Lovering, John. 1989. "The Restructuring Debate." In *New Models in Geography,* vol. 2, edited by Richard Peet and Nigel J. Thrift. Winchester, Mass.: Unwin-Hyman.

Luria, Daniel D., and Joel Rogers. 1999. "Metro Futures." In *Metro Futures: Economic Solutions for Cities and Their Suburbs,* edited by Daniel D. Luria and Joel Rogers, 3–40. Boston; Beacon Press.

Mailer, Norman. 1968. *Miami and the Siege of Chicago: An Informal History of the Republican and Democratic Conventions of 1968.* New York: World Publishing Company.

Mari Gallagher Research and Consulting Group. 2006. *Examining the Impact of Food Deserts on Public Health in Chicago.* Chicago: Mari Gallagher Research and Consulting Group.

Markusen, Ann. 1994. "Studying Regions by Studying Firms." *Professional Geographer* 46, no. 4: 477–90.

———. 2003. "Fuzzy Concepts, Scanty Evidence, Policy Distance: The Case for Rigour and Policy Relevance in Critical Regional Studies." *Regional Studies* 37, no. 6/7: 701–17.

———. 1985. *Profit Cycles, Oligopoly, and Regional Development.* Cambridge, Mass.: MIT Press.

Markusen, Ann, Peter Hall, Scott Campbell, and Sabina Deitrick. 1991. *The Rise of the Gunbelt: The Military Remapping of Industrial America.* New York: Oxford University Press.

Markusen, Ann, and Greg Schrock. 2006. "The Artistic Dividend: Urban Artistic Specialisation and Economic Development Implications." *Urban Studies* 43, no. 10: 1661–86.

Massey, Douglas, Jorge Durand, and Noland J. Malone. 2003. *Beyond Smoke and Mirrors: Mexican Immigration in an Era of Economic Integration.* New York: Russell Sage Foundation.

Massey, Doreen, and Richard Meegan. 1979. "The Geography of Industrial Reorganisation." *Progress in Planning* 10:155–237.

———. 1982. *The Anatomy of Job Loss: The How, Why, and Where of Employment Decline.* New York: Methuen.

McMillen, Dan, and Thomas W. Lester. 2003. "Evolving Subcenters: Employment and Population Densities in Chicago, 1970–2020." *Journal of Housing Economics* 12:60–81.

McTaggart, Jenny. 2005. "Being el Super." *Progressive Grocer* 84, no. 12: 26–37.

Mehta, Chirag, Ron Baiman, and Joe Persky. 2004. *The Economic Impact of Wal-Mart: An Assessment of the Wal-Mart Store Proposed for Chicago's West Side.* Chicago: University of Illinois at Chicago Center for Urban Economic Development.

Mehta, Chirag, and Nik Theodore. 2000. "Winning Union Representation for Temps: An Analysis of the NLRB's M. B. Sturgis and Jeffboat Ruling." *WorkingUSA* 4, no. 3: 37–58.

———. 2005. *Undermining the Right to Organize: Employer Behavior during Union Campaigns.* Chicago: University of Illinois at Chicago Center for Urban Economic Development.

———. 2006. "Workplace Safety in Atlanta's Construction Industry: Institutional Failure in Temporary Staffing Arrangements." *WorkingUSA* 9:59–77.

Mehta, Chirag, Nik Theodore, and Marielena Hincapié. 2003. *Social Security Administration's No-Match Letter Program: Implications for Immigration Enforce-*

*ment and Workers' Rights.* Chicago: University of Illinois at Chicago Center for Urban Economic Development.

Mehta, Chirag, Nik Theodore, Iliana Mora, and Jennifer Wade. 2002. *Chicago's Undocumented Immigrants: An Analysis of Wages, Working Conditions, and Economic Contributions.* Chicago: University of Illinois at Chicago Center for Urban Economic Development.

Milkman, Ruth. 2006. *L.A. Story: Immigrant Workers and the Future of the U.S. Labor Movement.* New York: Russell Sage Foundation.

———. 2010. Introduction to *Working for Justice: The L.A. Model of Organizing and Advocacy,* edited by Ruth Milkman, Joshua Bloom, and Victor Narro, 1–19. Ithaca, N.Y.: ILR Press.

Mishel, Lawrence, Jared Bernstein, and Sylvia Allegretto. 2006. *The State of Working America 2006/2007.* Ithaca, N.Y.: Cornell University Press.

Mollenkopf, John H., and Manuel Castells, eds. 1991. *Dual City: Restructuring New York.* New York: Russell Sage Foundation

Muellereile, Christopher M. 2009. "Financialization Takes Off at Boeing." *Journal of Economic Geography* 9, no. 5: 663–77.

Muñiz, Karina. 2010. "The Janitorial Industry and the Maintenance Cooperation Trust Fund." In *Working for Justice: The L.A. Model of Organizing and Advocacy,* edited by Ruth Milkman, Joshua Bloom, and Victor Narro, 211–31. Ithaca, N.Y.: ILR Press.

Nathalie P. Voorhees Center. 2012. *Evaluating Chicago's Response to Food Deserts: Do 'Discount' Supermarkets Offer Varied and Affordable Fresh Food?* Chicago: Nathalie P. Voorhees Center, University of Illinois at Chicago.

National Employment Law Project. 2003. *Undocumented Workers: Preserving Rights and Remedies after Hoffman Plastics Compounds vs. NLRB.* New York: National Employment Law Project.

National Immigration Law Center. 2004. *Michigan Supreme Court Vacates Order Granting Motion to Appeal in Workers' Compensation Case.* Los Angeles: National Immigration Law Center.

Ness, Immanuel. 2005. *Immigrants, Unions, and the New U.S. Labor Market.* Philadelphia: Temple University Press.

Nicholson, Tom. 2006. "Big Home Centers' Influence Sways the Broader Materials Market: Smaller Contractors Are Starting to Bite, but Big Fish Are Elusive." *Engineering News Record* 256, no. 11: 29.

Nicodemus, Aaron. 2007. "Workers Sue Michael Bianco Inc. for Overtime Wages." *New Bedford Standard-Times,* May 16.

Nissen, Bruce. 2004. "The Effectiveness and Limits of Labor–Community Coalitions: Evidence from South Florida." *Labor Studies Journal* 29:67–88.

Organization for Economic Cooperation and Development. 2011. "Divided We

Stand: Why Inequality Keeps Rising." Paris: Organization for Economic Cooperation and Development.
Paral, Rob. 2006. "Latinos of the New Chicago." In *The New Chicago*, edited by Koval et al., 105–14. Philadelphia: Temple University Press.
Palladino, Grace. 2005. *Skilled Hands, Strong Spirits: A Century of Building Trades History*. Ithaca, N.Y.: Cornell University Press.
Passel, Jeffrey S. 2006. *The Size and Characteristics of the Unauthorized Migrant Population in the U.S. Estimates Based on the March 2005 Current Population Survey*. Washington, D.C.: Pew Hispanic Center.
Passel, Jeffrey S., and D'Vera Cohn. 2011. *Unauthorized Immigration Population: National and State Trends, 2010*. Washington, D.C.: Pew Hispanic Center.
Peck, Jamie. 1996. *Work-Place: The Social Regulation of Labor Markets*. London: Routledge.
Peck, Jamie, and Nik Theodore. 1998. "The Business of Contingent Work: Growth and Restructuring in Chicago's Temporary Employment Industry." *Work, Employment, and Society* 12, no. 4: 655–74.
———. 2001. "Contingent Chicago: Restructuring the Spaces of Temporary Labor." *International Journal of Urban and Regional Research* 25, no. 3: 471–96.
Perkins, Jim. 2004. *Beyond Bodegas: Developing a Retail Relationship with Hispanic Customers*. Ithaca, N.Y.: Paramount Market Publishing.
Perry, David C., and Alfred J. Watkins. 1977. "People, Profit, and the Rise of the Sunbelt Cities." In *The Rise of the Sunbelt Cities*, edited by David C. Perry and Alfred J. Watkins, 277–305. Beverly Hills, Calif.: Sage.
Persky, Joe, Marc Doussard, and Wim Wiewel. 2009. "Export Orientation and the Limits to Local Sovereignty." *Urban Studies* 46, no. 3: 519–36.
Pew Hispanic Center. 2007. "Fact Sheet: Construction Jobs Expand for Latinos Despite Slump in Housing Market." Washington, D.C.: Pew Hispanic Center.
Philips, Peter. 2003. "Dual Worlds: The Two Growth Paths in U.S. Construction." In *Building Chaos: An International Comparison of Deregulation in the Construction Industry*, edited by Gerhard Bosch and Peter Philips. London: Routledge.
Pongracz, Petra. n.d. *Attracting Supermarkets to Underserved, Urban Markets: A Case Study in a Low-Income Neighborhood in Durham, North Carolina*. Chapel Hill: University of North Carolina.
Porter, Michael. 1995. "The Competitive Advantage of the Inner City." *Harvard Business Review* 73, no. 3: 55–71.
Pothukuchi, Kameshwari. 2005. "Attracting Supermarkets to Inner-City Neighborhoods: Economic Development Outside the Box." *Economic Development Quarterly* 19, no. 3: 232–44.
Pothukuchi, Kameshwari, and Jerome L. Kaufman. 2000. "The Food System: A Stranger to the Planning Field." *Journal of the American Planning Association* 63, no. 2: 113–24.

Progressive Grocer. 2006. "A Leaner Marsh." *Progressive Grocer* 85, no. 4: 12–13.

Rangaswamy, Padma. 2006. "Asian Indians in Chicago." In *The New Chicago*, edited by Koval et al., 128–140. Philadelphia: Temple University Press.

Rast, Joel. 1999. *Remaking Chicago: The Political Origins of Industrial Change.* DeKalb, Ill.: Northern Illinois University Press.

Reynolds, Jonathan, and Steve Wood. 2010. "Location Decision Making in Retail Firms: Evolution and Challenge." *International Journal of Retail and Distribution Management* 38, no. 11/12: 828–45.

Royko, Mike. 1971. *Boss: Mayor Richard J. Daley of Chicago.* London: Barrie and Jenkins.

Ruckleshaus, Cathy, and Sara Leberstein. 2011. *NELP Summary of Independent Contractor Reforms New State and Federal Activity November 2011.* New York: National Employment Law Project.

Ruggles, S., T. Alexander, K. Grenadek, R. Goeken, M. B. Schroeder, and M. Sobek. 2010. "Integrated Public Use Microdata Series: Version 5.0" (machine-readable database), Minnesota Population Center website, http://usa.ipums.org/usa.

Sassen, Saskia. 1998. *Globalization and Its Discontents.* Princeton, N.J.: Princeton University Press.

———. 2001. *The Global City: New York, London, Tokyo.* 2nd ed. Princeton, N.J.: Princeton University Press.

Sayer, Andrew, and Richard Walker. 1992. *The New Social Economy.* Oxford: Blackwell.

Schaffer, Richard Lance. 1973. *Income Flows in Urban Poverty Areas: A Comparison of the Community Income Accounts of Bedford-Stuyvesant and Borough Park.* Lexington, Mass.: Lexington Books.

Sellers, Jeffrey M. 2002. *Governing from Below: Urban Regions and the Global Economy.* New York: Cambridge University Press.

Short, Anne, Julie Guthman, and Samuel Raskin. 2007. "Food Deserts: Oases, or Mirages? Small Markets and Community Food Security in the San Francisco Bay Area." *Journal of Planning Education and Research* 26, no. 3: 352–64.

Sites, William. 2007. "Beyond Trenches and Grassroots? Reflections on Urban Mobilization, Fragmentation, and the Anti-Wal-Mart Campaign in Chicago." *Environment and Planning A* 39, no. 11: 2632–51.

Sites, William. 2003. *Remaking New York: Primitive Globalization and the Politics of Urban Community.* Minneapolis: University of Minnesota Press.

Smith, Michael Peter. 2001. *Transnational Urbanism.* Oxford: Blackwell.

Spirou, Costa. 2006. "Urban Beautification: The Construction of a New Identity in Chicago." In *The New Chicago*, edited by Koval et al., 295–302. Philadelphia: Temple University Press.

Stephens, Duncan G. 1998. *The Unofficial Guide to Hiring Contractors.* New York: MacMillan General Reference.

Storper, Michael, and Richard Walker. 1989. *The Capitalist Imperative: Territory, Technology, Growth.* Oxford: Blackwell.

Suchar, Charles S. 2006. "Chicago's Central Area." In *The New Chicago,* edited by Koval et al., 56–76. Philadelphia: Temple University Press.

Tarnowski, Joseph. 2006. "Safeway, Inc." *Progressive Grocer* 85, no. 1: 54.

Tattersall, Amanda. 2005. "There Is Power in Coalition: A Framework for Assessing How and When Union–Community Coalitions Are Effective and Enhance Union Power." *Labour and Industry* 16, no. 2: 97–112.

Theodore, Nik. 2003. "Political Economies of Day Labour: Regulation and Restructuring of Chicago's Contingent Labour Markets." *Urban Studies* 40, no. 9: 1811–28.

Theodore, Nik, and Nina Martin. 2007. "Migrant Civil Society: New Voices in the Struggle over Community Development." *Journal of Urban Affairs* 29, no. 3: 269–87.

Theodore, Nik, and Jamie Peck. 2002. "The Temporary Staffing Industry: Growth Imperatives and Limits to Contingency." *Economic Geography* 78, no. 4: 463–93.

Theodore, Nik, Abel Valenzuela Jr., and Edwin Meléndez. 2009. "Worker Centers: Defending Labor Standards for Migrant Workers in the Informal Economy." *International Journal of Manpower* 30, no. 5: 422–36.

Therborn, Goran. 2011. "End of a Paradigm: The Current Crisis and the Idea of Stateless Cities." *Environment and Planning A* 43:272–85.

Tiebout, Charles. 1956. "A Pure Local Theory of Expenditures." *Journal of Political Economy* 64, no. 5: 416–24.

Tilly, Charles. 1984. *Big Structure, Large Processes, Huge Comparisons.* New York: Russell Sage Foundation.

Tilly, Chris. 1996. *Half a Job: Bad and Good Part-Time Jobs in a Changing Labor Market.* Philadelphia: Temple University Press.

———. 2006. "Wal-Mart and Its Workers: NOT the Same All over the World." *Connecticut Law Review,* May.

TradeDimensions. 2000. *Market Scope: the Desktop Guide to Category Sales.* Wilton, Conn.: TradeDimensions.

———. 2001. *Market Scope: the Desktop Guide to Category Sales.* Wilton, Conn.: TradeDimensions.

———. 2002. *Market Scope: the Desktop Guide to Category Sales.* Wilton, Conn.: TradeDimensions.

———. 2003. *Market Scope: the Desktop Guide to Category Sales.* Wilton, Conn.: TradeDimensions.

———. 2004. *Market Scope: the Desktop Guide to Category Sales.* Wilton, Conn.: TradeDimensions.

———. 2005. *Market Scope: the Desktop Guide to Category Sales.* Wilton, Conn.: TradeDimensions.

———. 2006. *Market Scope: the Desktop Guide to Category Sales.* Wilton, Conn.: TradeDimensions.

Turock, Art. 2005. "Teflon Retailing." *Progressive Grocer* 84, no. 7: 22–24.

U.S. Bureau of Labor Statistics. 2006a. Consumer Expenditure Survey, 2006. Bureau of Labor Statistics website, http://www.bls.gov/cex.

———. 2006b. Quarterly Census of Employment and Wages, 2005. Bureau of Labor Statistics website, http://www.bls.gov/cew.

———. 2007. National Compensation Survey, 2006. Bureau of Labor Statistics website, http://www.bls.gov/eci.

U.S. Census Bureau. 1990. Guide to the 1987 Economic Census and Related Statistics. U.S. Census Bureau website, http://www2.census.gov/econ1987/Guide_to_the_1987_Economic_Censuses.pdf.

———. 1995. Economic Census, 1992. U.S. Census Bureau website, http://www.census.gov/epcd/www/92result.html.

———. 2000a. Building Permits Survey, 2000. U.S. Census Bureau website, http://www.census.gov/construction/bps.

———. 2000b. Economic Census 2007. U.S. Census Bureau website, http://www.census.gov/epcd/www/econ97.html.

———. 2000c. Value of Construction Put in Place, Private Construction, 2000. U.S. Census Bureau website, http://www.census.gov/construction/c30/privpage.html.

———. 2001. Value of Construction Put in Place, Private Construction, 2001. U.S. Census Bureau website, http://www.census.gov/construction/c30/privpage.html.

———. 2002. Value of Construction Put in Place, Private Construction, 2002. U.S. Census Bureau website, http://www.census.gov/construction/c30/privpage.html.

———. 2003a. Nonemployer Statistics, 2002. U.S. Census Bureau website, http://censtats.census.gov/cgi-bin/nonemployer/nonsect.pl.

———. 2003b. Value of Construction Put in Place, Private Construction, 2003. U.S. Census Bureau website, http://www.census.gov/construction/c30/privpage.html.

———. 2004a. Nonemployer Statistics, 2003. U.S. Census Bureau website, http://censtats.census.gov/cgi-bin/nonemployer/nonsect.pl.

———. 2004b. Value of Construction Put in Place, Private Construction, 2004. U.S. Census Bureau website, http://www.census.gov/construction/c30/privpage.html.

———. 2005a. Economic Census 2002. U.S. Census Bureau website, http://www.census.gov/econ/census02.

———. 2005b. Nonemployer Statistics, 2004. U.S. Census Bureau website, http://censtats.census.gov/cgi-bin/nonemployer/nonsect.pl.

———. 2005c. Value of Construction Put in Place, Private Construction, 2005. U.S. Census Bureau website, http://www.census.gov/construction/c30/privpage.html.

———. 2006a. Building Permits Survey, 2006. U.S. Census Bureau website, http://www.census.gov/construction/bps.

———. 2006b. Nonemployer Statistics, 2005. U.S. Census Bureau website, http://censtats.census.gov/cgi-bin/nonemployer/nonsect.pl.

———. 2006c. Value of Construction Put in Place, Private Construction, 2006. U.S. Census Bureau website, http://www.census.gov/construction/c30/privpage.html.

———. 2007. County Business Patterns, 2005. U.S. Census Bureau website, http://www.census.gov/econ/cbp/download/05_data/index.htm.

U.S. Congress. 2002. "Economic Outlook." Hearing before the Joint Economic Committee, Congress of the United States, Washington, D.C., November 13.

United Food and Commercial Workers. 2007. Private database on pay rates and benefits provisions by job, seniority, and firm, provided to author.

Valenzuela Jr., Abel. 2003. "Day-Labor Work." *Annual Review of Sociology* 29, no. 1: 307–33.

Valenzuela Jr., Abel, Janette A. Kawachi, and Matthew D. Marr. 2002. "Seeking Work Daily: Supply, Demand, and Spatial Dimensions of Day Labor in Two Global Cities." *International Journal of Comparative Sociology* 43, no. 2: 192–219.

Valenzuela Jr., Abel, Nik Theodore, Edwin Melendez, and Ana Luz Gonzalez. 2006. "On the Corner: Day Labor in the United States." Los Angeles and Chicago: UCLA Center for the Study of Urban Poverty / University of Illinois at Chicago Center for Urban Economic Development.

Van Kempen, Ronald, and Peter Marcuse. 1997. "A New Spatial Order in Cities?" *American Behavioral Scientist* 41, no. 3: 285–98.

Wage Theft. 2012. "State, City, County." Wage Theft website, http://wagetheft.org/wordpress/?page_id=1634.

Waldinger, Roger, and Michael I. Lichter. 2003. *How the Other Half Works: Immigration and the Social Organization of Labor.* Berkeley: University of California Press.

Washington State Department of Labor and Industries. 2007. *Protect Yourself When Hiring a Contractor.* Olympia: Washington State Department of Labor and Industries.

Weil, David. 1991. "Enforcing OSHA: The Role of Labor Unions." *Industrial Relations* 30, no. 1: 20–36.

———. 2005. "The Contemporary Industrial Relations System in Construction: Analysis, Observations, and Speculations." *Labor History* 46, no. 4: 447–71.

———. 2009. "Rethinking the Regulation of Vulnerable Work in the USA: A Sector-Based Approach." *Journal of Industrial Relations* 51, no. 3: 411–30.

Weil, David, and Carlos Mallo. 2007. "Regulating Labour Standards via Supply Chains: Combining Public/Private Interventions to Improve Workplace Compliance." *British Journal of Industrial Relations* 45, no. 4: 791–814.

Wilson, David. 2011. "Performative Neoliberal-Parasitic Economies: The Chicago Case." *International Journal of Urban and Regional Research* 35, no. 4: 691–711.

Wolch, Jennifer. 1990. *The Shadow State: Government and Voluntary Sector in Transition*. New York: The Foundation Center.

Wright, Eric Olin, and Rachel Dwyer. 2003. "The Patterns of Job Expansions in the USA: A comparison of the 1960s and 1990s." *Socioeconomic Review* 1, no. 3: 289–325.

Yerak, Becky. 2006. "Supervalu Still in Jewel Hunt." *Chicago Tribune*, January 20.

Zabin, Carol, Arindrajit Dube, and Ken Jacobs. 2004. "The Hidden Public Cost of Low-Wage Jobs in California." Berkeley: University of California Institute for Labor and Employment.

Zatz, Noah D. 2008. "Working Beyond the Reach or Grasp of Employment Law." In *The Gloves-off Economy: Workplace Standards at the Bottom of America's Labor Market*, edited by Annette Bernhardt, Heather Boushey, Laura Dresser, and Chris Tilly, 31–64. Champaign, Ill.: Labor and Employment Relations Association.

Zook, Matthew, and Mark Graham. 2006. "Wal-Mart Nation: Mapping the Reach of a Retail Colossus." In *Wal-Mart World: The World's Biggest Corporation in the Global Economy*, edited by Stanley D. Brunn, 15–25. New York: Routledge.

# Index


Abu-Lughod, Janet, 10
aerospace industry, 23, 45
AFL-CIO, 208
African American neighborhoods, 60, 63, 67, 81, 90, 98, 102–3
Albany Park Work Center (APWC) (Chicago), 66–67; broker role, 174, 191, 195, 196–97; geographical focus of, 207; political connections, 208, 211; as research site, 77; shape-ups as organizing sites, 190–91; wage theft intervention, 194, 195
Aldi, 90
Alinsky, Saul, xi
antiunion activities, 33. *See also* employer retribution for union campaigns
Assembly Bill 633 (California), 215
auto industry, 45, 241n4

Beauregard, Bob, 63
bidding process, 46, 73, 166, 182–85, 245n5
Big-Box Bill campaign (Chicago), 67
big-box retailers: competition with chain grocery stores, 94; economies of scale, 90, 242n1; employee compensation, 88; expansion of, 69, 242n5; market share, 83, 98; organizing aimed at, 67; and price-based competition, 111; and United States as international outlier, 12
Bluestone, Barry, 14
Blumenfeld, Hans, 13
bodégas. *See* midsize supermarkets
Boeing, 23
border crossing debt, 34, 36, 106, 119, 132, 233
Boston, 216, 223
breaks. *See* employer retribution
Brenner, Neil, 10, 56
bulk purchasing. *See* economies of scale
Bureau of the Census, 73, 74
Bureau of Labor Statistics, 73
business models. *See* employer strategies
business-to-business services, 46

Cameron, Angus, 226
capital investment, alternatives to: and job degradation, 38, 43–44, 81–82, 106; and residential construction industry instability, 149; and residential remodeling, 59
capital mobility: dominant narrative focus on, 14, 24; and global cities theory, 23; and market fragmentation, 45; and organizing strategies, 30–31
Carré, Francoise, 243n6

Casa de Maryland, 207
Centro Comunitario Juan Diego, 67
chain grocery stores: big-box retailer competition with, 94; consolidated ownership in, 85–86; employee compensation, 82–83, 88–89, 113, 243n4; and ethnic solidarity, 104, 105, 137–38; expansion of, 69; and food desert issue, 97–98; and limitations of Fordist model, 88, 95, 110, 113–14; management, 117; midsize supermarket competition with, 15, 82, 98–100, 104, 110, 125; and price-based competition, 83–84, 111, 243n2; profit margins, 139; suburban expansion, 84–85; unions, 86, 88, 95, 113
change strategies. *See* organizing strategies
Chiapas case study, 125–29, 243n7
Chicago: African American neighborhoods, 60, 63, 67, 81, 90, 98, 102–3; Big-Box Bill, 67; deindustrialization in, 52–53; food retail industry overview, 69–71, 242n5; as Fordist paradigm, 52, 53, 96–97; housing boom, 23–24, 59–60, 160; as ideal research location, 53–54, 96–97; immigrant population, 53, 60–63, 65, 89–90, 97, 242nn1,2; legal-realignment strategies, 215–16; outer neighborhood transformation, 60–65; political machine in, 54, 58–59, 66, 67; residential construction industry overview, 71–73; unions, 168; Washington administration activism, 58–59, 67; workers' organizations in, 65, 66–68. *See also* Albany Park Work Center; Chicago, economic inequality in
Chicago, economic inequality in: growth of, 54–56, 57; and Loop investment, 58, 59; and neighborhood-level transformation, 56–58; symbols of, 49–50; unique nature of, 53–54
Chicago school, 52
coethnic workers, 103–4, 119, 243n7. *See also* ethnic solidarity
collective bargaining. *See* unions
command-and-control centers, 7, 50
Community Labor Coalition of the Lower East Side (New York), 220
community–labor organizations. *See* union campaigns; workers' organizations
competition. *See* cost-based competition; employer strategies
construction industry: and downtown investment, 59; general contractor model, 164, 165–66; heterogeneity within, 20; industry codes, 73–74, 244n2, 245n7; labor-intensive models in, 38, 151; organizing challenges, 40–41; research methods, 76–77, 78; subcontracting, 59, 73, 149; unions, 13, 59, 166, 168, 169, 177, 180. *See also* day labor; residential construction industry
consumer pressure, 221, 222–23. *See also* public pressure
contingent work, 1–2, 32, 191, 194, 205
corporate structure, 6–10, 23
cost-based competition: food retail industry, 85, 88, 106, 139–40; and low-income markets, 106; pressures toward, 38, 39–40, 44, 46; vs. quality-based competition, 42–45, 83–84, 106; residential construction industry, 154

Daley, Richard M., 23, 24, 54, 58–59, 66, 67
Daley, Richard J., 58
Davis-Bacon Act, 13, 59, 146, 167
day labor, vii–viii, ix–x, 1–2; benefits of, 169–70, 171–72, 197–99; contingent nature of, 1–2, 191, 194; and contractor networks, 196–97; and deskilling, 177–80, 201–2, 245nn3,4; employee compensation, 173, 174–77, 191, 245n2; and employee misclassification, 245n14; and employer official invisibility, 210, 244n4; employer strategies, 29; hiring process, 195–96; history of, 12, 144, 150, 154, 171; homeowners as employers, 180–81, 197, 246n9; immigrant worker role in, 155, 157–58; job search strategies, 196–97; and labor contracting model, 159, 245n6; and managerial flexibility, 150, 172–73, 197–99; and multiple worker roles, 244n5; participant observation, 77; and research methods, 76; self-imposed work speed, 192–93; shape-ups as organizing sites, 41, 190–91; speed/hours conundrum, ix, 143, 192; traffic safety concerns, 208; uncertainties of, 143–44; worker centers as brokers for, 145, 174, 190–91, 195, 196–97, 208, 223, 246n9. *See also* residential construction employer strategies; residential construction industry; worker centers
degraded work. *See* job degradation
deindustrialization: Chicago, 52–53; and construction industry, 24; and corporate structure, 6–7; dominant narratives on, xii, 4–6, 13–14; during 2000s economic expansion, 55; and organizing strategies, 41–42; and urban poverty, 5–6. *See also* service sector growth
*Deindustrialization of America, The* (Bluestone and Harrison), 14
Department of Labor, 74
deskilling, 149–50, 171; and day labor, 177–80, 201–2, 245nn3,4; and labor contracting model, 164; and premanufactured housing components, 163; and price-based competition, 70–71
disinvestment. *See* food desert issue
Doeringer, Peter, 47, 232
Domestic Worker Bill of Rights (New York), 214, 218
dominant narratives: analytical neglect of locally oriented industries, xi–xii, 8–9, 10, 13–14, 19, 21, 227, 243n6, 246n1; on Chicago as Fordist paradigm, 52, 53; on cost- vs. quality-based competition, 42–43, 44, 83–84, 154; on deindustrialization, xii, 4–6, 13–14; on economic expansion, 144; on economic inequality, xi, 2, 4, 56, 225–26, 229; global cities theory, 2, 6–10, 23, 50, 54, 56; global focus of, 18, 54, 226, 227; on job degradation as inevitable, 39–40, 154, 227–28; on low wages as intrinsic to locally oriented industries, 10, 11, 12, 13, 25, 47; and multifaceted nature of employer strategies, 140; on service sector growth, xii, 2, 7–9; on undocumented immigrants, viii, 37, 51, 107; on urban space, 5–6, 56; and wages vs. income, 63; on workers' organizations, 65
Dominick's, 70, 97
dual city theory, 2

Dunlop, John, 148–49
Dwyer, Rachel, 5

Eagle Industries case, 30–31
economic development theory, 13, 19, 42, 44
economic inequality: Chicago as unique, 53–54; dominant narratives on, xi, 2, 4, 56, 225–26, 229; and downtown investment, 49–50, 58, 59; during economic expansion, 55; growth of, 1, 5, 54–56, 57, 225; as inevitable, 226; job degradation as cause of, 2–3, 9; and neighborhood-level transformation, 56–58; service sector growth as cause of, xii, 2, 227; symbols of, 49–50, 54; urban concentration of, 6; and wages vs. income, 63, 242n1
Economic Policy Institute, 5
economic restructuring theories: analytical neglect of locally oriented industries, 11, 13–14, 19; on capital investment, 43; on corporate structure, 6–7; and cost- vs. quality-based competition, 140; on deindustrialization, 41–42; on employer strategies, 18–20; and process-based approach, 79–80; on residential construction industry, 200–201
economies of scale, 90, 93, 112, 114, 115–16, 117–18, 125, 242n1
Emanuel, Rahm, 54, 66
employee compensation: big-box retailers, 88; chain grocery stores, 82–83, 88–89, 113, 243n4; day labor, 173, 174–77, 191, 245n2; during economic expansion, 51, 71, 144, 154–55; existing studies of, 16–17; food retail industry comparisons, 114–15, 243n5; low wages as intrinsic to locally oriented industries, 10, 11, 12, 13, 25, 47; midsize supermarkets, 25, 95, 113, 116, 125–26, 135; minimum wage, 33, 116, 131, 203, 241n3; two-tier wage agreements, 88; United States as international outlier, 12; wages vs. income, 63, 242n1; wage theft, 77, 188–90, 191–92, 193–95, 210, 215, 218
employee misclassification, 166–67, 218–19, 245n14
employer retribution, 25, 121, 126–28, 132, 136. *See also* employer retribution for union campaigns; job degradation
employer retribution for union campaigns: Chiapas case study, 127–28; extent of, 83, 244n10; Illinois Foods case study, 133–34, 244n11; and organizing strategies, 30, 207; and origins of job degradation, 34; and public pressure, 213; and undocumented immigrants, 34, 37, 107–8, 214; worker toleration of, 122, 124
employer strategies: and cost- vs. quality-based competition, 42–43, 44–45, 83–84, 106; economic restructuring theories on, 18–20; importance of analyzing, x–xi, xii–xiii, 3, 16, 17–18, 19, 21–22, 29–30, 230–31; lockouts, 88–89; multifaceted nature of, xiii, 10–11, 15–16, 20, 65, 139–41, 227–29, 230–31. *See also* job degradation; midsize supermarket employer strategies; residential construction employer strategies
ethnic solidarity as employer strategy, 70, 81; and African American neighborhoods, 102–3; and chain

grocery stores, 104, 105, 137–38; Chiapas case study, 134; and co-ethnic workers, 103–4, 119, 243n7; and firm location, 101–2; and market fragmentation, 64–65; and organizing strategies, 106, 108, 133, 137–38, 213; and wholesale/distributor access, 104–5

Fair Labor Standards Act, 15, 122, 131, 216. *See also* labor regulations
Federal Trade Commission (FTC), 85
Filipino Worker Center (Chicago), 207
finance, insurance, and real estate (FIRE) sector, 2, 50, 53. *See also* global cities theory
Fine, Janice, 66, 205–6
Food 4 Less, 69, 90
food desert issue, 68–69, 81, 82, 89, 97–98, 141
food retail industry, 81–106; Chicago overview, 69–71, 242n5; employee compensation, 114–15, 243n5; food desert issue, 68–69, 81, 82, 89, 97–98, 141; Fordist model, 51, 84–86, 95; global cities theory on, 9; Greengrocer Code of Conduct, 15, 141, 211, 217, 219–22; industry codes, 73; limitations of Fordist model, 86–89, 94–96, 98–100, 110, 242n1; limited-assortment stores, 90, 242n4; market fragmentation, 70, 86, 89–90, 228; store format market share, 83, 90, 92, 98, 242n2; study of, 68–69; unions, 86, 88, 95, 113. *See also* big-box retailers; chain grocery stores; midsize supermarkets
food stamps, 95
footloose industries. *See* capital mobility
Fordism: Chicago as paradigm of, 52, 53, 96–97; and consolidated ownership, 38; creation of, xii; day labor within, 150; in food retail industry, 51, 84–86, 95; and labor regulation enforcement, xii, 13, 38, 232–33; limitations of, 86–89, 94–96, 110, 113–14, 242n1; repeal of, 203; in residential construction industry, 12–13, 167–68; in retail industry, 11. *See also* dominant narratives
Friedmann, John, 7

Gallagher, Mari, 69
general contractors: bidding process, 166, 182–84, 245n5; traditional model, 164, 165–66. *See also* labor contracting model
Gini coefficient, 5
global cities theory, 2, 6–10, 23, 50, 54, 56. *See also* dominant narratives
*Global City, The* (Sassen), 8
globalization: as focus of dominant narratives, 18, 54, 226, 227; and management, 117. *See also* deindustrialization; global cities theory
Greengrocer Code of Conduct (New York), 15, 141, 211, 217, 219–22
Greenspan, Alan, 160

Harrison, Bennett, 14
Harvey, David, xii, 7
H. E. Butt, 105
Hispanic people, 60, 89–90, 97, 98. *See also* immigrants
*Hoffman Plastics Compounds v. NLRB*, 37, 107–8, 214
Home Depot effect (materials availability), 163, 179, 181, 182, 185–86, 201
homeowners: as employers, 180–81,

197, 246n9; and information asymmetries, 46, 73, 161–62, 181, 182, 183–84
hospitality industry, viii, 41, 59; Restaurant Opportunities Centers United, 40, 207, 209, 211, 222
hot cargo provision, 216
household work, 38
Hudson, Ray, 42–43

Illinois Day Labor and Temporary Services Act, 211, 214, 217, 218
Illinois Foods organizing case study, 130–35, 138–39, 243n8, 244nn9,10,11
immigrants: Chicago population, 53, 60–63, 65, 89–90, 97, 242nn1,2; as consumers, 51, 64, 91, 92–93, 103, 109–13; household income, 62–63, 242nn1,2; as low-income markets, 103, 106, 109–13, 132; and market fragmentation, 89–90; residential construction industry roles, 155–59, 162–63. *See also* ethnic solidarity as employer strategy; undocumented immigrants
immiseration. *See* job degradation
Industrial Areas Foundation, xi
industry codes, 73–74, 244n2, 245n7
industry organizing focus. *See* sectoral campaigns
Initiative for a Competitive Inner City, 241n5
injuries. *See* safety issues
institutional-formation strategies, 212, 216–22; Greengrocer Code of Conduct, 15, 141, 211, 217, 219–22
Interfaith Worker Justice network, 67
international economy. *See* globalization
International Grocery Corp., 129

janitorial industry, viii, 38; Justice for Janitors campaign, 31, 40, 212–13, 215, 222; Maintenance Cooperation Trust Fund, 216
Jenkins Remodelers, 175–76, 180, 185, 245nn2,4
Jewel, 70, 97
job degradation, viii–ix; advantages of, 125–30; analytical neglect of, viii, 24–25, 79, 229–30, 246n1; and bidding process, 73, 184–85; vs. capital investment, 38, 43–44, 81–82, 106; as cause of economic inequality, 2–3, 9; as competitive necessity, 46, 116, 145, 184, 185–86; and contingent work, 1–2, 32; day labor as example of, viii, ix–x, 1; defined, ix; and downtown investment, 59; during economic expansion, 12, 13, 51–52, 72, 144, 169–70; employee misclassification, 166–67, 218–19, 245n14; existing studies of, 16–17, 27, 28; extent of, 1, 25–26, 27–29, 122–24; idea transmission, 35; as inevitable, 39–40, 154, 227–28; and labor contracting model, 186, 245n6; midsize supermarket specifics, 25, 83, 121, 123, 128–29, 141; multiple uses of, 29, 43–44; nonwage aspects, ix–x, 1–2, 26–27, 128–29, 197–99, 229–31; origins of, 32–35; as place based, 47–48; and pressures toward cost-based competition, 38, 39–40; residential construction industry specifics, ix–x, 71–72, 145, 186–91; safety issues, 33–34, 132, 186, 187–88, 244n9; scheduling, 83, 121, 122, 124, 126, 135–36, 243nn6,7, 244n13; verbal abuse,

25, 132, 133, 187; wage theft, 77, 188–90, 191–92, 193–95, 210, 215, 218; worker toleration of, 122, 124, 130, 187, 234. *See also* deskilling; organizing strategies
Justice for Janitors campaign, 31, 40, 212–13, 215, 222
just-in-time scheduling, 83, 121, 122, 124, 126, 135–36, 243nn6,7

Korean Immigrant Worker Advocates (Los Angeles), 207

labor barons, 159, 164. *See also* labor contracting model
labor contracting model, 159, 164–66, 167, 176, 177, 180, 186, 245n6
labor costs. *See* cost-based competition; employee compensation
labor intensification, 118–19, 123, 124, 172. *See also* job degradation
labor-intensive models, 38, 81–82, 91–92, 151
labor law violations: extent of, 25–26, 27, 33, 121–22, 233. *See also* employer retribution for union campaigns; job degradation; organizing strategies; wage theft
labor market segmentation, 47, 128, 130, 141, 232–35
labor regulation enforcement: and deconcentrated nature of locally oriented industries, 38–39; Fordist model, xii, 13, 38, 232–33; and institutional-formation strategies, 216, 220–21; and legal-realignment strategies, 214–15, 216; political barriers to, 203; union role in, 34, 65, 168, 233; weakening of, 33–34, 65, 107, 164, 167–69, 194, 209, 233, 245n15; and worker organization political connections, 210–11
labor regulations: top-down nature of, 15; undocumented immigrants' limited knowledge of, 36, 119–20, 131, 241n3; and wage theft, 218; weakening of, 33; weakness for undocumented immigrants, 36–37, 107–8, 214. *See also* labor law violations; labor regulation enforcement
Latino Organization of the Southwest Side, 67
legal-realignment strategies, 212, 213–16, 221
limited-assortment stores, 90, 242n4
locally oriented industries: analytical neglect of, xi–xii, 8–9, 10, 13–14, 19, 21, 227, 243n6, 246n1; deconcentrated nature of, 38–39, 151, 219, 241n4; economic restructuring theories on, 18–20; expansion of, 64; firm location in, 45–47, 99, 100–101; heterogeneity of, 226–27; instability of, 148–49, 227, 245n6; labor-intensive nature of, 38; low wages as intrinsic to, 10, 11, 12, 13, 25, 47; urban domination of, 14, 21. *See also* market fragmentation; midsize supermarkets; research methods for locally oriented industries; residential construction industry; service sector growth
lockout strategy, 88–89
Logan Square Neighborhood Association, 67
Los Angeles, 54, 67, 168, 213, 215. *See also* Justice for Janitors campaign
low-income markets, 106, 109–13, 114, 134–35
low-income workforce: and firm

location, 114; and market fragmentation, 46–47; and organizing strategies, 132, 194; overlap with consumer population, 64, 114
low-wage job growth. *See* service sector growth

Mailer, Norman, 52
Maintenance Cooperation Trust Fund, 216
manufacturing: consolidated ownership in, 241n4; labor-intensive models in, 38; market fragmentation in, 45, 86; predictability of, 149; and temp industry, 29. *See also* deindustrialization; dominant narratives; Fordism
market fragmentation, xiii; Chicago overview, 91; and ethnic solidarity, 64–65; and firm location, 45–46, 241n5; food retail industry, 70, 86, 89–90, 228; and Fordist model, 86; and low-income markets, 106; and low-income workforce, 46–47; and quality-based competition, 44–45; residential construction industry, 73
Markusen, Ann, 13, 45
Marxian theory, xii, 6, 20. *See also* dominant narratives; economic restructuring theories
materials availability (Home Depot effect), 163, 179, 181, 182, 185–86, 201
meat-packing industry, job degradation in, 25
Mexico Solidarity Network, 67
midsize supermarket employer strategies, 98–106; advantages of job degradation, 125–29; bulk purchasing, 117–18, 125; Chiapas case study, 125–29, 243n7; and competition with chain grocery stores, 15, 82, 98–100, 104, 110, 125; and cost- vs. quality-based competition, 106, 140; deskilling, 70–71; employee compensation, 25, 95, 113, 116, 125–26, 135; employer retribution, 25, 121, 126–28, 132, 136; ethnic solidarity, 70, 81, 101–5, 134, 140, 243n7; extent of job degradation, 122–24; firm location, 46, 99, 100–102; immigrants as consumers, 91, 92–93, 103, 109–13; job degradation as competitive necessity, 116; job degradation specifics, 25, 83, 121, 123, 128–29, 141; labor intensification, 118–19, 123, 124; labor-intensive models, 81–82, 91–92, 95; labor law violations, 69, 83, 93, 121; lean management, 116–17; low-income markets, 109–13, 114, 134–35; multifaceted nature of, 139–41; niche products, 70, 83–84, 91, 101; nonunion status, 113–14; nonwage aspects, 116; post-Fordist nature of, 94–96, 110; price-based competition, 70–71, 83–84, 93, 106, 111–13, 115–16, 134–35; and price variations, 124–25; store openings, 136, 244n13; and undocumented immigrants, 107–8, 119–20; wholesale/distributor access, 104–5, 112–13, 223
midsize supermarkets: expansion of, 51, 69–70, 81, 98, 242n5; and legal-realignment strategies, 215–16; owner ethnicity, 243n7; research methods, 75, 78; and sectoral approach, 211; union campaigns, 122, 124, 126, 127–28, 131, 243n8. *See also* midsize supermarket employer strategies

Milkman, Ruth, 159
mimetic isomorphism, 31–32
minimum wage, 33, 116, 131, 203, 241n3

National Day Laborer Organizing Network, 208, 209, 210, 211
National Domestic Workers Alliance, 209
National Labor Relations Act, 15, 30
National Labor Relations Board (NLRB), 33, 168. *See also* labor regulations; union campaigns; unions
Neighborhood Food Basket, 129, 135–39, 244nn12,13
neoclassical economics. *See* dominant narratives
New Deal, xii, 15, 232. *See also* labor regulations
niche products, 70, 83–84, 91, 101. *See also* ethnic solidarity as employer strategy; undocumented immigrants
no-match letters, 108
nonpayment. *See* wage theft

Obama administration, 33
Occupational Safety and Health Act, 15
Occupational Safety and Health Administration (OSHA), 33–34, 167. *See also* labor regulations; safety issues
Occupy Wall Street, 242n4
on-the-job injuries. *See* safety issues
*On the Waterfront* (film), 12, 150
organized labor. *See* unions
organizing strategies, xiii, 207–9; activity classification, 212; bottom-up focus, 15, 204; and capital disorganization, 217–18; and capital mobility, 30–31; city government resistance to, 66, 67; consumer pressure, 221, 222–23; day labor brokering, 145, 174, 190–91, 195, 208, 223, 246n9; day laborer bidding/contracting skills, 244n5; day labor shape-ups as organizing sites, 41, 190–91; deal-making framework, 67–68, 242n4; and deconcentrated nature of locally oriented industries, 219; and dominant narratives, 10; and downtown investment, 58; Eagle Industries case, 30–31; and ethnic solidarity, 106, 108, 133, 137–38, 213; and food desert issue, 141; Illinois Foods case study, 130–35, 138–39, 243n8, 244nn9,10,11; and importance of analyzing employer strategies, xi, xii–xiii, 3, 16, 19, 29–30, 230–31; institutional-formation strategies, 15, 141, 211, 212, 216–22, 217; Justice for Janitors campaign, 31, 40, 212–13, 215, 222; and labor market segmentation, 235; legal-realignment strategies, 212, 213–16, 221; and local market dependence, 3–4, 21, 24–25, 31, 227, 235–36; local nature of, 40–41, 66–68, 204–5; and low-income workforce, 132, 194; mimetic isomorphism, 31–32; and multifaceted nature of employer strategies, xiii, 140–41; need for conceptual framework, 41–42; Neighborhood Food Basket case study, 135–39, 244nn12,13; and permitting, 41, 215–16, 223; political barriers to, 203, 217; and political connections, 58–59, 66, 67, 208–9, 210–11, 220, 221; and price-based competition, 134–35, 138–39, 223; public pressure, 31, 41, 207, 211, 213,

215; sectoral approach, 209–11, 215; strikes, 88–89; and undocumented immigrants, 131; wage theft intervention, 77, 191, 194–95, 215, 218. *See also* union campaigns; workers' organizations
orthodox analysis. *See* dominant narratives
O'Sullivan, Terry, 169
overtime. *See* wage-and-hour violations

Palan, Ronan, 226
*parada, la. See* day labor
participant observation, 77–78
part-time employment, 12. *See also* contingent work
Peck, Jamie, 47
permitting strategies, 41, 215–16, 223
Personal Responsibility and Work Opportunities Reconciliation Act (1996), 33
Piore, Michael, 47, 232
polarization. *See* economic inequality
Pomona Economic Opportunity Center (California), 207
Porter, Michael, 69, 241n5
postwar economy. *See* Fordism
premanufactured housing components, 163
price-based competition, 93, 106; chain grocery stores, 83–84, 111, 243n2; and consumer short-term focus, 176, 245n12; and deskilling, 70–71; food retail industry comparisons, 83–84, 87, 114–16; and low-income markets, 93, 106, 111–13; and nonunion labor, 113–14; and organizing strategies, 134–35, 138–39, 223; residential remodeling, 161, 176, 184–85, 245n12. *See also* low-income markets
primary vs. secondary labor markets. *See* labor market segmentation
*Profit Cycles, Oligopoly, and Regional Development* (Markusen), 45
*Progressive Grocer,* 78
public pressure, 31, 41, 136–37, 207, 211, 213, 215

quality-based competition, 42–45, 83–84, 106

Reagan administration, 54, 164, 168, 225
regulatory frameworks. *See* labor regulations
reputation-based strategies. *See* public pressure
research methods for locally oriented industries, 73–80; challenges, 73–74, 146–47, 244nn3,4,5; Chicago as ideal location, 53–54, 96–97; and elusive nature of job degradation, 79; interviews, 75–77; participant observation, 77–78; process-based approach, 79–80; relational focus, 147; secondary data sources, 74–75, 78
residential construction employer strategies: bidding process, 46, 73, 166, 182–85, 245n5; and contractor networks, 195–97; deskilling, 149–50, 163, 171, 177–80, 201–2, 245nn3,4; employee misclassification, 166–67, 218–19, 245n14; general contractor model, 164, 165–66; job degradation as competitive necessity, 145, 184–86; job degradation specifics, ix–x, 71–72, 145,

186–91; labor contracting model, 159, 164–66, 167, 176, 177, 180, 186, 245n6; labor-intensive models, 151; and managerial flexibility, 150, 172–73, 197–99; motivations for, 169–70; and supply chain dynamics, 46, 166, 200–201; wage theft, 188–90, 191–92, 193–95. *See also* day labor
residential construction industry: Chicago overview, 71–73; consumer information asymmetries, 46, 73, 161–62, 181, 182, 183–84; consumer short-term focus, 176, 245n12; economic vulnerability of, 148, 152–54; employer official invisibility, 74, 147, 191–92, 210, 244n4; ethnic identifications, 246n7; Fordism in, 12–13, 167–68; Home Depot effect, 163, 179, 181, 182, 201; and housing boom (2002–7), 23–24, 51, 59–60, 71, 73, 144, 153–55, 159–63; immigrant worker role in, 155–59, 162–63; instability of, 72, 148–49, 245n6; invisibility of, 146–47, 151–52, 153, 244nn3,4; and labor regulation enforcement, 167–69, 245n15; male domination of, 246n8; market fragmentation, 73; multiple worker roles in, 147, 159, 244n5, 246n6; remodeling, 59, 150–52, 156, 160–62, 184–85, 245nn7,8,12; and sectoral approach, 210; segments of, 152, 199–200, 201; specialty contractors, 175–76, 180, 185, 245nn2,4; union weakness, 180. *See also* residential construction employer strategies; worker centers
Restaurant Opportunities Centers United, 40, 207, 209, 211, 222
Retail Action Project, 222
retail industry, viii, 11–12, 25–26, 243n6. *See also* food retail industry

safety issues, 33–34, 132, 186, 187–88, 244n9
Sandburg, Carl, 49
San Lucas Worker Center, 67, 211, 218
Sassen, Saskia, 7, 8, 9, 43, 59, 160
Save-A-Lot, 69, 90
Sayer, Andrew, 43
scheduling, 83, 121, 122, 124, 126, 135–36, 243nn6,7, 244n13
Schrock, Greg, 13
Scott, 105
sectoral campaigns, 209–11, 215
Service Employees International Union (SEIU), 211, 214–15; Justice for Janitors campaign, 31, 40, 212–13, 215, 222; Maintenance Cooperation Trust Fund, 216
service sector growth: as cause of economic inequality, xii, 2, 227; dominant narratives on, xii, 2, 7–9; and global cities theory, 7–8. *See also* locally oriented industries
shadow state, 65–66
shape-ups. *See* day labor
sick leave. *See* employer retribution
skilled trades. *See* deskilling; subcontracting
Smith, Michael Peter, 226
Social Security Administration, 108
Southern California grocery lockout (2003–4), 88
specialty food retailers, 90, 114
spot markets. *See* day labor
Storper, Michael, 44–45
strikes, 88
strong vs. weak competition, 44–45

subcontracting, 59, 149; and bidding process, 73, 184–85; labor contracting model, 159, 164–66, 167, 176, 177, 180, 186, 245n6; and managerial flexibility, 197–99; and supply chain dynamics, 166, 200–201; traditional general contractor model, 164, 165–66

supermarkets. *See* food retail industry

*supermercados*. *See* food retail industry

supply chain dynamics, 215, 216; and economies of scale, 88; Home Depot effect, 163, 179, 181, 182, 185–86, 201; and labor contracting model, 166, 200–201; and market fragmentation, 46. *See also* labor contracting model

sweating labor. *See* job degradation

Taft-Hartley Act, 216

Target. *See* big-box retailers

Targeted Industries Partnership Program, 217

Tattersall, Amanda, 212

temp industry, 46, 211, 214, 218, 242n3

three-strikes systems. *See* employer retribution

Tiebout, Charles, xi

Tilly, Chris, 243n6

Tommy's, 129

Trader Joe's, 90

two-tier wage agreements, 88

underclass, 5–6

undocumented immigrants, vii; dominant narratives on, viii, 37, 51, 107; immigration law enforcement weakness, 107, 120; and labor market segmentation, 233–34; and labor regulation enforcement, 34, 107–8, 214; limited knowledge of labor regulations, 36, 119–20, 131, 241n3; low-income status of, 34, 132, 233; no-match letters, 108; number of, 35, 241n2; and organizing strategies, 131; residential construction employer preference for, 72; vulnerability of, 34, 36–37, 107–8, 119–20, 131–32, 203. *See also* immigrants

union campaigns, 206–7, 212–13, 243n8; and capital mobility, 30–31; Justice for Janitors, 31, 40, 212–13, 215, 222; midsize supermarkets, 122, 124, 126, 127–28, 131, 243n8. *See also* employer retribution for union campaigns

Union of Needletrades and Industrial Textile Employees, 220

unions: chain grocery stores, 86, 88, 95, 113; coalitions with worker centers, 208; construction industry, 13, 59, 166, 168, 169, 177, 180; and deconcentrated nature of locally oriented industries, 39; food retail industry, 86, 88, 95, 113; and institutional-formation strategies, 216–17; and research methods, 75; roles in labor regulation enforcement, 34, 65, 168, 233; two-tier wage agreements, 88; UNITE HERE!, 30–31; weakening of, 33, 164, 179, 233. *See also* Fordism; union campaigns

United Auto Workers, 232–33

United Food and Commercial Workers, 223

United States as international outlier, 12

UNITE HERE!, 30–31, 41

urban space, 57–58, 231; dominant narratives on, 5–6, 56. *See also* Chicago

Valenzuela, Abel, Jr., 159, 245n14
verbal abuse, 25, 132, 133, 187

Wage and Hour Division, U.S. Department of Labor, 33, 167, 216
wage-and-hour violations: Chiapas case study, 126; extent of, 25–26, 33, 121–22; hot cargo provision, 216; and institutional-formation strategies, 211; Neighborhood Food Basket case study, 135, 244n12
Wage and Hour Watch Program (New York State Department of Labor), 210–11
wages. *See* employee compensation; wage-and-hour violations
wage theft, 77, 188–90, 191–92, 193–95, 210, 215, 218
Walker, Richard, 43, 44–45
Walmart. *See* big-box retailers
Warehouse Workers Alliance, 209
Washington, Harold, 58, 67
Washington Alliance of Technology Workers, 207
Weil, David, 217
welfare, 33
*When Work Disappears* (Wilson), 5–6
Whole Foods, 90, 114
Wilson, William Julius, 5–6
Worker Adjustment and Retraining Notification Act, 218
worker centers, 15, 66–67, 204–6; broker role, 145, 174, 190–91, 195, 196–97, 208, 223, 246n9; and contractor networks, 195–97; day labor shape-ups as organizing sites, 41, 190–91; geographical focus of, 207; political connections, 66, 208–9, 210–11; as research sites, 77; and sectoral approach, 210; wage theft intervention, 191, 194–95, 210. *See also* workers' organizations
*Worker Centers* (Fine), 205–6
workers' organizations, 14–15; challenges for, xi, 15–16, 24, 40–41, 130; Chicago overview, 65, 66–68; diversity of, 204; dominant narratives on, 65; labor law violation documentation, 121–22; multiple roles of, 65–66; origins of, 209; and research methods, 75; wage theft intervention, 194–95. *See also* organizing strategies; unions
*Work Place* (Peck), 47
world systems theory, 6
Wright, Eric Olin, 5

**MARC DOUSSARD** is assistant professor of urban and regional planning at the University of Illinois at Urbana–Champaign.